MODERN NOVELISTS

MODERN NOVELISTS

Published titles

ALBERT CAMUS Philip Thody
FYODOR DOSTOEVSKY Peter Conradi
WILLIAM FAULKNER David Dowling
GUSTAVE FLAUBERT David Roe
E. M. FORSTER Norman Page
ANDRÉ GIDE David Walker
WILLIAM GOLDING James Gindin
GRAHAM GREENE Neil McEwan
HENRY JAMES Alan Bellringer
D. H. LAWRENCE G. M. Hyde
DORIS LESSING Ruth Whittaker
MALCOLM LOWRY Tony Bareham
MARCEL PROUST Philip Thody
BARBARA PYM Michael Cotsell
SIX WOMEN NOVELISTS Merryn Williams
JOHN UPDIKE Judie Newman
EVELYN WAUGH Jacqueline McDonnell
H. G. WELLS Michael Draper

Forthcoming titles

MARGARET ATWOOD Carol Ann Howells
SAUL BELLOW Peter Hyland
IVY COMPTON-BURNETT Janet Godden
JOSEPH CONRAD Owen Knowles
GEORGE ELIOT Alan Bellringer
F. SCOTT FITZGERALD John S. Whitley
JOHN FOWLES James Acheson
ERNEST HEMINGWAY Peter Messent
CHRISTOPHER ISHERWOOD Stephen Wade
JAMES JOYCE Richard Brown
NORMAN MAILER Michael Glenday
THOMAS MANN Martin Travers
IRIS MURDOCH Hilda Spear
V. S. NAIPAUL Bruce King
GEORGE ORWELL Valerie Meyers
ANTHONY POWELL Neil McEwan
PAUL SCOTT G. K. Das
MURIEL SPARK Norman Page
GERTRUDE STEIN Shirley Neuman
PATRICK WHITE Mark Williams
VIRGINIA WOOLF Edward Bishop

MODERN NOVELISTS
ANDRÉ GIDE

David H. Walker

St. Martin's Press
New York

First published in the United States of America in 1990

Printed in Hong Kong

ISBN 0–312–04037–7

Library of Congress Cataloging-in-Publication Data
Walker, David H.
    André Gide / David H. Walker.
        p.   cm.—(Modern novelists)
    Includes bibliographical references.
    ISBN 0–312–04037–7
    1. Gide, André, 1869–1951—Technique.   2. Narration (Rhetoric)
I. Title.   II. Series.
PO2613.I2Z93   1990
848′.91209—dc20
                                                          89–27574
                                                               CIP

Contents

Acknowledgements

Part of the chapter on *Les Faux-Monnayeurs* appeared in a slightly different form in *French Studies*. I am grateful for permission from the editors to reproduce it here.

The author and publishers wish to thank the following for permission to use copyright material: Alfred A. Knopf, Inc. for extracts from *The Immoralist* by André Gide, trans. Dorothy Bussy. Translation copyright © 1930, renewed 1958 by Alfred A. Knopf, Inc.; Alfred A. Knopf, Inc. for extracts from *The Counterfeiters* by André Gide, trans. Dorothy Bussy. Copyright © 1927, renewed 1955 by Alfred A. Knopf, Inc.; Martin Secker & Warburg for extracts from 'Prometheus Misbound' in *Marshlands and Prometheus Misbound* by André Gide, trans. George D. Painter, 1953; and with Alfred A. Knopf, Inc. for extracts from *Strait is the Gate* by André Gide, trans. Dorothy Bussy. Copyright © 1924, renewed 1952 by Alfred A. Knopf, Inc.

Every effort has been made to trace all the copyright holders, but if any have been inadvertently overlooked the publishers will be pleased to make the necessary arrangement at the first opportunity.

General Editor's Preface

The death of the novel has often been announced, and part of the secret of its obstinate vitality must be its capacity for growth, adaptation, self-renewal and even self-transformation: like some vigorous organism in a speeded-up Darwinian ecosystem, it adapts itself quickly to a changing world. War and revolution, economic crisis and social change, radically new ideologies such as Marxism and Freudianism, have made this century unprecedented in human history in the speed and extent of change, but the novel has shown an extraordinary capacity to find new forms and techniques and to accommodate new ideas and conceptions of human nature and human experience, and even to take up new positions on the nature of fiction itself.

In the generations immediately preceding and following 1914, the novel underwent a radical redefinition of its nature and possibilities. The present series of monographs is devoted to the novelists who created the modern novel and to those who, in their turn, either continued and extended, or reacted against and rejected, the traditions established during that period of intense exploration and experiment. It includes a number of those who lived and wrote in the nineteenth century but whose innovative contribution to the art of fiction makes it impossible to ignore them in any account of the origins of the modern novel; it also includes the so-called 'modernists' and those who in the mid- and late twentieth century have emerged as outstanding practitioners of this genre. The scope is, inevitably, international; not only, in the migratory and exile-haunted world of our century, do writers refuse to heed national frontiers – 'English' literature lays claim to Conrad the Pole, Henry James the American, and Joyce the Irishman –

but geniuses such as Flaubert, Dostoevsky and Kafka have had an influence on the fiction of many nations.

Each volume in the series is intended to provide an introduction to the fiction of the writer concerned, both for those approaching him or her for the first time and for those who are already familiar with some parts of the achievement in question and now wish to place it in the context of the total *oeuvre*. Although essential information relating to the writer's life and times is given, usually in an opening chapter, the approach is primarily critical and the emphasis is not upon 'background' or generalisations but upon close examination of important texts. Where an author is notably prolific, major texts have been selected for detailed attention but an attempt has also been made to convey, more summarily, a sense of the nature and quality of the author's work as a whole. Those who want to read further will find suggestions in the select bibliography included in each volume. Many novelists are, of course, not only novelists but also poets, essayists, biographers, dramatists, travel writers and so forth; many have practised shorter forms of fiction; and many have written letters or kept diaries that constitute a significant part of their literary output. A brief study cannot hope to deal with all these in detail, but where the shorter fiction and the non-fictional writings, public and private, have an important relationship to the novels, some space has been devoted to them.

NORMAN PAGE

List of Abbreviations

The French text of works by Gide can be found in the following, to which page numbers refer:

André Gide, *Romans, Récits et Soties, Oeuvres Lyriques* (Paris: Bibliothèque de la Pléiade, 1958).

References to editorial material contained in this volume are indicated by the abbreviation *RRS*.

Other sources are indicated as follows. Full details are given in the Bibliography.

JI	*Journal 1889–1939*
JII	*Journal 1939–1949. Souvenirs*
OC I, II, III . . .	*Oeuvres complètes d'André Gide* (15 volumes)
W	*Les Cahiers d'André Walter*
NJP	*Ne Jugez pas*
BAAG	*Bulletin des Amis d'André Gide*
J1, 2, 3, 4	*The Journals of André Gide* (4 volumes)

English versions of the texts are taken from the standard translations listed in the Bibliography. Where these translations contain inaccuracies, omissions or turns of phrase which exclude a nuance present in the French and germane to my argument, I have introduced modifications which are in italics.

Page references to both French and English versions are given wherever possible, in the form of a pair of numbers separated by a semi-colon. A colon following such numbers indicates an explanation of the source, date, etc. Thus (*JI*, 69; *J2*, 264: 1921) refers to an entry for 1921 appearing on page 69 of the French text, *Journal 1889–1939*, and on page 264 of the second volume of the English text, *The Journals of André Gide*.

Where no page reference is given for an English version,
the translation is my own.

For Lesley

1

Gide and Narrative

In the mid 1930s, after a career spanning some forty-five years, André Gide went through a phase during which he took stock of his achievements. He came to a conclusion which at first sight may seem surprising: 'I am not cut out for the novel'.[1] But this had been the case from the start of his writing career. He was unfortunate enough to reach the age of twenty in 1889, in an era which was not propitious for the novel. As Michel Raimond has shown, the generation of 1890 unanimously scorned the genre, which had become associated with realism and naturalism, and was fit only for the allegedly facile – and dull – transcription of everyday reality.[2] More than this, the novel had become the handmaiden of the positivist philosophy which rose to pre-eminence in the nineteenth century. By common consent its role was to provide sociological and psychological documents from which the researcher could construct a scientific understanding of Man. Indeed, from Balzac to Zola, novelists themselves had been intent on writing narratives that bore out, or derived authority from, scientific theories. Balzac was inspired by the Natural History of Geoffroy Saint-Hilaire, Zola adopted the 'experimental' methods expounded by the physiologist Claude Bernard and the theories of scientific determinism popularised by Hippolyte Taine. In the late 1880s, however, realism and naturalism gave way to symbolism. Taking their inspiration from the work of the poet Stéphane Mallarmé, young artists refused to accept scientifically-observed reality as the whole, or even the most significant aspect, of reality. Rather, it was the domain of the accidental and the insignificant. Truth, for the symbolists, lay in a realm accessible only to intuition. Poetic or aesthetic emotion was the key to an ideal world in

1

comparison with which the world of experience was an imperfect, indeed dispensible, substitute. Thus the novel, in concerning itself with the details of observable reality, was concentrating on inessentials. Furthermore, in relying on a narrative form that aped the scientific logic of cause and effect and remained shackled to chronology, the genre was denying the reader the possibility of aesthetic insights and an intuitive understanding of a higher reality. The poet Paul Valéry, a member of the same generation as Gide, notoriously summed up his aversion to the novel by declaring that he could never bring himself to write: 'La marquise sortit à 5 heures'; and Gide himself endorsed his friend's sentiment.[3] In later life, he offered this summary of his position at the age of twenty:

> Influenced by Mallarmé . . . and at the height of the reaction against naturalism, several of us dreamed of accepting nothing but absolutes. We dreamed at that time of works of art outside time and 'contingencies'.[4]

Poetry was the privileged vehicle of symbolism, and from an early age the young Gide had decided that he too had a vocation to be a poet. However, his first efforts in this direction revealed no significant poetic gifts;[5] and it is a fact that his major inclination was towards the novel. He certainly rejected the genre as it had been conceived by his predecessors; but this did not preclude the attempt to create a new form of novel more in keeping with the preoccupations of the new age. In January 1891, he wrote to Valéry: 'I am a symbolist, I would have you know. . . . So Mallarmé for poetry, Maeterlinck for drama – and though alongside those two I feel a bit puny, I add Me for the novel.'[6]

Gide's allegiance to symbolism was the result more of a discovery than of a conscious decision. He completed his first book, *Les Cahiers d'André Walter*, in 1890, and realised in early 1891 that its chief themes and artistic concerns fitted exactly with those of the disciples of Mallarmé. He had written this work largely to give expression to his youthful uncertainties, to his aspirations, and above all to his love for his cousin Madeleine, who he hoped would be persuaded by the book to accept his proposal of marriage. In fact large sections of this work consist of extracts from the diary Gide had been keeping for some time already.[7] It is ostensibly posthumous, comprising, as the title suggests, the notebooks of one André Walter who, it is revealed, has died as a result of a cerebral fever. In fact he has driven himself mad in trying to rise above an intolerable reality and unite his spirit with that of Emmanuèle, the young woman he loves. Separated from her, first by his mother's dying wish that they abandon their plans to marry, and later by the death of Emmanuèle herself, André Walter retreats into an intense solipsism within which he seeks to intensify his subjective emotions and bring his love to fruition through a communion of souls. Turning his back on external reality, Walter seeks to create an inner vision, a higher reality which will fulfil his dream: in this he is the epitome of the symbolists of the 1890s. Gide's first hero plunges into madness, driven further and further into a mental impasse by the conflict between his spiritual aspirations and his sexual urgings, which inspire him with horror. Gide was later to say that the tone of *Les Cahiers d'André Walter* exasperated him, and he all but disowned the work in a preface he wrote for its re-edition in 1930. But what is of particular interest from the point of view of the young Gide's attitude to narrative is that in this book he creates a text which deliberately eschews normal narrative chronology and virtually does away with incident. The plot is minimal, and the text consists of disjointed fragments, diary entries incorporating transcriptions of an earlier diary Walter kept during a previous phase of his relationship with Emmanuèle; the reader has to work to unify these and other elliptical notes in accordance with thematic affinities and allusive cross-references.[8] In practice, the book calls for a reading which is essentially poetic, breaking with the order of narrative the better to recreate a state of mind and an inner drama. Many of André Walter's notes reveal him struggling with the very patterns of language, seeking to bend syntax and orthography to make them conform to the experience he has to express.[9] He is planning to write a novel, sketches and extracts for which are reproduced in the text of the novel we read – producing an internal mirroring effect, the so-called *mise 'en abyme'*, which will become a hallmark of Gide's later self-reflexive fiction. But at the same time these notes suggest an aesthetics of the novel which will inform some of Gide's subsequent development. Essentially, what Walter is seeking is a 'forme immatérielle' through which his emotion may be 'perceptible intuitivement' (152; 129); in other words, he is concerned that the structure of his text should itself be a vehicle for its meaning: we will read the text not just for what it says through the progressive analysis and development of character, for instance, but for what it suggests by indirect means. 'Intuitive knowledge is the only knowledge necessary. One must go beyond phenomena *with their* contingent pluralities and contemplate ineffable truths' (*W*, 105; 89), Walter writes. He seeks 'not a realistic truth, inexorably contingent, but rather a theoretical truth, which is absolute' (*W*, 92; 77). The logic his novel will mobilise will not arise from the depiction of particular events; it will not be that of narrative cause and effect, but will be akin to poetic association and the lyrical distillation of emotional essences: 'The evolution of the passions must be so cleverly plotted that they stand out and illuminate each other, as if by a mutual reflection . . . so that a part will reveal the whole' (*W*, 105; 89). In fact he envisages no external manifestations of events, since '*the drama is intimate*, no part of it appears on the surface'; there will be no picturesque elements and no décor, no specific location or chronology; all will be 'beyond time and space' (92; 77–8). While the conventional narrative ingredients are thus drastically reduced, Walter plans a form which will hold the elements of the text tightly together. Though he hopes to communicate at the level of the 'indicible', he none the less wants a structure of 'geometrical lines . . . rigid lines', asserting that 'A novel is a theorem' (*W*, 92; 79). In this he is attacking realist narrative from another angle: the notion of the novel as a 'baggy monster', as an inartistic genre, incapable of aesthetic form because condemned to mimic the shapelessness of reality, is banished.

Gide thus emerged from writing *Les Cahiers d'André Walter* with a ready-made aesthetics for the symbolist novel he aimed to make his own.[10] He declared his official allegiance to symbolism by publishing *Le Traité du Narcisse*, subtitled *Théorie du symbole*, in 1891. This version of the well-known myth has Narcissus watching the river flow by, seeing in it the passage of phenomena from the future, through the present, to the past; and musing about Paradise, that perfect crystallisation of essences where all is immobile, where nothing flows or changes because everything is, definitively, in its pristine purity. But Adam, in this paradise, is bored, and longs for something to happen. 'Hang it all! a little something unexpected!' he declares (6; 8), and snaps a twig on the tree Ygdrasil, thus precipitating disaster, destroying the equilibrium of Paradise and plunging the whole of creation into the irrevocable and unceasing flow of phenomena. The poet's task, says Gide, is to contemplate these fleeting, imperfect forms and to turn them into symbols which restore some part of the original lost paradise:

> When he, the visionary, has caught sight of the Idea . . . which sustains the imperfect form, he seizes it, and then, regardless of that transitory and temporal form which clothed it, he is able to restore it to an eternal form, its own veritable form, in fact, its Fatal form, – Paradisiac and crystalline (9–10; 13–14).

Hence the work of art becomes itself a partial paradise 'where, as in the vanished Eden, a normal and necessary order has arranged all forms in a reciprocal and symmetrical interdependence' (10; 14).

From the point of view of Gide's novelistic ambitions *Le Traité du Narcisse* presents an intriguing ambivalence. Adam in the Garden of Eden has no story to tell – until he breaks the twig and precipitates the flow of time; but the function of the artist is to reverse Adam's gesture and restore something of the initial immobility and timelessness of things. The work of art must therefore be in some measure inimical to narrative, as its purpose is to annul the effect of time, to unify diversity and to arrest the flow of incidents. The poetic symbol freezes reality into a fixed artistic pattern, putting an end to change and processes which operate chronologically. The linear nature of narrative runs counter to this aspiration; and it is a fact that the vigour with which Adam's impatience is depicted leaves one wondering which side Gide is really on. Set against the impassive, measured prose of the rest of the treatise, Adam emerges as a character looking for a novel to figure in: 'And then after all, so much the worse! this harmony with its constant perfection of the common chord exasperates me. A gesture! a little gesture, just to know, – a discord, what the deuce!' (6; 8). He is positively anecdotal, and his desire for 'imprévu' opens the way to the most unsystematic and formless torrent of incident. It is perhaps no accident, therefore, that the first edition of *Le Traité du Narcisse* carried the announcement: 'I shall write the little treatise on contingency.'[11] Gide was already planning to address himself more closely to the contingent, accidental forms which are the primary manifestations of reality and which the symbolist movement was inclined to disdain.

This complementary treatise was to see the light of day as *Paludes, Traité de la contingence*, published in 1895. But during the intervening four years Gide's aesthetic was to undergo a significant evolution.[12] In 1893 he published a symbolist allegory, *Le Voyage d'Urien*, which can be seen as an illustration of André Walter's plan to depict the passions in a form 'so cleverly plotted that they stand out and illuminate each other, as if by a mutual reflection' (*W*, 105; 89). Indeed it is a deliberate attempt on Gide's part to give to symbolism the novel it lacked, as he was to explain many years later: 'It seemed to me that symbolism, the actual theory of symbolism, could lend itself to a quite new form of novel, in which events would be representative . . . I left to the description of the landscapes what others would have left to accounts of events'.[13] Urien and his fellow pilgrims weigh anchor in their ship the *Orion* for a dream journey. They sail across the 'Océan pathétique', calling at the luxuriant islands of desire where they are exposed to a variety of sensual temptations; are becalmed on the 'Mer des Sargasses', on whose stagnant waters they experience all the ennui of which the *fin-de-siècle* imagination was capable; and finally attain the 'Mer glaciale' and the polar regions, through which they trek in search of an icy transcendence. Having discovered in the ice a corpse in whose hand is a piece of paper bearing a message, they decline to seek further and kneel to adore 'the reflection of the sky I imagine'. An 'Envoi' concludes by declaring that the journey never took place. The symbolic character of the

landscapes, encounters and of the journey as a whole is plain
to see – as is a certain impatience on the part of the narrator
with the schematic, not to say anaemic and jejune, forms
which as a symbolist he is restricted to:

> I was afraid I would have shouted too loud
> And spoilt the poetry
> If I had told the Truth
> The Truth which must be heard
> Preferring to lie yet again
> And to wait, – wait, wait . . .

By this stage in his career Gide was seriously concerned about
the inhibiting influences on his life: his religious upbringing,
sustained still by his strict Protestant mother, had generated
a complex of moral, psychological and aesthetic obstacles to
his proper development both as a man and as a writer. In
October 1893, in an effort to break free, he set off on a
momentous journey to North Africa the consequences of which
were to transform his existence. The series of trips to North
Africa during the following six years, and the adventures they
entailed, have been widely chronicled, and we have no need
to go into them here: but it is important to recall that as Jean
Delay points out,

> His inner revolution came about not from the effects of his
> trip and hedonistic experiences but *before* . . . Nothing
> was more considered and more premeditated than Gide's
> departure toward the 'fruits of the earth'. It corresponded
> to a complete change in his moral and aesthetic attitudes,
> opposing a pagan ethics to Christian ethics and an art close
> to life to an art far from life. [Italics in original.][14]

In this sense, then, there is a fundamental continuity in the
way Gide's aesthetic develops over these years.

The most significant development sees Gide modifying his
stance in relation to symbolism. He was later to say that the
great mistake of the symbolists lay in their turning their back
on reality out of a horror of 'contingence', instead of, as Gide
puts it, seeking to 'extract some beauty and some truth of a

general order out of the inextricable medley presented at that
time by "realism" '.[15] The notes in his *Journal* for this period
show however that, rather than rejecting symbolism, he is
intent on redefining its aesthetic for his own purposes. He
writes: 'A well-composed work is necessarily symbolical.
Around what could the parts group themselves? What could
guide their arrangement except the idea of the work, which
creates that symbolic arrangement? . . . The symbol is the
thing around which a book is composed' (*JI*, 94; *JI*, 76–7).
Hence the symbol becomes above all a compositional element
of the work. It may not be necessary to subscribe to the belief
that the symbol offers access to a higher, transcendent reality;
essentially what it serves to do is guarantee the form of the
work of art. To this extent Gide remains a symbolist, even
when – or especially when – he turns to the novel as the
domain of the contingent. For as an aspiring novelist, Gide
remains committed to the aesthetic ideals of symbolism and
clearly opposed to the *laisser-aller* of a certain kind of realist
narrative. In 1894, while working on *Paludes*, he declares
his dissatisfaction with the famous description of the novel
proposed by Stendhal and writes,

> Today the novel must prove that it can be something other
> than a mirror carried down the road – that it can be superior
> and a priori – that is, deduced, that is, *composed* . . . it will
> show that it can be a work of art, composed through and
> through, whose realism does not derive from the small
> contingent facts, but is of a higher sort . . . Each part of a
> work must prove the truth of every other in their very
> relationship.[16]

The novel as he envisages it, then, carries echoes of André
Walter's theories still; it will compel the reader's assent, not
by claiming to reflect the accidental happenings occurring in
the real world, but by virtue of the internal coherence of its
structure. Gide is perceiving something of what prompted
Flaubert to aspire to write a book about nothing, which would
sustain itself by virtue of its style; and he is in a sense
anticipating those structuralist critics who would demonstrate
that it is not truth to fact which carries conviction in the

novel, but verisimilitude – itself the product of a formal composition. Composition will remain the central principle of Gide's work; it is an ideal he returns to again and again. He writes: 'I hold that the composition of a book is of the first importance . . . It is through composition that a painter gives depth to his canvas. Without composition a work of art can only offer a superficial beauty.'[17] Few writers have pursued so intensely as Gide the systematic construction of internally coherent texts – texts in which every detail is weighed and related to the whole, in which no reference, however apparently trivial or *contingent*, is there by chance.

The effect of this type of composition is to offer the reader perspectives in depth which can easily escape him or her on a first reading. Gide explicitly wrote in order to be re-read, and the intricate and meticulous internal correspondences and mirrorings in his texts constitute a virtually inexhaustible basis for repeated reading. His works stand as notable examples of what the critic Joseph Frank has called 'spatial form', whereby the temporal dimension normally considered inseparable from the process of reading narrative is subsumed by, and converted into, a perception of the text as analogous to a painting, in which all the components of the work are simultaneously present to the viewer's attention.[18] Such, arguably, was the ideal of André Walter, who hoped to attain a timeless perception of a unified whole through the structure of his projected novel. Certainly the type of attention to textual detail required of a reader by this kind of structure is one purposely cultivated by Gide.

He does so, on his own admission, because of what he considered as his disabling lack of any real talent for telling stories. 'Not having any gift whatsoever at telling stories', as he puts it, he was concerned to appeal to 'intense attention . . . without which one cannot penetrate my writings' (*JI*, 690–1; *J2*, 264). On occasion he was not above rationalising his weakness and asserting that in any case the kind of attention that is demanded by straightforward narrative – 'half listless and discursive . . . that one is most inclined to lend' (*JI*, 690; *J2*, 264) – is too facile to be of any real interest to him. Frequently we find him criticising certain novels in terms such as 'I have been unable to get interested in

this purely linear narrative (I mean without depth), solely
discursive' (*JIII*, 221–2; *J4*, 198). However, like many other
modern writers, Gide is acutely aware that writing novels
places upon the author an obligation to satisfy this very basic
expectation of every reader: it is elementary, and the serious
novelist may jib at it, but the novel must tell a story and hold
the reader's attention.[19] In reality, no amount of bids for
another kind of reading could distract Gide from this require-
ment. The fact is that from an early age he had been brought
up to read aloud to people – a habit that he never abandoned.
From reading other people's books to a variety of listeners –
his family, wife, friends – he acquired a keen sense of what
held their interest and what did not. This element in Gide's
development as a novelist has not been much discussed by
critics, but he himself pointed to its importance (*JI*, 690–1,
716–17; *J2*, 264, 286–7); and if further proof were necessary,
we need only note the fact that throughout his life he always
made a point of reading aloud drafts of his own work to family,
friends and fellow-writers in order to test its effect on other
people. 'My great habit of reading aloud permits me to feel
very rapidly and exactly the reader's impression – and these
try-outs are very useful to me. I was able to note all the holes,
false notes, etc,' he declared after one such session.[20] Thus,
however he may rail against the tyranny of the reader,
sometimes deliberately refusing to write what he felt was
expected of him and, as we shall see, resorting to a variety of
strategies in order to make the reader collaborate more actively
in the narrative, he certainly understood the complex nature
of 'that collaboration which the reader will supply only when
the writer has already been able to secure it' (*JI*, 1050; *J3*,
166). In very real ways, the reader is inscribed in Gide's
narratives. We could take as an example a feature of his texts
which has often been remarked upon, though by no one more
vehemently than Roger Martin du Gard, Gide's close friend
and fellow novelist. Many of Gide's narratives end abruptly,
the final sequence taking up only a few pages where the reader
might expect a more leisurely and expansive conclusion. The
explanation Gide offers is that 'that contraction or shrinking
of the end of [his] books' is due to 'the fear of not being able
to retain the reader's attention'; the author's lack of confidence

in his ability to sustain interest through his story leads him
to try to get to the end as soon as possible once it is in sight:
'Just a moment more, gentlemen, and I shall have finished',
he can hear himself saying (*JI*, 691; *J2*, 264: 1921).[21]

Whether or not we take this explanation at face value, we
must consider, when reading Gide's narratives, the role played
in them, and the form assumed, by the relationship between
narrator and listener which often figures explicitly, and which
can be taken as a figure of that more subtle construction of
the narratee, or 'reader in the text', which has received much
attention from literary critics in recent years.[22] The importance
of this feature is highlighted when we reflect that Gide did go
through periods – most notably in 1898 – when he felt he was
a voice speaking in a wilderness: 'In the whole of France I
haven't a dozen good readers,' he complained. 'My mistake
lay in setting too great a store by the reader; today my mistake
lies in scorning him too much. I no more know today than I
did yesterday whom I am really writing for.'[23] Indeed, in a
much wider sense Gide was concerned to find a readership.
In a lecture with the eloquent title 'The Importance of the
Public', given in 1903, he dismisses as dangerously mistaken
those artists who claim that they can – or must – do without
a public, and asserts: 'When the public is absent, what does
[the artist] do? He invents it'.[24] This is exactly what Gide
sought to do – in the larger world, through his dealings with
reviews like *L'Ermitage* and *La Revue Blanche* and the founding
of the *Nouvelle Revue Française*,[25] and in the private world of his
texts by taking care to cater for the kind of reader he hoped
for.

Already in the 'Envoi' to *Le Voyage d'Urien* Gide addresses
the reader as 'Madame' – his chief and most significant reader
at this point being his cousin Madeleine, whom he had
unsuccessfully wooed through *Les Cahiers d'André Walter* by
giving her a copy in which the heroine's name is crossed
out and replaced by that of Madeleine herself. *La Tentative
Amoureuse* (*The Lovers' Attempt*), written in 1893, recounts
another unsuccessful romance – unsuccessful, ostensibly, in
order to demonstrate the futility of surrendering to desire and
the preferability of a platonic companionship. The narrator
repeatedly interrupts his story in order to address his reader –

'Madame', once again – and it becomes noticeable that his attitude to his story, as well as to his listener, changes as the narrative progresses. 'Madame – this story is intended for you . . . I have tried to find in it what gifts love brings us; and if I have found nothing but tedium, it is my fault; you have disenchanted me with happiness', he declares (77; 29). When describing how his hero and heroine experienced what he refers to as the tedious happiness of those who satisfy each other's sexual desires, he adds: 'They did not know the impulse that leads one to repel the very thing one longs to clasp – as we did, ah, Madame! – from fear of possession and love of pathos' (77; 29). It is clear that the narrative is a pretext for a dialogue between story-teller and listener – between narrator and narratee – in the course of which a negotiation (in this case an amorous negotiation) is taking place over the respective moral and psychological stance of each. In fact the point is reinforced by a *mise 'en abyme'* when Luc, the hero of the story, conveys his dissatisfaction to the heroine Rachel by telling *her* stories about which they too talk (80–1, 83; 33–4, 37–8). An awareness of this dimension of the text's workings makes the reader particularly sensitive to its ironies. As Luc and Rachel grow weary of their life together, the narrator interjects 'But, Madame, do not let us talk of them too much, for here we are almost beginning to like them' (79; 32) – the implication being that if the lassitude of satisfied desire is akin to the tedium that follows from repression of desire then nothing is to be lost through the former, just as nothing is to be gained from the latter. 'Madame, this story is boring me' (82; 36), declares the narrator as his narrative ceases to carry conviction and he momentarily contemplates departure: 'Think, think of the joys of travel' (84; 39). But he must, dutifully, complete his story in accordance with the logic that impelled him to begin it. 'So Luke and Rachel parted . . .' (82; 36) – and the 'so' evokes a logic that stems from the transaction between teller and listener, rather than from the story itself: Luc and Rachel must part because their story must illustrate a moral the teller and listener have agreed on beforehand. 'It is a necessary separation, for only a like past is able to make souls that are alike . . . There are some, as you know – as we know, Madame – who travel along parallel lines and will never be

able to approach each other' (82; 36). But this very agreement
has been strained by the story itself, so that it is with some
relief that the narrator can declare: 'I have finished telling
you this story which we found so tedious' (84; 38).

La Tentative Amoureuse, then, enacts the narrator–narratee
relationship, offering it as a spectacle to the actual reader. But
it is not fundamentally different from a text where the narrator–
narratee relationship remains implicit, since the actual reader
is at liberty to decline to occupy the role inscribed for him or
her in any such narrative and merely to observe the narratee
as an effect of the text – just as here we perceive 'Madame'
as a character in the text rather than a position we adopt as
we read.[26] What emerges from this brief text is the way in
which Gide establishes narrative as at once a contract, based
on an understanding and implied agreement between author
and reader as to certain premises – for instance a shared
belief – which will determine the manner in which the story
is conducted and the outcome to be expected from it; and at
the same time as a transaction, a process which may effect a
shift in the nature of this relationship and the respective
stances of the 'contracting parties'.[27] *Les Nourritures Terrestres*
(*Fruits of the Earth*), which Gide wrote during the years 1893–
97, presents another notable example of a reader-oriented
text. One of the most striking features of this book is that it is
addressed throughout to a reader who is actually named as
Nathanaël: 'My Nathaniel, whom I have not yet seen . . .
these things are no more false than this name I call you by,
not knowing what yours will be – yours, Nathaniel, who will
one day read me' (153; 13). *Les Nourritures Terrestres* is arguably
not a narrative at all: it consists of a heterogeneous collection
of fragments, lyrical passages, descriptions of nature, and
moral precepts. However, on the strength of certain sections
which evoke the narrator's experience in the course of his
youth and of his travels (which account for the exotic character
of much of the book), it is possible to infer a narrative sequence
underpinning the text. In fact, the device of the narratee called
Nathanaël serves to involve the reader in the search for
precisely such a narrative coherence – as well as in the
perception of recurrent motifs and formal parallels which unify
the disparate, disjointed elements in a structured composition

of a kind Gide's declared aims would lead us to expect.[28] More
than this, however, the narratee of *Les Nourritures* is cajoled,
persuaded, ordered and even seduced into espousing the
moral and philosophical attitudes of the narrator: the text
is punctuated by insistently repeated statements such as
'Nathaniel, I would teach you fervour' (171; 37). Mysterious
possibilities are held out as tantalising attractions to induce
the young man to accept the narrator's invitation:

> Nathaniel, I would like to bestow on you a joy no-one else
> has ever bestowed. I do not know how to bestow it and yet
> that joy is mine . . . Nathaniel, I will inflame your lips with
> a new thirst and then I will put to them cups of a cooling
> drink. I have drunk of them. I know the springs where hot
> lips can quench their thirst   (156–7, 215; 19, 93).

The narrator aims to lure Nathanaël away from his customary
habits of mind, accompany him on an imaginary journey
through the world's sensual delights, and leave him with a
taste for 'vagabondage' and 'volupté'.[29] The basis for this
lyrical adventure has much in common with the structure and
techniques of narrative, which manipulates enigmas and
suspense to induce the reader similarly to set out on a journey
through the text. Though he will rarely resort to such direct
means in his narratives, the example of *Les Nourritures Terrestres*
shows the importance for Gide of the relationship between
speaker and listener in his books. There can be little doubt,
then, that when it comes to involving the reader in his texts,
whether they be narrative or not, Gide means business: 'I call
a failure any book which leaves its reader intact,' he was later
to write.[30]

The writing of *Les Nourritures Terrestres* coincided with –
indeed overlapped with – that of *Paludes* (*Marshlands*), Gide's
so-called 'Treatise on Contingency'. Having savoured the
fruits of the Earth during his journeys to North Africa and
elsewhere, he was ready to report on the real world of physical
phenomena which continued to pose a problem so far as his
aesthetics of the novel were concerned. *Les Nourritures Terrestres*
was a direct call to enjoy the physical presence of the world;
in *Paludes* Gide confronts the issues obliquely, through satire.

The narrator and main protagonist of *Paludes* is a writer, working on a text called *Paludes* – which cannot be a novel, since, having symbolist allegiances, its author points out, 'My aesthetic principles are opposed to my conceiving a novel' (146; 90). In effect, from the fragments we are given to read, we may infer that his book will be something on the model of *Le Voyage d'Urien*. The writer suffers from the error Gide himself had fallen into and would later denounce thus: 'Far from understanding that art can only live and have its being in the particular, I held that it should be removed from all contingencies, considered any definition of outline to be contingent and aspired only after the quintessential.'[31] He is seeking to reduce the world around him to a few significant symbols which will sum up reality, and has fixed on an account of a character, Tityre, who lives contentedly amid marshlands. When Tityre goes fishing, the draft of the narrative, quoted in the text, is interspersed with the pointer '(symbole)' (94, 95; 19–20) – which of course defeats the object, if this object is to communicate intuitively and do away with the need for analytical commentary. His studied efforts to avoid precision in his text, and his repeated exasperated – and largely unsuccessful – attempts to explain the meaning of his book to his acquaintances who are impatient to find out, highlight his dilemma.

Paludes is a satire, this much is clear. In the dedication to the book, Gide refers to it as 'this satire on – what?' (88; 10). It is a subtle, elusive text, with corrosive, all-pervading comic and ironic elements. But within it there is a confrontation between realism and idealism, in both the aesthetic and the moral spheres. The narrator-protagonist is seeking to escape the 'boredom, emptiness, monotony' which characterise his life and that of the people around him (95; 20); he wants to break free from predictable routine and demonstrate to others the futility of their existence. The fact that his extreme intellectualism, neurasthenic temperament and obsession with writing defeat all his attempts to achieve something in the real world is a major source of the book's manifold ironies. He undertakes a journey into the suburbs in an effort to shake off inertia (he really dreams of going to Biskra, as Gide himself had done, and this is the next best thing). The outing is a complete fiasco; but he comments: 'It is just as well, after all, that this little journey has been a failure', since this failure has provided him with the opportunity to write an elegant sentence summing up – symbolically, of course – 'the impression made by our journey' (138; 79–80). Writing not only compensates for failure, but also subtly invites it. In the final analysis, the writer is not crucially involved with the moral questions he raises: 'I don't mind it, because I'm writing *Marshlands*', he asserts (98, 102; 25, 30). But the conversations the writer has with his friend Angèle and his other acquaintances also call into question the principles underlying his aesthetic. His insistence on evoking an ideal narrative, with its own inner logic, corresponding to symbolic truths, is criticised by Angèle. He has noted, when Tityre goes fishing, the 'Inevitability of never catching anything', to which Angèle retorts: 'But supposing he did catch something?' (94; 19). In reality, nothing happens out of necessity; events are contingent – they occur in a random way, and alternative patterns can easily be envisaged. Our narrator's projected narrative presents incidents which had to happen, to conform to the desired structure, which generates the intended symbolic significance. In fact the discussion extends beyond the particular issue of symbolism, since of course the inner logic of narrative itself transforms the random nature of events as they occur in reality into a significant pattern in which every detail has a role to play.[32] 'But it's not a question of truth at all, since you arrange the facts to suit yourself', complains Angèle. And the writer, for all his principled aversion to the genre, is obliged to invoke the conventions of the novel in justification: 'I arrange the facts in such a way as to make them conform more closely to truth than they do in real life .. the events are appropriate to the characters; that is what makes a good novel' (94; 19). Hence the novel's effect essentially is to idealise reality, to make it symbolically significant. The novel and the real are in fact incompatible. The novel is a work of art, and the novelist is bound to put artistic principles first. But this puts in doubt the referential value of the form – the criterion of a novel's worth, conventionally, being its truth to fact. Hence when the writer tells Angèle the identity of the man who is the model for his character Tityre – 'in real life he is

married – a father of four' – she protests that he had depicted
Tityre as a batchelor: 'There now, you see perfectly well that
your story isn't true!' The author's response is again to invoke
the 'artistic device' and to declare: 'If one uses actual events
in a story, they never preserve the interrelated values they
had in real life. To keep their truth one has to rearrange them'
(105; 35). The truth of narrative is not the same thing, then,
as the faithful adherence to reality as such. This may seem
an obvious remark; but the acuity with which the idea is
experienced by Gide will be crucial in his refinements of
narrative technique. When the writer in *Paludes* does attempt
to confront reality, in the pseudo-heroic prologue to his 'petit
voyage' when he abandons selectivity or choice in the interest
of fidelity to fact – 'Let us look upon everything with equal
insistence', he cries – the product is a droll list of incongruous
notes:

– Three vegetable-hawkers passing.
– An omnibus, already.
– A doorkeeper sweeping in front of his door. (136–37;
76–7)

and so on. We are tempted to add 'La marquise sortit à cinq
heures'. The narrator bursts into tears – 'it takes me like that
whenever I make lists of things' – at this reminder of the sheer
intractability of reality which, despite all his efforts, remains,
in its very banality and triviality, beyond his artistic grasp.

As Vinio Rossi demonstrates, *Paludes* marks a significant
point in the development of Gide's aesthetic.[33] This emerges
most clearly during an argument in Angèle's *salon* between
the narrator and a sceptical critic in the course of which the
writer sets out the appropriate function of specific detail in a
work of art:

Art consists in depicting a particular subject with sufficient
power for the generality on which it depended to be
comprehended in it ... you will, assuredly, take my
meaning, if you think of all the enormous landscape that
passes through a keyhole, as soon as the eye gets near
enough to the door. A person who sees nothing there but a

keyhole, would see the whole world through it, if only he thought of bending down. It is enough that there should be the possibility of generalization; to make that generalization is the part of the reader, the critic.   (118; 51–2)

A properly selected and adequately presented particular will invite generalisation. The trouble with the symbolist was that he tried to describe the particular *as if* it was already general, avoiding 'tout contour précis' and seeking primarily a portentous effect, foregounding the invitation to generalise through what has been called an 'effect of allusion': straining, in other words, to hide the particular behind a veil of potential significance. It is a fault for which the narrator of *Paludes* is satirised. Gide, for his part, would repudiate the notion of symbols altogether, eventually writing: 'Let no-one see "symbols" here but simply an invitation to generalize.'[34]

At this point, we might say, Gide has completed his remodelling of the symbolist aesthetic to enable him to move on to the novels he hoped to write. From symbolism he has retained the importance of composition, the ordering and focusing of the work's structure to permit a reading which is not merely linear; and also the possibility of an artistic stance which would integrate the depiction of the particular and general truths. This will produce, as we shall see, the first set of Gide's narrative masterpieces, those works he theorised as a priori novels.[35] But a niggling doubt remains, unresolved by this aesthetic synthesis. It is expressed, again, in the preoccupations of the narrator in *Paludes*. For all his commitment to artistic form and the appropriate aesthetic arrangement of reality, what he wants to achieve above all is an action or event which escapes all systems of thought or representation. We have referred to his horror of life's monotony; he is continually seeking a reality beyond the confines of narrow routine: 'the very surprise of it is my goal – the unforeseen – do you take my meaning? – the unforeseen!' (110; 40). We could recall Adam, in Paradise: we meet here once more the impulse which is inimical to artistic structure, to narrative logic and formal necessity.[36] The philosopher in *Paludes* interprets this impulse as the urge to commit 'un acte libre', that is, one which breaks out of set patterns of mental or social habit, which is without precedent: which constitutes 'la contingence' (115; 48). This key theme is not resolved by the artistic solution. As we have already noted, the very triviality of the contingent world remains beyond the compass of artistic visions. The fact that the failed journey is redeemed by the fine sentence does not change the real failure into a real success; and it is also clear that while the writer, occupying front of stage, so to speak, goes through his artistic debates and proclaims his moral anguish, reality passes him by. It is his friend Hubert who abandons everything and goes off to North Africa; our 'littérateur's' activities do not impinge on reality at all. After completing *Paludes*, he embarks on a sequel entitled *Polders*: which in effect shows him choosing literature and renouncing life.

The conclusion to *Paludes* reaffirms the radical split between literature and reality, even while the text in places suggests the possibility of an artistic compromise between the two. The debate between these two positions will continue throughout Gide's work. The duality associated with this problem, as well as other issues we have discussed in this chapter, are crystallised in a characteristic device which Gide conceptualised during this period of his literary apprenticeship and which was to become one of his hallmarks. This device is the *mise en abyme*, which he discussed in his diary shortly after completing *La Tentative Amoureuse*.[37] It consists in the reproduction in miniature, within the work, of the subject of the work itself. Thus we have seen the story of Adam within the *Traité du Narcisse*; the unsatisfactory relationship between the narrator and 'Madame' in *La Tentative Amoureuse* is mirrored in that between Luc and Rachel – and within their story is a further story told by Luc to Rachel. Similarly, *Les Cahiers d'André Walter* contains indications of André Walter's attempts to write a novel which will reflect his own predicament; and *Paludes* contains the story of a man seeking to write a novel called *Paludes*. A striking effect of this device, which Gide chooses to single out, is its role in clarifying the form of the work: 'Nothing throws a clearer light upon it or more surely establishes the proportions of the whole,' he writes (*JI*, 41; *JI*, 29–30). It highlights, therefore, the *composition* of the text; the reader sees at a glance – since s/he is contemplating a miniature – its overall shape, which enhances that perception of 'spatial form' we referred to earlier. Furthermore, the concentration of the content in the *mise en abyme* highlights the thematic concerns of the work; it has the effect of pressing our eye to the keyhole, as it were, and enabling or encouraging us to generalise from the particular within the book, just as we are invited to extend our gaze from the work to the world in an analogous movement. The spectacle, within the novel, of characters listening to or reading narratives, reminds us further of our own role in the narrative process. However, when this happens, the *mise en abyme* can be said to open up a critical perspective. When what is reduplicated is a text within the text or a novelist within the novel, then the novel as a whole is relativised, and the gap between the work and the world is highlighted. When we see that André Walter's novel *Allain* is and yet is not connected to his own life; when we see that the pages of *Paludes* in the novel of that name are qualitatively different from the existence which is depicted in the book we are leafing through, we are given an insight into what literature leaves out; or rather we are reminded that literature and reality are not the same thing. The recurrence of the *mise en abyme* in Gide's subsequent narratives thus betokens his fidelity to the issues we have so far sketched.

2

First-Person Narratives

Symbolism's attacks on the novel did not actually discourage writers from turning their hand to the genre; but the effect of their profound dissatisfaction with the form was to generate a great multiplicity of mutually contradictory experiments amongst aspiring novelists during the 1890s.[38] Gide himself would soon declare: 'The novel as a literary genre lacks clear outline and is multiform and omnivorous.'[39] His aesthetic instincts, as we have seen, could hardly be satisfied with such a state of affairs; and his notion of the a priori novel was one solution to the problem. It could be viewed, in fact, as the culmination of André Walter's assertion that 'a novel is a theorem' (*W*, 92; 79). In this perspective, the inner logic of the narrative, the principle which gives the novel its formal coherence, depends upon a deductive process whereby from an initial premiss the story develops logically a certain set of consequences. It could be argued that the 'experimental' fiction of Zola and the naturalists claimed to do much the same thing; but they were concerned above all with the *inductive* laws of science which draw their conclusions from empirical observation. Whereas their experiments set out to illustrate theories of scientific determinism – in other words, to confirm the inevitability of what scientists had already asserted was the case – Gide's theory of narrative was aimed at exploring possibilities as yet uncharted. His fictions were to be governed by the logic of ideas, rather than by enslavement to contingent fact which was inherent in the naturalists' empirical methods of documentation.

Gide's method was also motivated by a reaction against symbolism's avoidance of moral issues. Having turned their back on the world, the symbolists did not find it necessary to

ask questions about any other form of action which might be
contemplated: 'It seemed to me that the doctrine of "Art for
Art's sake" owed its failure solely to its refusal to embrace
moral questions,' Gide was later to write.[40] Gide's Protestant
background and upbringing predisposed him to take moral
matters very seriously; and he could eventually congratulate
himself on his deliberate decision to exploit 'so rich a material'.[41] But by thus inviting the label 'moralist', Gide risked
being neglected as an artist. It is a fact that still today Gide
is frequently referred to as a moralist; but an over-simplistic
use of the term misrepresents the nature of his narratives –
and indeed, of his own attitude towards the issues the
label raises. A further complicating factor is, of course, the
autobiographical material which is the starting point for much
of Gide's work. Gide may have been tormented by moral
problems as a young man, and the contradiction between
sincerity and morality concerned him throughout his life; but
as he puts it in a preface he wrote for *L'Immoraliste*, 'in art
there are no problems – that are not sufficiently solved by the
work of art itself' (367; vii). Moral questions are the stuff of
his fictions, but Gide does not moralise. Rather, he stands in
the same relationship to moral matters as does the sculptor
to the stone from which he will carve a statue. Morality, for
Gide, is merely 'an appendage of aesthetics'.[42] Gide had
decided long before he wrote the works for which he is best
known that he was not directly interested in right and wrong,
nor in the truth or falsehood of a given idea. A character in
Les Faux-Monnayeurs puts the point very clearly: 'Nothing is
good for everyone, but only relatively to some people; . . .
nothing is true for everyone, but only relatively to the person
who believes it is' (1089; 176). In a letter of 1894 Gide stresses
this notion, crucial to a proper appreciation of his fiction, of
the relationship between a given set of ideas and the person
who holds them: 'The psychological truth of such thoughts *in
relation to the person* who expresses them interested me much
more than their absolute truth.'[43] Gide is interested primarily
in those subtle features of personality and psychological
context which cause a given person to adopt certain ideas.
His narratives trace, then, the progression of an idea within a
mind which will be peculiarly predisposed towards it.[44] It is

in this sense that his novels are theorems developing the logic of ideas. The experimental element in these texts comes from the fact that Gide is testing out the implications of ideas in a variety of contexts: 'At the time of . . . my *Immoralist* and *Strait is the Gate*, I was almost solely concerned to circumscribe a position, a moral datum, to bring out its harmonics to the best of my ability, to develop my proposition to absurd lengths, to exhaust its implications.'[45] He invents, therefore, characters who will take these ideas to the lengths he wishes to push them to, while he, Gide, stands back and watches. He has deliberately disabled his protagonist beforehand, in the interest of the experiment: 'I take care that each of my heroes lacks that modicum of common sense that keeps me from taking certain ideas as far as they do.'[46] The last thing Gide wants the reader to do, therefore, is to identify uncritically with the character whose story he is reading: we must instead attend to the relationship between the ideas expressed and the person expressing them. Furthermore, in the 'absurd' extension of a given idea which it is the purpose of the narrative to expound, we would be well advised to look out for 'the delicate moment when *thought breaks down*', as André Walter puts it (*W*, 144; 122); that point at which a certain view on reality, developing logically from an initial situation, begins to veer into delusion, excess or incoherence.

What enables Gide to conduct his experiments with the subtlety they call for is his perfection of a method of first-person narration. It is the protagonist himself or herself who tells the story. Gide formulated the principles underlying his use of this technique at a very early stage in his career:

An angry man tells a story; there is the subject of a book. A man telling a story is not enough; it must be an angry man and there must be a constant connection between his anger and the story he tells. (*JI*, 41; *J1*, 30; 1893)

This statement points to the complex imbrication which Gide will exploit between the various levels of a narrative. The basic level of interest, in a conventional narrative, lies in the 'histoire', the fabula or diegesis, in modern critical terms:[47] we learn about or can piece together a certain sequence of events. But Gide's formulation stresses the fact that it is an 'histoire racontée', which foregrounds the process of story-telling. Thus we are required to examine what the narrator has done to the events in order to turn them into a story. For example, the narrator may be recreating his or her experiences retrospectively, as is the case of Michel in *L'Immoraliste* and Jérôme in *La Porte Etroite*, whereas Alissa's diary in *La Porte Etroite* records events more or less as they occur. On the other hand, the pastor of *La Symphonie Pastorale* sets out to recreate events which have already taken place but as these incidents continue to have repercussions on the present, his account is explicitly transformed into a diary too. This chronological distance – or lack of it – between narrator and the story being told will give rise to variations in the degree of involvement of the narrator. It may determine the selection of events he or she will choose to recall repeatedly or at length or pass over briefly or in silence, and it may also affect the order in which events are recounted and the way their progression is shaped. Michel and Jérôme know how their story finishes before they begin it; Alissa does not; the pastor appears undecided as to how his story will end, and ultimately events themselves will dictate a conclusion. Above all, the narrator, as Gide's formula emphasises, is not a detached, impartial observer; he is 'angry'. In essence this illustration refers to some emotional involvement or a particular state of mind which impinges on the telling of the story. The events in which the narrator was involved have affected him psychologically; and this will be evident in his narration. Indeed the very re-telling of events may reinforce the initial frame of mind. This accounts for the 'constant connection' Gide seeks to indicate between the 'anger' of the narrator and the story being told. Thus, as readers, we will find that the actual text of the narrative will repay close scrutiny, since the linguistic markers of which it is in part composed will chart not simply the progression of a set of incidents, but also the presence of a mental disposition, a complex of intellectual or emotional attitudes to what is being recounted.

All these factors produce in an alert reader a highly complex response to Gide's first-person narratives. We read what the narrator says and recounts; and we simultaneously infer what he or she is unable or unwilling to reveal. Our rôle is therefore crucial, and Gide stresses its importance: 'The reader will take a sort of interest from the mere fact of having to *reconstruct*. The story requires his collaboration in order to take shape properly.'[48] The fact that we are never able or willing to take the narrator's words at face value is attributable to the ironic stance which Gide's narrative technique has constructed for us. For Gide all his works are ironic in this sense, and they offer thereby a critical appraisal of the positions they present:

> All my books are *ironic* books; they are books of criticism. *Strait is the Gate* is the critique of a certain mystical tendency; ... the *Symphonie pastorale*, of a form of self-delusion; *The Immoralist*, of a form of individualism.[49]

L'Immoraliste (*The Immoralist*)

The narrator-protagonist of *L'Immoraliste* has come close to death during a journey to North Africa following his marriage to Marceline. His return to health after his serious illness is like a rebirth to him, and makes him view his former existence as misguided and based on a false set of values. He seems to have discovered, behind the person he was before his illness, another self he had ignored during his adult life: 'From the depths of my past childhood, there now awoke in me the glimmerings of a thousand lost sensations. ... Yes; my reawakened senses now remembered a whole ancient history of their own – recomposed for themselves a vanished past' (390; 27). He suddenly sees his life in terms of a narrative, and realises that his early success and subsequent established reputation as a scholar of ancient history were actually a parenthesis; this aspect of his life was in fact a diversion from the main story-line. The true narrative coherence in his existence, he now feels, derives from the life of his senses. It is evident that in his vulnerable, convalescent state Michel is experiencing what in psychoanalysis is referred to as the 'return of the repressed'. Part of the process of achieving adulthood consists of socialising or repressing the instinctual drives of infancy and childhood; but these urges, though unconscious, continue in later life their striving to break through the barriers of censorship.[50] In Michel's eyes, the importance he attaches to these primal impulses is justified by the logic of narrative; they offer a convincing perspective of continuity, a plausible story, in connecting his present with a distant past. As a historian he is accustomed to explaining matters through narrative; and of course the French word 'histoire' stresses the story in history. Hence one of Michel's first reactions to his state of mind during his convalescence is to retrace it, not to the illness it immediately stems from, but to an origin which he perceives in the 'true self' of childhood. Thus he is rewriting the story of his life, essentially seeking to realise and vindicate in his narrative a self which he had been accustomed to repress. In so doing, of course, he is following a procedure very close to the mode of therapy and explanation operated in psychoanalysis; but as the critic Peter Brooks has shown, the parallel between psychoanalytical and narrative strategies demonstrates that 'it is not so much simple coherence and mere plausibility that make our narrative persuasive. Narrative sequences and scenarios must accord with the complex, twisting, subversive patternings of desire'.[51] In *L'Immoraliste*, as we shall see, the gratification of desire through narrative is a prominent motif; but at the same time, the use of narrative as an instrument for self-assertion and self-justification also characterises Michel's undertaking.

The motif of writing is an important feature of this work. Michel's ambition to rediscover his authentic self is conceived as analogous to the efforts of the scholar seeking to reconstitute the original text of a manuscript on which the writing has been effaced to make room for a second text:

> And I compared myself to a palimpsest; I tasted the scholar's joy when he discovers under more recent writing, and on the same paper, a very ancient and infinitely more precious text. What was this occult text? In order to read it, was it not first of all necessary to efface the more recent one?   (399; 39).

Here is a crucial *mise en abyme*, reproducing the thematic content of the novel. Michel is opposed to spurious, artificial writings which obscure or betray the true forces in life: his distaste for the novelists and poets in Paris, for example, stems from the fact that in his eyes 'most of them . . . did not really live – contented themselves with appearing to live, and were on the verge of considering life merely a vexatious hindrance to writing' (423; 75).

However, the text in which Michel himself figures is not exempt from the flaws he is at pains to denounce. At the outset we learn that Michel's life has come to a standstill – occasioned, we later discover, by the death of his wife Marceline – and that he has appealed to his friends to join him so that he can tell them his story. His narrative is in a real sense, therefore, a substitute for a life he has lost, an attempt to give coherence to an existence which has ceased to have a meaning or purpose for him (471; 139). Moreover, it is not Michel who has written this text; its author is in fact one of the listening friends who has transcribed what Michel recounted. This is not the first time that Michel has used a written text to expound his thought while evading responsibility for it: his first published work appeared under his father's name. Its success brought praise for its supposed author; but his father's name endowed the text with a special prestige. Recalling this imposture, Michel's attitude is significant. 'As for me, I was a little abashed by the success of this deception. But my reputation was made'. (373; 3) It is a fact that we can see him persisting with this procedure which initially proved so successful. By recounting his story orally, he obliges his listeners to become involved in it to an unusual degree, while he himself remains uncommitted. Indeed, the text we read is presented as a plea addressed to the Prime Minister on Michel's behalf by the friend who has written down Michel's words. In assuming authorship of Michel's story, the friend has become an accessory to Michel's behaviour. Merely listening to Michel's narrative has imbued this amanuensis with a sense of guilty complicity:

We did not speak either, for we each of us had a strange feeling of uneasiness. We felt, alas, that by telling his story, Michel had made his action more legitimate. Our not having known at what point to condemn it in the course of his long explanation seemed almost to make us his accomplices. We felt, as it were, involved.'　(470; 139)

Hence in recounting his story in this way, Michel has achieved a number of effects. First, he has used essential features of narrative to manipulate and compel acquiescence from his listeners, disarming their critical senses and suspending their moral judgement. The 'ghost-writer' has been unable to perceive what we have referred to as 'the delicate moment when thought breaks down', with the result that the sheer linear coherence of Michel's story carries the force of a moral vindication. Second, Michel has exploited the relative anonymity of the text which transmits his experiences in order to escape personal censure, eluding thereby the guilt and social disapproval which his very real misdeeds call for. It is true that in some measure he might be said to have escaped the cycle of writing's inauthenticity by inserting his oral narrative in between the 'text' of his previous existence and the text composed by his friend.[52] However, his narrative itself is so intensely criss-crossed by allusions to the intertextual space that surrounds it and with which it engages that it is difficult to imagine how it might be said to constitute an authentic gesture that avoids being trapped in writing – which is itself, as Frederic Jameson has pointed out in a deconstructive discussion of the implications of Michel's palimpsest image, a 'prison-house' permitting no escape and offering no fixed centre.[53]

Far from being a direct, straightforward report on his experiences, therefore, Michel's story is dense with complexities which run directly counter to his avowed aim of stripping bare the original text of his being. This is attributable to the uncertainty about what constitutes his authentic being – a question which the novel asks in spite of Michel's apparent conviction that he has one. If we consider, for example, his initial contacts with the young Bachir, we see that he actually rewrites elements of his narrative as it progresses. It is unfortunate that much of the impact of this is lost in the English translation, which uses the past tense for both the episodes in question, whereas in the original the first encounter is narrated in the present tense: Michel as narrator has the vicarious experience, through the narrative process, of becoming once more the character he was at the time of which he speaks. He is at first 'embarrassed' by the presence of the young Arab boy; he notes a gesture which reveals the child's 'bare arms', he observes that 'under his thin white gandourah . . . he was naked'. Soon he forgets his embarrassment as he surveys the boy's bare feet; he describes his ankles and wrists as 'charmingly turned'. 'His gandourah, which had slipped down a little, showed his delicate little shoulder,' he remarks, 'I wanted to touch it' (381–2; 14–15). The repetition and prominence of key emotive terms points to the specifically sexual attraction which draws him to Bachir, an attraction the nature of which Michel is unwilling or unable to acknowledge fully, and which will take possession of him in subsequent parts of the story.

At Michel's insistence, the boy pays a second visit to his apartment; this encounter is presented rather differently. The narrative tense here is the past historic which in French, as Roland Barthes points out, is the tense of artifice, the tense which indicates the substitution of rationalisation for existential immediacy.[54] Sure enough, the spontaneous impulses which were in evidence in the previous evocation are suppressed; a gap opens up within the first-person of the text between the narrator and the protagonist, and this permits Michel to distance events, to obliterate the primary 'text' of his instinctual self with a spurious secondary text that concludes with the assertion: 'That was what I had fallen in love with – his health. The health of that little boy was a beautiful thing' (382; 15).

While this is a particularly striking example of the relevance of the palimpsest image to the narrative process itself, the whole of *L'Immoraliste* is marked by similar interactions between Michel as narrator and Michel as protagonist: indeed they are potentially constitutive of narrative irony in any first-person novel. The writing of this novel constantly folds back upon itself by virtue of the narrative structure it embodies. In sum what we are induced to explore is the archaeology of the text, made up as it is of various psychological or chronological strata. At the very point at which Michel introduces the palimpsest image and offers his reflections on its implications, he is compelled to break off and acknowledge: 'I did not think all this at the time, and my description gives a false idea of me' (399; 40). Elsewhere, when Michel recalls his convalescence, his narrative is accompanied by comments or other discursive markers in the prose (words like *peut-être* (perhaps), *donc* (therefore), *sans doute* (no doubt), *en effet* (indeed)) which draw attention to the text as a process of progressive elaboration in the present, as well as a reconstruction of the past. This means that Michel is liable to distort the sense of what he is recounting, under the influence of what he has lived through since or what he is experiencing at the moment he speaks. He says, for instance: 'I think, when I come to reflect on it today, that, in addition to my illness, I was suffering from a general nervous derangement. I cannot otherwise explain a series of phenomena which it seems to me impossible to attribute entirely to a simple condition of tuberculosis' (386; 21). Such interventions are, of course, to be expected in any retrospective account; but we should not lose sight of the need to justify himself which motivates, in part at least, Michel's narrative. One the one hand he announces he is going to 'speak at length of [his] body' in order to demonstrate that his rediscovery of life was no mere intellectual exercise: 'You will think at first that I have forgotten my soul. This omission, as I tell you my story, is intentional; out there, it was a fact.' Hence in the interests of authenticity he will deliberately suppress in his narration those aspects of his being which as protagonist he quite spontaneously lost sight of. Any moral shortcomings illustrated in the narrative are thus attributable to a person Michel implies he has ceased to be; but beneath this disclaimer he grants himself a licence to relive that person's experiences. On the other hand it is important for him to suggest that this convalescence was out of the ordinary in that it contributed to physiological benefits and moral insights which are themselves very far from morbid and which have enduring relevance: 'Any very keen sensibility may, I believe, according as the organism is robust or weakly, become a source of delight or discomfort' (387; 22).[55] Having thus derived an implicit moral justification for himself in the present from the invalid he induced us to suspend judgement on in relation to the past,

Michel can afford to disown this 'witness for the defence' whom he describes witheringly as alternately covering himself up, then throwing off the covers, *'overreacting ridiculously'* (386; 21).

His exploitation of the oscillation between sympathy and ridicule for the various persons Michel has been is accompanied by another dimension which also emerges at such points in the narrative. Consider Michel's remarks about learning to sleep with the window open: '. . . directly the window was shut, I felt stifled. Later on, with what rapture *shall I* feel the night wind blow, the moon shine in upon me . . .', he declares, in a narrative metalepsis which the published English translation misrepresents by putting the verb into the conditional tense – which, admittedly, narrative convention would normally dictate here – instead of the future which Gide actually wrote. In doing this, the author shows Michel injecting into his narrative an experience which is less the experience of the protagonist during or since his illness than the experience of the story-teller himself, reliving what he is recounting and anticipating what he has yet to tell. Indeed, as narrator, Michel suddenly grows impatient, declaring: 'I am eager to have done with these first stammerings after health'. The next sentence announces a coincidence in the narrative – marked by the phrase 'en effet' (indeed) – which corresponds precisely to the wishes of the narrator: 'Indeed, thanks to constant attention, . . . I soon began to improve' (387; 22). It is clear that the narrative is not in fact dictated by the logic of the diegesis, that the reality which is being set down is very far from being one-dimensional. The plot of this narrative, here as in the previous cases we have examined, is obeying the devious promptings of desire, its 'latent, cunning life' (390; 27) in the narrator.

Hence the alleged facts of Michel's story, which the reader is implicitly invited to re-establish in accordance with one of Gide's aims, tend to disappear behind an accumulation of features which at first sight may be judged ancillary. We are compelled to ask whose is the voice we are hearing: that of the friend acting as intermediary, certainly, but how much of this ventriloquism we read corresponds to the Michel from immediately before his illness, a self which survives in spite of everything? We do hear the Michel who speaks after the death of Marceline: is he experiencing guilt, or laying claim to the moral liberty of the élite individualist who sees himself as above such matters?

It is difficult, in fact, to define the specific experience in which the autobiographical elements of the narrative might be said to originate. In the first part of his story, Michel tells how one morning he read and learned by heart 'three lines of the *Odyssey*' to commemorate the importance of the sensations which he felt awakening in him (391; 27). Later, on his return to North Africa, he tries to remember what it was he had been reading on the previous occasion: 'What was it I read there? . . . Homer; I have not opened the book since' (465; 132). This latter incident, narrated from a present-tense standpoint, blends once more narrator and protagonist but implies at the same time a distinction between the memory of the protagonist, who must cast around in his past before retrieving the reminiscence, and that of the narrator, who at this moment is reliving the initial incident for the fourth time. The same remarks apply to the recollections of the verses from the Scriptures which Michel reads in part 1 and is reminded of in part 3 (397; 36. 467; 134). This very device of attaching memories to written texts which we are then invited to reread with hindsight presents in some senses a telling parallel to the type of complex rereading which *L'Immoraliste* dictates. Any intrinsic meaning the lines from Homer or the quotation from the Scriptures may be held to express is secondary to the significance they acquire by means of the dynamic system of interconnections which Michel's narrative establishes. Around the different levels of experience which Michel sets out to chart is woven a variety of levels of narration and a multiplicity of textual implications, such that we are confronted, at the end of the novel, by a palimpsest far more complex and challenging than the one Michel originally evoked. Further- more, the *mise 'en abyme'* that occurs with the introduction of Ménalque within Michel's story adds yet another layer of text whereby Michel relays, i.e. 'writes over' Ménalque's story (a mirror-image of his own) much as the anonymous intermediary reconstitutes Michel's. The slippage and uncertainty intro- duced into the narrative through such features as these mean that the self Michel is seeking to retrieve in an effort to vindicate his actions is fragmented and dispersed throughout the text. *L'Immoraliste* illustrates in some respects Lacan's view on the subject as a victim of the workings of desire in language: pursuing an ever-inaccessible self-identity and self-completion through an endless process of difference and absence.[56]

From the reader's point of view, the fact that it is an anonymous scribe who has assumed responsibility for the document we read also calls into question the precise status of the narrating function which would usually provide a fixed point of reference for our efforts to decipher the text. Like Michel's listeners, we find ourselves confronted by an enigma since we cannot decide how to view his story, and his essential impassivity offers no clues:

> He finished the story without a quaver in his voice, without an inflection or a gesture to show that he was feeling any emotion whatever; he might have had a cynical pride in not appearing moved or a kind of shyness that made him afraid of arousing emotion in us by his tears, or he might not in fact have been moved. Even now I cannot guess in what proportions pride, strength, reserve, and want of feeling were combined in him.   (470–1; 139)

In operating this suspension of certainty at our expense, the narrative has replicated an experience which Michel himself undergoes in the course of his adventures. One morning in Biskra, the child Moktir visits Michel's apartment. While Michel, leaning on the mantelpiece reading a book, has his back turned, Moktir steals a pair of scissors. In fact Michel is able to watch the theft in the mirror above the fireplace; but he says nothing, taken aback by the spontaneous surge of joy that overcomes him at the spectacle and inwardly delighted at the implicit bond between himself and the boy which he establishes by later explaining away the disappearance of the scissors rather than denouncing Moktir to Marceline (394–5; 32–3). That a secret complicity in this furtive challenge to propriety should affect Michel in this way gives the reader a foretaste of that complex motivation which will lead later to his colluding in poaching on his own land (452; 114). An

equally telling aspect of this incident emerges on another
occasion, however. Later, in Paris, Michel encounters
Ménalque, who in the interval has found himself retracing
some of Michel's footsteps in North Africa and in particular
has become acquainted with Moktir. He confronts Michel
with the pair of stolen scissors he has acquired from the boy
and tells him that Moktir 'saw you were watching him in the
glass and caught the reflection of your eyes looking at him'
(427–8; 81). At this moment the tables are turned on Michel;
from having believed he had a privileged point of view on
the crime which enabled him to enjoy the spectacle while
remaining aloof from it, he now discovers *he* is the one who
was being watched while he gratified his furtive impulses. The
whole episode carries strong overtones of voyeurism;[57] but the
special interest lies in the reversibility of perspective which
the presence of a mirror facilitates. The roles of voyeur and
victim are in effect shown to be interchangeable. It is significant
too that Michel's voyeurism is associated with his reading a
book; this detail invites us to draw parallels with our reading
of *L'Immoraliste*. Certainly Michel's listeners are shifted, in the
course of his narrative, from a morally and psychologically
secure position as 'spectators' to a stance of something
resembling culpable complicity in his misdeeds (470; 139).
Similarly, it might be said that Gide's readers are implicated
in the story if only because we have re-enacted in our
imagination all the text recounts; and when confronted like
Michel's friends with the need to form a judgement on his
actions, their unease is a pointer to what we may feel; 'We
felt, as it were, involved'. To this extent, then, the reader in
L'Immoraliste also has the tables turned on him or her; once
tricked into collusion with the text, we are confronted by a
reflection of ourselves as voyeurs and are thereby denied the
comfortable moral superiority offered by a conventional text
which permits the straightforward gratification of voyeuristic
fantasies.[58]

    This aspect of the reader's implication in the text of
L'Immoraliste reinforces that uncertainty of perspective we have
associated with the palimpsest motif. Both features of the book
are connected with the various types of unconscious desire
which can be seen to constitute the driving force of the

narrative. The transmission and renewal of such impulses is highlighted particularly by virtue of the fact that the novel presents Michel's story as 'framed', that is relayed, by the discourse of the anonymous intermediary while Michel's story in turn serves as a channel for that of Ménalque. In this respect, *L'Immoraliste* provides a striking illustration of the parallel drawn by Peter Brooks in a work to which we have already alluded, between the narrative transaction linking text and reader, and the phenomenon of transference which occurs between patient and therapist in Freudian psychoanalysis.[59] The novel exemplifies Brooks's notion of 'narrative as a process of dynamic exchange' between teller and listener, between text and reader; and in the final analysis it is this exchange or transaction which is the stuff of the narrative, rather than an autonomous diegesis. The meaning of the text is, precisely, the reader's inability to sum up or definitively assess Michel's project. If this is a frustrating conclusion, it is also a mark of the reader's dialogic implication in the text; and this in turn reproduces a figure which is perhaps the text's own most telling statement about its sense. We should not forget that Michel issues the appeal to his friends following Marceline's death; with her disappearance he has been reduced to a monologue, whereas throughout his story he has repeatedly confronted his point of view, implicitly or explicitly, with that of Marceline. Even when he is concerned to keep from her the psychological evolution he is undergoing, this is done in full cognisance of her presence and awareness as potentially an obstacle to his new inclinations: 'My very dissimulation increased that love,' he says, speaking of his love for her, and he points out that this strategy 'kept me incessantly occupied with Marceline' (403; 46). Her very entry into his life has been marked as the beginning of a dialogue he will henceforth be dependent upon: 'And now at last I realized that the monologue had come to an end' (376; 6).

The structure of the novel, with its complex and systematic symmetry between the first half and the second half of Michel's story, actually constructs a framework which highlights the central dialogic principle underlying the text.[60] The first and third parts, both situated in Africa and Italy and offering several examples of 'reflexive reference',[61] frame a central section which takes place in France: but this section in turn contains two parts evoking Normandy (with parallels and contrasts in the farm boys Michel frequents) and a middle element centred on Paris. In this sequence too, three meetings in Paris between Michel and Ménalque furnish further symmetries, the first and third taking place in Ménalque's hotel while the second occurs at Michel's home. We note, further, that this encounter also comprises three phases: the first has Michel uneasily introducing Ménalque to his wife, while the third depicts him agreeing to leave the ailing Marceline alone and spend an evening with Ménalque. This means that we are at the pivotal point in the text during the crucial second confrontation when Michel, in answer to Ménalque's denunciation of social conformism and moral pusillanimity, replies using the very admonition which Marceline had uttered earlier when he, Michel, had expressed sentiments identical to those Ménalque is now voicing: 'But, my dear Ménalque, you can't expect each one of them to be different from all the others.' (432; 87. 423; 75). Thus we find, at the apex of the book's structure, a confrontation made all the more significant by the subtly devised edifice which gives it prominence: a representation of the dialogue Michel's entire narrative is at pains to sustain, between the 'voice' of Marceline, reasoning and caring, and the 'voice' of Ménalque, aggressive and independent.

If dialogue is therefore the chief value the book embodies – and we should perhaps recall that Gide referred to himself as 'a creature of dialogue'[62] – then the point of no return in Michel's story – 'the delicate moment when thought breaks down' – occurs when Marceline's death becomes inevitable and the other voice is silenced. This might be associated with her miscarriage while Michel has abandoned her to visit Ménalque: after it she is to Michel 'a thing that had been spoiled' (439; 96), the full force of which expression emerges from the implicit cross-reference to the furniture, ruined by their visitors, which Michel has earlier referred to thus: 'things stained were things touched by disease, with the mark of death on them' (430; 84). It is true that Marceline will remain as an essential landmark in his existence – the light in her window guides him back to his home after his nocturnal outings with the unsavoury Bute

(449–50; 110), for instance – but he is henceforth driven to disregard her interests and what she stands for. Thus, when, increasingly weak herself, she points out that his doctrine 'does away with the weak', he replies, 'And so it should' (460; 124). It could be objected, however, that Gide's aim was to chart the progression of an idea, rather than a sequence of events. If we consider the text from this point of view, then the failure of dialogue might be said to be initiated at the moment when, as G. W. Ireland and Germaine Brée have persuasively argued, Michel elevates the egoism of the convalescent into a moral code and an obligation:[63] 'My recovery was to be my one and only concern; my duty was my health; I must think good, I must call right everything that was salutary to me, forget everything that did not contribute to my cure' (384; 18). Principled egoism is, of course, the very antithesis of dialogue; and it is significant that immediately following the formulation of this resolution, Michel gives vent to an outburst of irritation aimed at Marceline when the food he is offered does not suit him (385; 18). From whichever of the two perspectives we view the narrative, then, both the logic of ideas and the logic of events suppress dialogue.

The gradual stifling of dialogue in Michel leaves him a prey to that anarchic impulse, the 'démon' (459; 124) which has arisen within him and which ultimately exposes the delusion in his claim to be pursuing an ideal. The very fact that his ideas are expounded in the form of a narrative shows them to be unstable, shifting, subject to circumstance and essentially pretexts for his desires. A telling illustration is Michel's reference to the Roman emperor Athalaric, whom he at first sees as a reflection and vindication of his own outlook: 'I recognized in this tragic impulse towards a wilder, more natural state, something of what Marceline used to call my "crisis" ' (407; 53). At the same time he perceives a cautionary element in the young emperor's terrible death. Later, however, as the frenzy of his urges increases, 'if the youthful Athalaric himself had risen from the grave to speak to me, I should not have listened to him' (457; 121). It is not a corpus of ideas Michel is espousing, so much as an insatiable 'stubborn perseverance in evil' (467; 134) which generates intellectual rationalisations for itself.

But even this is not the whole truth: for we see in Michel a
peculiar reluctance to acknowledge explicitly the ideas which
drive him on. Despite the defiant note of the lectures he gives
in Paris, he himself is made uneasy by Ménalque's words,
'*which anticipated my thoughts too much* . . . I should have liked
to hang back, to stop him' (436; 92). It is not until he finds
himself back in Biskra that Michel admits to himself: 'That
then was my goal' (465; 132). The irony of a supposed
advance into unexplored moral territory which in fact brings
Michel back to his point of departure highlights his deep-
seated motivation: the urge to return to the Arab boys of
North Africa such as Ali (472; 140). Here is the instinct
Michel could not name; here is the force which unconsciously
drove him to seek out and sympathise with all that convention
and society rejected, in the unacknowledgeable pursuit of a
gratification which itself fell outside the bounds of permissible
behaviour. This inability to confront the true focus of his
yearnings denies all value to his ideological or moral pretensions, which are revealed as rationalisations of his frustrated
sexuality. His defeat is compounded by another circular irony
which emerges as we consider the nature of the 'new self'
(399; 40) Michel has been claiming to retrieve from beneath
the stifling layers of social convention. The fact is that in
spite of both illness and his supposed moral crusade Michel's
personality has changed precious little from the individual he
was before his marriage: he is still marked, for example, by
the 'austérité' he inherited from his strict upbringing (373; 3).
His need to disguise self-indulgence as strenuous moral
effort similarly derives from his early years: 'My puritanical
childhood has left me, I think, a hatred of any surrender to
. . . weakness – cowardice, I call it' (378; 9). The '*uncommon
fervour*' (374; 3) which accounted for his extraordinary schol-
arly accomplishments re-emerges in his dedication to the
recovery of his health (401; 42–3) and the pursuit of the 'vieil
homme' ('old Adam') (398; 39). All in all, we can see the
seeds of his subsequent development already present in the
picture his friends recall of him, 'the learned Puritan of old
days, whose behaviour was made *clumsy* by his very *conviction*'
(370; x). In the final analysis, Michel is not the stuff of which
great individuals are made; his story points a moral which

can be bluntly put: 'Let us not urge on to individualism that which has nothing individual about it; the result would be pitiful'.[64]

If Michel has nothing notably individual about him, his case is none the less – or all the more – representative. In particular, his story explores, as we have seen, the workings of impulses the protagonist himself does not understand. The force of psychological undercurrents in the narrative is enhanced through Michel's relationship to the landscapes he is placed in. Vestiges of Gide's symbolist theories can be discerned in the systematic evocation of appropriate contexts for events; as he himself puts it, 'the depiction of the countries themselves, of the landscapes, served me well, for it illustrates admirably the state of mind in which Michel happens to find himself'.[65] Albert Guérard emphasises Gide's achievement in this novel in combining the 'symbolic', indeed psychoanalytic, function of landscape and imagery with realistic techniques of presentation: 'Gide's significant images also serve as casual images – *and so serve because never explained*'.[66] However, what this view neglects is the strategies by means of which Gide achieves the effect of significance, in response to what he calls 'a certain desire for meaning which went well beyond the material or physical meaning'.[67] Some of these descriptions are far from being 'casual'; they exude a portentous sense of hidden meanings, an impression which can be seen to be deliberately cultivated. The unavowed desires and impulses for which Michel's story is a pretext find parallel expression in these descriptions, whose very pregnancy invites speculation as to their implicit content. A telling example occurs on the morning when Marceline leads Michel into one of the gardens of the oasis: 'She led the way along a path so odd that I have never in any country seen its like . . . a sudden turning as you enter it and you lose your bearings; you cease to know where you came from or where you are going. . . . I walked on in a sort of ecstasy', the passage begins (391–2; 28–9). The path provides a way into a walled garden which 'seemed beyond the touch of time'; and far more than conventional exoticism is present in this mythical, mysterious spot. Is this a *mise en abyme* of the labyrinthine text we are exploring? Or are we to seek archetypal images of regression to the womb, with

Marceline as a mother-figure? Clearly this is a passage which
seeks to signify more than a literal meaning. Other descriptions
of nature may be seen as more conventionally reflecting
Michel's state of mind: 'This African land . . . was now
awaking from its winter sleep, drunken with water, bursting
with the fresh rise of sap; throughout it rang the wild laughter
of an exultant spring which found an echo, a double, as it
were, in my own heart' (395; 34). The fertile plains and
pregnant cows of Normandy provide a backdrop as Michel
contemplates impending fatherhood, responsible husbandry,
and 'the scientific and perfect utilization of a man's self by a
controlling intelligence' (411; 59). Later, on his frenzied
flight into the desert, 'land of mortal glory and intolerable
splendour', Marceline will point the moral as she declares,
'You like what is inhuman' (468; 135). But in these latter
cases, the text itself annexes the landscapes and gives them
an explanation. The example we started from remains unexplained and perhaps resistant to explicit interpretations.
Another case occurs in the second part of the book, when
Michel joins in efforts to catch eels during the draining of the
pond. The draining away of the water brings to the surface
certain disturbed creatures which normally inhabit the depths
and are never seen in the light of day; and when the first eels
are spotted, the young Charles can restrain himself no longer
and plunges into the mud to help catch them, followed closely
by Michel himself: 'I called him after a moment to help me
catch a big eel; we joined hands in trying to hold it . . . at the
end of the day I became aware I was saying *tu* to Charles,
without having any clear idea when I had begun' (413–14;
61–2). Opaque suggestions such as these have become banally
transparent since Freud, but it is still worth singling them out
since they illustrate the operation, alongside the conscious
rationalisations which Michel provides elsewhere, of unconscious elements he is, or chooses to be, unaware of. 'The force
which calls the tune in Michel's novel is the unconscious,'
declares Germaine Brée with some justification.[68] The 'vie
latente et rusée' that stirs in Michel and leads him to disaster
is, as we have seen, quite plainly composed in part at least of
ill-understood sexual desires which, being repressed and
hidden, subconsciously drive Michel to reject society and

civilisation and plunge into the dark side of his nature in an effort to realise these obscure impulses: 'I cannot say where my folly showed more triumphantly. Was it in this pursuit of a trivial mystery, which constantly eluded me – or had I even invented the mystery by the mere force of my curiosity?' (449; 109–110). Even if we do not understand the language of the unconscious, we are aware that a hidden presence is expressing itself through the allusive language of much of the text; and these obliquely expressed, self-generating impulses reinforce the double meanings and thereby the ironic dimension of the novel.

La Porte Etroite (*Strait is the Gate*)

The story of *La Porte Etroite* can be summed up fairly simply, and can be seen to conform to Gide's conception of the a priori narrative. Two young people, Alissa and Jérôme, are united by a pious spiritual ambition inspired by a sermon preached on the theme: 'Enter ye in at the strait gate: for wide is the gate and broad is the way that leadeth to destruction' (505; 18: Matthew, VII, 13–14). Thus are sown in them, at an impressionable age, the seeds of a doctrine of renunciation which induces them to turn away from worldly pleasures in pursuit of spiritual salvation, expressed in the conclusion to the verse of the Scriptures: 'Strait is the gate, and narrow is the way, which leadeth unto life, and few there be that find it' (505; 18). From this premiss, in the quest for ever greater austerity, Alissa will eventually determine to forgo Jérôme's love, frustrate his and their families' wish to see them married, and will reduce her own existence to the level of a monastic frugality, ultimately bringing about her own death by the severity of her self-imposed sacrifices. Jérôme, inspired by the example of her renunciation, will seek to emulate her, partly in an attempt to preserve something of their relationship; but he will finally find himself alone, his life empty and unfulfilled, and mystified by the failure of a youthful love and a shared fervour which promised so much.

The progression of this narrative can be charted in terms of an inexorable logic arising from the initial premiss. The text of the sermon offers the status of an élite few to those who can follow its precept and seek, through effort, to confront difficulties on the road to salvation. Alissa narrows down the élite to the individual with her assertion: 'We must each of us find God by ourselves' (510; 24), relating to her view of the narrowness of the path: 'The way Thou teachest, Lord, is a narrow way – so narrow that two cannot walk in it abreast' (587; 129). Difficulty as a criterion of worth will cause Alissa to resist her natural inclinations and will dictate choices such as the enforced separation she persuades Jérôme to agree to, as an 'épreuve' appropriate to their aspirations (550; 78. 506; 19). Later, Alissa will derive from her need to preserve difficulty the principle that mere happiness is not to be valued: 'We were not born for happiness,' she tells Jérôme, and when he protests, 'What can the soul prefer to happiness?' she replies, 'Holiness' (563–4; 97). Hence satisfaction is to be avoided in the interests of saintliness and salvation; which leads to deliberate self-denial and a commitment to frustration itself, justified by the Biblical phrase, 'These all received not the promise, God having provided some better thing for us' (578; 116. 587; 128). The pursuit of saintliness involves a rejection of humanity itself, since human nature is inherently imperfect and inadequate, and cannot therefore present a goal worth pursuing: 'Cursed be the man that trusteth in man' (543; 68. 545; 71). The pursuit of God on the other hand, since it involves renouncing all human pleasures, brings no reward: 'The soul that loves God steeps itself in virtue out of natural nobility, and not for the hope of reward' (570; 105. 585; 125). Ultimately, therefore, Alissa is reduced to denying herself Jérôme's love without knowing why; she is a prisoner of privations for which she has no reason except an unjustifiable commitment to God: 'The reasons which make me fly from him? I no longer believe in them . . . And yet I fly from him, sadly and without understanding why I fly' (587; 129).

At this point, it might be argued that Alissa discovers the existential void at the heart of human reality. Certainly Gide was to be increasingly concerned with the fundamental gratuitousness of human endeavour and the consequent difficulty in grounding moral choices, and in this respect was a precursor of Sartre and Camus. But what motivates Alissa's choices is less the logic of ethical reflection than a compulsive need to behave as she does, as her desperate efforts to maintain her stance indicate. As we have pointed out earlier, underlying the logic of the ideas the narrative articulates is another kind of logic which Gide is more interested in; the logic which predisposes certain people to adopt certain convictions or attitudes in keeping with deep-seated temperamental or psychological needs. To understand the characters in this perspective is to explore the ironies the narrative facilitates by offering implicit connections between moral choices and a psychological and social context. In doing so we unearth a number of influences operating on the two main protagonists in convergent directions.

The family background is prominent, and in particular the Mother figure looms large in the psyche of both Jérôme and Alissa. Jérôme's mother, always dressed in black and having herself been reproached by her son for once having been so bold as to wear a mauve-coloured ribbon (495; 5), censures Alissa's mother, the flighty Lucile Bucolin, for her red shawls and ample décolletés (497–8; 8). The opposition between open sensuality and austere restraint could hardly be more marked. Lucile inspires horror in Jérôme, who evinces a kind of disgust following her playful attempt at an erotic tease (500; 11–12). He speaks of the 'hatred' (501; 13) he feels for her following her scandalous infidelity and her abandonment of her husband and family: but his admissions of a 'peculiar discomfort . . . a feeling of uneasiness, of disturbance, mingled with a kind of admiration and a kind of terror' (499; 11) and an 'uncertain and complex feeling' (501; 13) are probably nearer the truth. When the revelation of Lucile's infidelity occurs, Jérôme says, 'I . . . made it a point of honour not to question my mother' (505; 17); and Alissa too swears him to silence on the matter (504; 17). Circumstances conspire, then, to highlight and then repress sexual drives; with the result that these drives work on the protagonists in ways they are unable to appreciate. It is possible to argue that Alissa's denial of Jérôme's love, and his inability to be more enterprising in his attempts to overcome her inhibitions, are both prompted by their fear of sexuality: it is after all the trauma of Lucile Bucolin's sexual misdemeanours which brings them together in the first place

(503–4; 16–17).[69] Jérôme inhabits a world peopled chiefly by
females who are emblems of austerity and moral purity; his
mother, Miss Ashburton, and Tante Plantier are all asexual
figures. The sexual female is denounced and rejected, and
Jérôme is ill-prepared for an encounter with female sexuality.
The problem is made more complex because Alissa resembles
both Jérôme's mother and her own mother, as is pointed out
by Miss Ashburton as well as by Alissa's father (515; 31. 585;
126). Jérôme too acknowledges her similarity to Lucile Bucolin
(501; 13): which means that he is confronted, in her, by a
woman reminiscent of his mother – a forbidding figure
inspiring inhibition – but who is also capable of provoking in
him precisely those feelings his mother disapproved. Alissa,
for her part, has to come to terms with the coexistence within
herself, registered by her resemblance to these two dissimilar
women, of a sexual as well as a spiritual being – a difficult
problem she is fully aware of, as she confides to her diary
following a key conversation during which her father has
spoken to her of Lucile (585; 126). But since sexuality is
associated in her mind with her mother's betrayal of herself
and her father, powerful inhibitions are operating on her
too. It is hardly surprising, therefore, if resistance to their
instinctive impulses is second nature to Jérôme and Alissa.
For all her aspiration to a higher, ever-deferred fulfilment and
refusal of ordinary satisfactions, the area of their relationship
is ironically the one where Alissa appeals to simple happiness
in an effort to dissuade Jérôme from pressing to go further,
into engagement and marriage: 'Are we not happy enough as
we are?' she says (521; 39).

The pious family environment conditions another reflex
which will be crucial to the development of the two protagonists. Jérôme points out that the pastor's sermon, with its
austere lesson, found in him a soul 'ready prepared and
naturally predisposed to duty', since, as he puts it, 'Self-
control was as natural to me as self-indulgence to others, and
this severity to which I was subjected, far from being irksome
to me, was soothing' (506; 20). This is a familiar problem in
Gide's universe. The insidious attraction of restraint, discipline
and austerity is that for certain types of personality they are
roundabout forms of self-indulgence. Far from going against

his true nature, self-denial in fact comes naturally to Jérôme. This paradox whereby privation is a source of gratification in the context of a certain puritanism might be held to remove any moral value from codes of conduct which find their justification in the difficulty associated with the pursuit of a given ideal. Alissa is haunted by the implications of such an insight, as when she asks herself why she feels compelled to refuse what all her being longs for: 'What! shall I dare to call that virtue which is the most natural inclination of my heart? . . . Can it be that I am secretly attracted by a charm more powerful and a sweetness greater still than that of love?' (586; 127–28). Jérôme will later denounce, with bitter hindsight, 'the snare of virtue' – the special kind of temptation that Alissa represents for him, and which is the reason why he goes along with her ruinous strategies: 'All heroism attracted and dazzled me . . . Any path, provided it climbed upwards, would lead me to her' (565; 99). But if Alissa effectively leads Jérôme into this trap, it is largely because she first falls into it herself.

Such then, are the factors in the equation which *La Porte Etroite* seeks to develop to the inevitable conclusion. Two personalities, brought up in a certain religious and psychological climate, will respond to a crisis involving a mixture of moral horror and doctrinal prescription by proceeding along parallel courses to the ruination of their lives. This dual demonstration might be said to recall the progression evident in *L'Immoraliste* – and justifies thereby the analogies between the two books which Gide was at pains to stress.[70] However, *La Porte Etroite* is more complex than the earlier work in a number of respects. For one thing, it involves more characters in more significant interactions with the main protagonists. Alissa's sister, Juliette, falls in love with Jérôme and the ensuing complications bring out several important features of Alissa's motives as well as furnishing a crucial element in the novel's plot. On discovering her sister's feelings, Alissa tries to discourage Jérôme's love for herself so that he can marry Juliette. She is prepared to sacrifice herself, as Jérôme's friend Abel puts it (537; 61), in order to facilitate the happiness of her sister and Jérôme. But Juliette senses the true nature of Alissa's manoeuvre and resents the implication that Alissa should presume to dispose of their lives in this way; and in a fit of pique, refusing to 'be outdone by her sister' (539; 63), she sacrifices herself instead by accepting the proposal of another suitor although she does not love him, mainly to spite Alissa. Juliette's wilful impulse, consummated in an atmosphere of virtual hysteria, precipitates her own illness and a crisis of conscience in her sister. Alissa will later write: 'The trial through which Juliette has just gone, has had its effect on me too' (543; 68). Furthermore, directly associated with this admission is Alissa's renunciation of human relations. She quotes Jeremiah: 'Cursed be the man that trusteth in man', and will make much of an adaptation of the verse by Racine: 'Children of mankind . . . What is the fruit of all your care?' (which she first attributes to Corneille, indicating thereby, perhaps, her unconscious urge to be a Cornelian heroine herself in putting what she conceives as duty before personal inclinations) (543, 544, 545; 68, 71, 72).[71] But arising as it does out of the disastrous consequences of her attempt to manipulate her fellow-humans and make them conform to a scheme she had devised for their spiritual well-being, this new resolution looks suspiciously like 'sour grapes', a rationalisation of her failure. Such a view is reinforced by an admission Alissa makes later, as she contemplates the happiness Juliette's marriage appears to bring in spite of everything:

> That happiness which I longed for so much, to the extent of offering my own in sacrifice to it, is painful to me, now that I see that she has obtained it without trouble . . . I see well enough that a horrible revival of egoism in me is offended at her having found her happiness elsewhere than in my sacrifice – at her not having needed my sacrifice in order to be happy. (582; 122)

Structurally as well as thematically, this episode is at the centre of the novel (in the fifth out of nine chapters); ideologically, it is the point of no return for Alissa and Jérôme, as she henceforth flees human involvement with a new-found determination stemming from this crisis. From this stage onwards, Alissa will gratify her need for self-sacrifice by directing all her efforts at dissuading Jérôme from loving her, with the intention of leaving Jérôme undistracted from salvation, and offering her own sacrifice to God – who, it may be implied, will prove more appreciative of her gesture than mere humans.

Another part of the problem in relations between Alissa and Jérôme is their preference for the imaginary over the real. Their agreed separation and regular letter-writing gives greater satisfaction to Alissa, at least, than Jérôme's physical presence: so much so that she fears their actual meetings, and does what she can to postpone or shorten them (549; 77. 554–5; 84–5). In this situation, reunions can easily go wrong, as does the encounter that follows Jérôme's travels in Italy and his military service. Alissa's response is to write to him after his departure: 'I know it will be so always. Oh! I beg of you, don't let us see each other again!' (558; 89). Jérôme confesses that he too derives a kind of pleasure from their separation (550; 77–8) and prolongs it 'out of fear, too, of an unsatisfactory meeting' (551, 79), recognising with Alissa that their correspondence has produced an imaginary relationship and that 'we have been so grievously hurt by our fall into reality' (560; 92). The conflict between the ideal and the real, a recurring theme in Gide's work, is clearly operative in this text too. It is a fact that the reflex illustrated here will account for much of the protagonists' behaviour, finding perhaps its clearest expression in Alissa's assertion: 'Our love made us foresee for one another something better than love. Thanks to you, my friend, my dream climbed so high that any earthly satisfaction would have been a declension' (578; 115).

At a point before she has achieved her transcendent solution to their problem, Alissa incriminates their letter-writing in the following terms: 'Our correspondence was nothing but a vast mirage . . . we were each writing, alas! only to ourselves' (559; 90). But in fact the difficulty can be traced to a more fundamental phenomenon which is set out obliquely but insistently throughout the narrative. Much of the communication between the two is accomplished only indirectly from the earliest stages in their story. Messages overheard or communicated via an intermediary are frequent occurrences. Jérôme overhears a conversation between Alissa and her father

on the subject of marriage and Jérôme's qualities, in the course
of which his compulsion to listen is indicative of his hope of
hearing something Alissa would not say to him directly (508–
9; 22–3). He explains elsewhere how they used Juliette as a
go-between: 'I told her what I dared not tell Alissa, with
whom excess of love made me constrained and shy' (516; 32).
More significantly, it is during a conversation with Juliette
that, suspecting Alissa may be able to hear from behind the
hedge which conceals her from sight, Jérôme demonstrates how
this indirect communication can produce an extraordinary
enhancement in his powers of expression as he lyrically evokes
the future he envisages for them (517–20; 33–7). Later,
following the crisis brought about by Juliette's dramatic
acceptance of the wholly unsuitable marriage proposal, Alissa
will write to Aunt Plantier a long letter in the hope that
she will show it to Jérôme and unblock the channels of
communication between them – once more, indirect means
are most effective (542–4; 67–70). We may perceive here a
parallel with *L'Immoraliste*, in that *La Porte Etroite* too drama-
tises a failure of dialogue. Jérôme and Alissa speak of each
other, see each other most easily, in the third person rather
than through the second person which installs between two
people an interaction, a dialogue which might have permitted
a relationship to generate mutual corrections of the extreme
tendencies they fall a prey to. The very fact that the book
which reveals their story takes the form of two monologues
within which each refers to the other in the third person is a
testimony to their sorry plight.

What is it which renders the characters thus incapable of
straightforward communication? Elements of an explanation
are hinted at precisely in the declaration Jérôme makes when
he suspects (correctly, as it turns out) that Alissa may be
listening behind the hedge: 'Oh, if only we could lean over
the soul we love and see as in a mirror, the image we cast
there!' (518; 35). This wish may be a fairly banal one, at
bottom; but it is given a particular pertinence in the *La Porte
Etroite* by virtue of the fact that the image of the mirror occurs
as a prominent feature of relationships between the characters.
Far from satisfying the narcissistic fantasy of having the loved
one see him as he wishes to be seen, the mirror motif is

associated with incidents involving profound discomfiture for the male protagonist. Jérôme's friend Abel Gautier, whose own hopes are dashed with the revelation of Juliette's love for Jérôme and her subsequent engagement to another, is reduced from his usual spirited resourcefulness to a highly uncharacteristic cowed resignation by an encounter with Juliette, in Alissa's room, when she addresses him via a mirror:

> I pushed open the door of the room. Juliette was there motionless, standing in front of the chimney-piece, her elbows on the marble, her chin in her hands; she was staring at herself in the glass. When she heard me she didn't turn round, but stamped her foot, crying, 'Oh, leave me alone!' so harshly that I went away again without asking for more' (538; 61)

The echoes of the crucial mirror episode in *L'Immoraliste*, whose importance we have already discussed, also contribute to endow this brief incident with significance; the more so as Jérôme encounters Alissa in precisely the same way, as he too, uninvited, opens the door to her room – that door and that room which are associated, from years earlier, with decisive moments in his life (503–4; 16–17):

> The fear of being obliged to leave before speaking to her sent me to her room a little before dinner. She was putting on a coral necklace, and, her arms raised to fasten it, she was bending forward, with her back to the door, looking at herself over her shoulder, in a mirror between two lighted candles. It was in the mirror that she first caught sight of me, and she continued to look at me in it for some moments without turning round.
> 'Why,' said she, 'wasn't the door shut?' (520–1; 38)

There are grounds for suggesting that such an encounter may well be intimidating, or at least unsettling, for one who is concerned with the image he creates, 'as in a mirror', in another's eyes. It activates in Jérôme a set of unconscious reflexes which can be seen at work in several other instances. Alissa watches, not Jérôme, but his image in the mirror –

which he cannot see, and therefore cannot tell what picture she has of him. On the other hand the 'specularity' here highlighted in the relationship conveys Jérôme's vulnerability to Alissa's scrutiny (underlined by the implied reproach in her comment about the door) and his sense of being seen by her as a third person, a 'he' rather than a 'you': which paralyses not only his initiative in his dealings with her, but also his powers of judgement when it comes to understanding Alissa's motives and responding rationally. Moreover, we may recall that his traumatic and determining encounter with sexuality in the person of Lucile has a mirror as an essential component:

> 'There, see if that doesn't look better!' and taking out her little mirror, she drew my face down to hers, passed her bare arm around my neck, put her hand into my shirt, asked me laughingly if I was ticklish – went on – further . . . (500; 12)

Small wonder that the experience of himself as a spectacle in a mirror is fraught with guilt and inhibition. A hint of the same complex emerges in a remark such as 'What suspicious instinct had put her on guard? Had she formerly detected in my words some reflection of my friend's advice?' (559; 91). Jérôme's insecurity concerning Alissa's view of him spontaneously expresses itself in terms of a reflection revealing more to her gaze than he can monitor. Hence, we may conclude, Jérôme's preference for situations in which he cannot be seen by Alissa with her 'look' which is insistently qualified as 'enquiring' (507; 21. 501; 14). Hence too the obstacles to communication between them: 'I offered . . . all up, mystically, to Alissa, and, indeed, invented a refinement of virtue by which I often left her in ignorance of what I had done only for her sake' (507; 21). Critics have frequently remarked on Jérôme's weak personality – he himself admits to being 'somewhat unenterprising'; but the inhibitions that govern his conduct with Alissa stem from this excessive self-awareness and the ensuing excessive readiness to feel guilty, or somehow wanting, in his dealings with her: 'And at that it was myself that I turned to upbraid, not wishing to give way to reproaches, and, indeed, hardly knowing what might be expected from her now, nor with what I could reproach her' (572; 107).

This brings us to what is perhaps Jérôme's major role in the novel: that of narrator.[72] Jérôme says at one point, 'I look back to the past and live it over again' (579; 117); and in the introduction to his narrative, he asserts that he is making no particular effort to elaborate on events, to give artistic shape to his memories, since 'any effort I might make to dress them up would take away the last pleasure I hope to get in telling them' (495; 5). We are to assume, therefore, that what governs his narrative is simply the desire to recall events and derive what melancholy consolation he can from the process. To take him too literally, however, would be disingenuous. He has as an important aim the pursuit of verisimilitude, as when he comments: 'As I put down our words I feel that they will seem very unchildlike ... What am I to do? Try to excuse them? No! no more than I will colour them to make them look more natural' (510; 25). He clearly has in mind the judgement of a reader, and as a result cannot be entirely spontaneous and unselfconscious. We have seen how Jérôme is haunted by the 'look', especially when it is that of Alissa; when preparing a text for a future reader we might expect him to be no less constrained by thoughts of the impression he is making. It is plain that Jérôme edits the material at his disposal: 'I copy out the part that throws light on my story', he says of one of Alissa's letters (542; 67. Cf.551; 79); but since we as readers do not yet know quite what the story will turn out to be, we are made aware that Jérôme does have a clear idea, and that it will involve the exclusion of material he considers irrelevant. But a different storyteller, with a different story, might have a different view on what is relevant: and, of course, this is the point made by the inclusion in *La Porte Etroite* of Alissa's diary alongside Jérôme's narrative, as we shall see.

Moreover, we cannot be sure that Jérôme is an entirely reliable narrator. On his own admission, what he writes may be inaccurate. 'Were those her words exactly? I cannot be sure for, I repeat, I was so full of my love that, beside it, I was scarcely aware of any expression but its own' (519; 37), Jérôme notes of a conversation with Juliette. This is a particularly subtle claim, in which the narrator contradicts his earlier undertaking not to resort to invention in order to 'patch' or 'connect' his memories (495; 5). We may, on the other hand, place this reported conversation alongside that he overhears between Alissa and her father, in which Jérôme repeatedly fails to hear – or perhaps more exactly, fails to record, what Alissa's father says (508–9; 22–3). Arguably Jérôme's justifications for the peculiarly one-sided dialogue he records (he does manage to make out Alissa's every word) still leave this page less convincing than the perhaps invented one he denounces as such: but they both make the same point that Jérôme missed details of the story he is telling. A question that arises is, can we distinguish between omissions and misunderstandings which occurred at the time of the events he recounts and those he perpetrates as he narrates? The process of narrating is as important in this novel as it was in *L'Immoraliste*, and as in the earlier novel we are kept aware of the narrating presence by interventions like those we have already mentioned, and others such as 'I write them down as I remember them, and without any after addition of either art or logic' (570; 105). An example which gives a particularly striking impression of immediacy occurs when Jérôme writes, 'The evening before – no, two evenings before my departure' (517; 33), a correction we might expect in speech – but which, in fact, seems odd in a written account where revisions normally supersede previous versions. The cumulative effect of these features is to heighten the dialogue in the present between story-teller and narratee – who is evoked some seven times, in statements such as: 'Robert . . . of whom I have so far told you very little' (541; 66). This pair relive events almost as they are happening – which is to say that, as in the example we analysed from *L'Immoraliste*, the present of narration sometimes slips into an anticipatory future as if it were the present of events in the narrative: '*Before speaking of the unhappy event which will shatter our family life . . . it is time that I told you about my cousin*' (501; 13). The great difference between the two novels in this respect is that while we are aware of the present state and circumstances of Michel as he tells his story, those of Jérôme are much less clear. As a result it is difficult to assess why he is telling his story – or whom he is telling it to.

Towards the end of the novel we learn that it is over ten years since Alissa died, but that Jérôme saw Juliette in the previous year. In fact what he writes is 'J'ai revu Juliette l'an passé' ('I saw Juliette again last year') (596; 141); and in the French text his abandonment of the past historic for the perfect tense – the single occasion on which it is used to denote an element in Jérôme's narrative – makes it clear that this encounter is still in his mind as he writes. Juliette has asked him to be the godfather of her new-born daughter, who is called Alissa: perhaps this is the trigger for his narrative, as old memories acquire a new lease of life. More than this, Juliette, in asking why he never married, enquiries: 'Then you think that one can keep a hopeless love in one's heart for so long as that?' (597; 143) in a manner which implies that she too has never succeeded in stifling what she felt for him; and for all her would-be bluffness in saying, as night falls, 'Come! . . . we must wake up', she slumps back in her chair, looking to Jérôme as if she is crying. This poignant ending evokes, then, an abiding set of relations, condemned to melancholy frustration, which extend on into the present in which Jérôme writes.

As for the 'vous' whom Jérôme addresses, this remains an anonymous presence whose significance, as Babcock puts it, lies not in its identity but in the fact that the device shifts attention from the diegesis to the narration of the novel.[73] On the other hand, Maisani-Léonard, in an exhaustive study of the linguistic markers in the text, concludes that the locus of the narration is elided: we cannot know more than we have indicated above about the circumstances in which Jérôme writes. This critic points to the consistent use of the past historic as indicative of an attempt to recount events as a fixed, preordained sequence and thereby evade the question of any responsibility on Jérôme's part for the tragic outcome; but certain present-tense sequences – the incident with Lucile Bucolin (500; 12), the revelation of the adultery and Alissa's distress which are decisive factors in determining Jérôme's life (503–4; 16–17), Juliette's anguished attempt to outdo her sister's self-sacrifice (539–40; 63–4) – all these betoken a renewal of emotion in Jérôme which calls into question his stance of resigned detachment (the effect is lost in the English version,

which relates these in the past tense just like the rest of the text).
He seems to hesitate, as Maisani-Léonard puts it, between a
desire to relive his past and a need to analyse it.[74] He has told
Juliette, just prior to beginning his narrative, of his desire to
remain faithful, not so much to Alissa, as to 'her idea of me . . .
I think I couldn't do otherwise' (597; 143). This seems to
indicate that he is still governed by that image he was concerned
to see in her eyes; and it is noticeable that through the narrative
he repeatedly portrays himself as in the grip of a moral and
psychological paralysis, as if hypnotised still by the impact
Alissa has had on him. Albert Sonnenfeld, in his studies of the
novel, has shown that this fascination can be attributed to
Alissa's strategies and in her writing to or for Jérôme; she is as
anxious as he to project a certain image.[75] To revert briefly to
the mirror scene, we may recall that even while keeping her
back turned to Jérôme, Alissa is projecting into the mirror an
image of herself which we can see – and the fact that she is
putting on a necklace indicates that a certain kind of vanity is
not foreign to her nature. So, for example, in indicating that
she has torn certain pages from her diary – having read them
first (588; 129) – she produces an effect on the reader which the
simple removal of the pages in question would have avoided.
Similarly, in letting Jérôme see that she has removed certain
works from her bookshelves (568–9; 103–4) she is making a
gesture of a kind which implies a spectator to give it meaning.
Most telling of all, she deliberately arranges for her diary to be
sent to Jérôme after her death. She writes in the final pages: 'I
had never written it except for him' and expresses the hope that
it may convey to him her desire to urge him 'to those heights of
virtue which I myself despaired of reaching' (594–5; 139). By
obliging him to read this document (communicated to him once
more by indirect means, and referring to him largely in the
third person) she is extending her influence over him. Moreover,
an implied wish to annex him to her ambition can be read
into her making him read sentences she has written such as:
'Sometimes as I listen to him talking I seem to be watching
myself think. He explains me and discovers me to myself' (584;
124). Not only is Jérôme entrusted with maintaining the image
she had of him; his very being becomes a repository for her own
self-image. This is the culmination of a process whereby the

convolutions of their mutual emulation blur the very source of moral initiative in their relationship and in their separate personalities.[76] By thus placing Jérôme in the rôle of narratee to her text, Alissa gives renewed impetus to this dynamic. At the same time, as Zvi Lévy has pointed out, the impact of her 'look' on Jérôme is doubled by his reading of her diary; it affects him first, as we have seen, in his experience as protagonist of the story he tells; and then again subsequently in his experience as narrator, recounting the story, and reading and transcribing Alissa's writings in order to do so. The effect on Jérôme of this double subjection to Alissa's influence is to bring him to a state of psychological and judgemental inertia.[77] Thus the tone of his introduction is that of a man who has been reduced to numbness by his experiences: 'The story I am going to tell is one which took all my strength to live and over which I spent all my virtue' (495; 5). In a sense he is led to abdicate responsibility for his narrative in a manner similar to that in which he allowed Alissa to take the psychological initiative in their relationship. Hence the 'vous' to whom he addresses his story is someone to whom he can appeal to provide the responses he has ceased to be capable of evoking on his own behalf: 'No doubt you can easily imagine with what transports of joy I read this letter, with what sobs of love' (547; 74). At the same time, of course, the device permits him actually to indulge his inability to rise to the challenge of re-reading pages from Alissa's diary: 'I transcribe them without commentary. You will imagine well enough the reflections I made as I read, and the commotion of my heart, of which I could but give a too imperfect idea' (580; 119).

To this extent, then, the impression we have of Jérôme is of a man who barely understands what has happened to him, and who was reduced to watching helplessly while Alissa inexplicably slipped beyond his grasp. But we should perhaps beware of confusing a helplessness projected through the narration with a supposed helplessness in Jérôme's actual dealings with Alissa. His account of their final meeting illustrates the need to keep the distinction in mind. Jérôme desperately takes Alissa in his arms in an effort to persuade her to give up her project:

I crushed my kisses on her lips. An instant I held her

unresisting, as she half lay back against me; I saw her look
grow dim . . .   (577; 115)

It seems that Jérôme is on the point of swaying Alissa, of
compelling her to respond to the physical desire which is a
component in their love. But she cries, 'Have pity on us, my
friend!' and Jérôme adds:

Perhaps she said too: 'Don't be cowardly!' or perhaps it was
I who said it to myself; I cannot tell now . . .   (577; 115)

The avowed uncertainty of the source of this utterance
illustrates the blurring of moral responsibility their relationship engenders, while leaving open the possibility that the
phrase has been imagined after the event by Jérôme – perhaps
invented for the purposes of his narrative, to explain and
justify retrospectively his falling to his knees and beseeching
her: 'If you loved me so, why have you always repulsed me?'
He is clearly anxious to forestall disapproval on the part of
his reader; which indicates that he sees the possibility of
another point of view, rather different from the one he is at
pains to maintain. Later in the same sequence, he says, in
response as it were to alternative possibilities:

But to have kept her, to have forced the door, to have
entered by any means whatever into the house, which yet
would not have been shut against me – no, even today,
when I look back to the past and live it over again – no, it
was not possible to me, and whoever does not understand
me *as I say this*, has understood nothing of me *up to that
point*.   (579; 117)

The 'alors' and 'à présent' in the French text of this declaration
are revealing, as signs of two chronological levels which
Jérôme's narrative is seeking to bring into congruence. It
becomes clear that Jérôme has composed his account in order
to render intelligible his action at this point in the story. If
we cannot appreciate that it was impossible for him to behave
otherwise, then we have not understood the story 'jusqu'alors':
all the past events which preceded this incident contributed

to a temperament and an outlook which could only surrender the initiative in a crisis. On the other hand, there is a close connection between what made him behave as he did then and what causes him to speak as he does now: we can appreciate and sympathise with his motivation in the past only if we understand him 'à présent', as the man he is now, having reviewed his past experiences and having come to the conclusion that it all had to be. He has therefore been confirmed in his stance by re-telling the story, and hopes that the narrative will persuade the reader to agree and thereby vindicate Jérôme in his present outlook.

This conclusion to the main body of Jérôme's narrative is not, of course, the conclusion of the novel: but the force with which it is put cannot be divorced from the fact that it precedes Alissa's diary in our reading of *La Porte Etroite*. In many respects Jérôme's narrative and the conclusion it leads us to are a preface to Alissa's diary, and the novel as a whole derives great poignancy from the contrast between Jérôme's retrospective recreation and the story which Alissa has to tell. The former is structured in terms of both chronological and moral closure – Alissa is now dead, the story is over and done with, and the lesson it illustrates has been confirmed; but the latter, being told in diary form, conveys the immediacy of an existential present continuously open to alternative possibilities and from which no definitive conclusion can be drawn. It is true that Jérôme has composed his narrative after reading Alissa's diary, and therefore his version of events may be expected to have incorporated any insights the diary may offer; but the fact that we read this document after Jérôme's text means that the position of the narratee has been constructed in such a way as to offer the possibility of judging Jérôme's narrative in the light of Alissa's diary – giving to her testimony the inevitable extra weight it has by virtue of coming after the rest.[78]

The first point to make about Alissa's diary is that it offers the same kind of ironic perspectives as does Jérôme's account; – and details provided by Jérôme's narrative furnish essential correctives to Alissa's views, just as her text generates a perspective that intersects with his and shows up its short-comings. The most obvious case in point is, of course, the fact that Alissa makes no mention of the circumstances of her mother's infidelity, without some knowledge of which her reference to her conversation with her father about Lucile, and her own fear that her sensuality confirms her resemblance to this scandalous figure, lose most of their impact (585–6; 125–7). The sermon on 'la porte étroite' is not recalled explicitly, but we make the connection between it and Alissa's meditation on the biblical text (587; 129); and in so doing confirm the significance of both testimonies. Elsewhere, perhaps we can impute to Jérôme a deliberate intention in that the background to Juliette's marriage which he gives shows up Alissa's commentary in a dubious light: 'Juliette is happy; she says so, seems so; I have no right, no reason to doubt it' (583; 123). We know that Juliette did violence to her feelings in accepting the proposal of Tessières; we may be inclined to feel that Alissa is too ready to accept the surface appearance of happiness she now sees. 'Such happiness is so practical, so easily obtained', she comments, discounting the distress it has cost Juliette – and then, having established this somewhat specious fact, she will go on to use it as a justification for her own patronising dismissal of such allegedly facile happiness: 'Oh, Lord! . . . Teach me to put off my happiness, to place it as far away from me as Thou art'. This cross-reference does not redound to her credit. However, in her version of the meeting when Jérôme notices she has removed from her room a number of pictures and books, she makes quite plain how false is her outwardly tranquil denunciation of so much that they have previously held dear. Referring in particular to a 'torturing conversation in which I succeeded in feigning indifference – coldness, when my heart was fainting within me!' (590; 132), she writes of her 'shameful, foolish words' on Pascal: all this in an effort to turn Jérôme's love away from herself and direct it towards God. In the light of this revelation we can appreciate the tragedy of Jérôme's having been taken in to the extent of feeling his heart rent by her words and crying in horror 'Alissa! why do you tear off your wings?' when he heard her voice these dismissive views on Pascal (568–71; 104–7). Typically, he is incapable of responding as he would wish: 'Perhaps my tears would have vanquished her; but I remained without saying a word', he says – which is all the more ironic as elsewhere in her diary Alissa says: 'Poor Jérôme! If he only knew that sometimes he would have but a single sign to make, and that sometimes I wait for him to make it . . .' (586; 127). A similar misunderstanding is evident in Jérôme's assertion, 'I do not think that Alissa . . . did anything for my sake or for me, though all my efforts were only for her. Everything in her unaffected and artless soul was of the most natural beauty' (507; 21). The truth is, as Alissa confesses, 'My virtue is all only to please him' (584; 124). Another passage of Alissa's diary which highlights Jérôme's lack of insight as well as his consequent failure to rise to the occasion concerns an evening when, as he reads over her shoulder, Jérôme's closeness inspires such a sensual arousal in Alissa that she has to go into another room to regain her composure (585–6; 126–7). Not the least significant aspect of this episode is that no trace of it occurs in Jérôme's narrative. Finally, the scene of their last leave-taking, which we have seen Jérôme striving to write up in a form vindicating his failure to overcome Alissa's resistance in spite of her own weakness, takes on renewed poignancy from details made available in Alissa's account. Whereas Jérôme is telling himself he could never force open the door behind which he remained sobbing after Alissa shut it, we learn that she later returned and opened it in the hope that he might still be there, or might have come back again (592–3; 136).

It is worth noting that while this device of intersecting narratives can tend to make us view each version of events with a critical, if not sceptical eye – and raises doubts about the veracity of narrative itself – it also furnishes what we may call a 'reality effect', achieving verisimilitude by apparently confirming that events referred to did actually take place even though interpretations or perspectives may differ. The novel acquires something of the texture of reality as each text corroborates the other: for instance we recognise in Alissa's diary a version of the quotation 'God having provided some better thing for us' (587; 128) which Jérôme reports her as having said to him (578; 116). Similarly, we may see her rehearsing a principle she is intent on impressing upon Jérôme when she writes in her diary, 'No, Jerome, no, it is not after a future recompense that our virtue is striving' (585; 125), since she will use very similar words later – in a conversation which, in fact, we have already read in Jérôme's narrative (570; 105). On the one hand, then, *La Porte Etroite* confirms the point illustrated by *L'Immoraliste* that the relationship between teller and tale is essential to a proper understanding of narrative. On the other hand, however, though the reality behind any given monologue may remain distanced and problematical, distorted by the narrator's temperamental idiosyncrasies, the particular narrative technique used in *La Porte Etroite* gives a new dimension to Gide's invitation to the reader to re-establish the facts behind his characters' depositions. The development of devices for producing such effects will be very much in evidence in Gide's subsequent works.

La Symphonie Pastorale (The Pastoral Symphony)

La Symphonie Pastorale is a deceptively simple work, and Gide himself was known to rank it less highly than others of his fictions. But it contains complexities of theme and technique which have been overlooked by many critics, and it repays detailed scrutiny. The text is in two parts, comprising a diary composed of two notebooks in which a pastor tells the story of his involvement with Gertrude, a blind orphan girl to whom he has given a home. The fact that we are reading a diary is signalled very clearly; the novel begins with a date, '10 février 189.' (877), and the text continues to be dated as a diary. The first notebook, for example, contains seven entries, running from 10 February to 12 March. This feature we may view as an invitation to consider what we read as a chronicle of a month in the life of the diarist, just as the dates in Alissa's diary enable us to locate the events she writes of in relation to the chronology of Jérôme's account. The striking fact about the pastor's diary, however, is that to begin with it makes very little direct reference to current events, apart from initial allusions to the snow which prevents him from going out on his rounds and leaves him with the leisure to write. The first notebook is made up of a retrospective account in which the pastor has decided, as he puts it, to 'think over the past and set down how I came to take charge of Gertrude' (877; 9). It presents a narrative starting some two and a half years previously and ending in the August of the preceding year, approximately six months before the date on which the pastor begins to write. We can reconstitute the chronology of Gertrude's stay at the pastor's house, from his narrative; but the chronology of events which occur as he writes is indicated only as a succession of dates heading each 'chapter' of his retrospective story. The journal frame foregrounds what is referred to in linguistic terms as the 'discursive situation',[79] and invites speculation as to current events occurring while the pastor writes; but the one thing we expect of a diary is tellingly absent. There is thus an enigma about this text, arising from the very special hybrid form which the narrative assumes: clearly there must be a link between the present during which the pastor writes and the past of which he writes.[80] We have seen that the precise status of narration in relation to story is a crucial problem in Gide's first-person narratives; in *La Symphonie Pastorale* the problem takes on a fascinating new dimension.

Amélie, the pastor's wife, explodes into indignation on seeing her husband bring back to the house the vermin-infested 'lump of flesh' (880; 12) he has found but which she will have to see to in the first instance; there are 'enough of us in the house already' (882; 15), she protests. What is noticeable in the evocation of this dispute is that it shows the pastor slipping from the past into the present, as he constantly does when commenting on his family. He writes, 'As always happens when we *are about to have a disagreement*, I began by telling the children . . . to leave the room' (880; 13). Elsewhere he points out that except for his daughter Charlotte, all his children 'have been well trained by their mother' (880; 13). The emphasis here falls not on how they were at the time of the events he is writing about, but on the present – the period during which he is writing. The pastor's wife, the woman who has had such an influence on their children's behaviour, is presented in a paragraph which breaks into the past-tense narrative of his return home with the blind waif to establish a similarly ambiguous impression of two different levels of chronology at work:

> My wife is a garden of all the virtues; and in the times of
> trouble we have sometimes gone through I have never for
> an instant had cause to doubt the stuff of which her heart
> is made; but it does not do to take her natural charity by
> surprise. She is an orderly person, careful neither to go
> beyond nor to fall short of her duty. Even her charity is
> measured, as though love were not an inexhaustible treasure.
> That is the only point on which we differ . . .   (880; 13)

This passage precedes the pastor's presentation of Amélie's
somewhat brutal reaction on seeing Gertrude arrive among
them; it is offered ostensibly as an explanation and extenuation
of what the reader might expect to find unsympathetic in her
behaviour. But the even-handedness of the treatment barely
conceals the strain which the pastor undergoes in compiling
this damning dossier of faint praise. The *points de suspension* in
the final line also betray a continuing 'point de conteste'.
While 'forcing himself' to be frank about events on his return
home – 'I have too much regard for the truth to pass over in
silence the unpleasant welcome I had to encounter on my
return home' (880; 13), he writes – and appearing to excuse
Amélie's behaviour by presenting explanations for it, the
pastor is in fact subtly pre-empting our judgement and
discrediting her.[81] When Amélie begins to 'protest that she
had absolutely nothing to say', her husband adds with more
than a hint of resentment: 'which is her usual prelude to the
lengthiest explanations' (882; 15). Later the pastor sourly
evokes 'her habit of letting people do things and of reserving
to herself the right to blame them afterwards' (897; 32). Such
repeated allusions to habitual patterns in domestic relations
clearly signal an accumulation of particular disputes. The
pastor's ostensibly retrospective narrative visibly frames a
situation which the narrator is in the process of living through
as he writes about the past. On occasion, indeed, he abandons
his chronicle in favour of a straightforward diatribe, in the
present tense, against his wife; on 8 March he writes in his
notebook: 'The only pleasure I can give Amélie is to refrain
from doing the things she dislikes . . . The degree to which
she has already narrowed my life is a thing she cannot realize'
(898; 33).

This novel contains a subtle psychological analysis of a married couple going through a difficult stage in their relationship. It is deft and all the more telling because it is presented implicitly, as the underside of what is supposed to be the main substance of the text: the story of the education of the blind girl. The book does signal the theme, however, for the pastor observes 'how two people who love one another and live practically the same life can yet remain (or become) as much of an enigma to each other as if they lived behind stone walls' (905; 42). But the equivocation of 'remain (or become)' merits further comment. We cannot properly assess the tensions in this marriage without some information as to what they stem from. Such an explanation would ordinarily be the stuff of a narrative, which puts events together in a linear succession of cause and effect relationships to demonstrate how a certain outcome arises as a consequence of certain previous events. However, the pastor's narrative seeks to skirt round the (hi)story of his life with Amélie by embedding the images of his wife as she appears to him today within his account of events which date back two and a half years. Have he and his wife been strangers to each other from the start and *remained* that way – or have they *become* estranged? Is there a story in their relationship, or is it merely the prolongation of an initial unsatisfactory state of affairs? To answer these questions we need to know more about the actual nature of the present which lies behind the narrative; we also need to establish what it is that connects the past of the narrator's story to the present that is manifestly reflected in it. If we can fill in these gaps we may then, for example, be able to explain an outburst like that of 8 March, when the pastor is ostensibly speaking of a concert in Neuchâtel which took place almost two years beforehand and could hardly account on its own for the vehemence of the pastor's attack on Amélie.

We can extract from the first notebook some illuminating clues to the present state of affairs concerning the protagonists. When the pastor refers to the music lessons he tried to give Gertrude, he speaks of 'the little harmonium of our chapel which is usually played by Mlle de la M . . . , with whom Gertrude is at present staying' (900; 36). So at present Gertrude is no longer living in the pastor's house; but we have

to read a little further before discovering that this is a result
of a clash between the pastor and his son Jacques. The young
man has fallen in love with Gertrude, and consequently the
pastor, in a fit of jealousy, has sent Gertrude to live with Mlle
de la M . . . while forcing his son to renounce his hopes of
marrying her as well as obliging him to leave home for the
rest of the holidays before returning to college in Lausanne.
Moreover, all this took place in the August preceding the
pastor's decision, taken on 10 February, to set down his
account. But this is not the whole picture; for the pastor's
narrative, which aims to be a retrospective chronicle, cannot
in fact recapitulate the whole story since the events he is
writing of have not yet reached a conclusion at the moment
when he starts to write.[82] Unlike Michel and Jérôme, who
have reached the end of their story before recounting it, the
pastor is still profoundly implicated in an unresolved conflict
of interests at the point when he begins to narrate.[83]

It is not until the beginning of his second notebook that the
pastor sketches in the current life of the principal characters.[84]
Here he recalls that since the previous autumn Gertrude has
been living with Mlle de la M . . . , 'a profoundly religious
woman', who is providing board and lodging for three other
young blind girls as well as the pastor's protégée. It is clear
that this charitable lady is very well off, having the wherewithal
to cater for the needs of her guests 'without putting herself
out in any way' (919; 58) – she is evidently not having to run
a household on a pastor's stipend, like Amélie. It emerges
from these pages that the pastor has developed a taste for the
ambience which prevails in this tranquil house: and as we
read them, it becomes obvious that he is actually inviting us
to make comparisons, point for point, to the detriment of his
own home. He could hardly be more systematic – nor more
devious, in omitting to indicate that this is what he is doing.
Thus there are the same number of people in each household,
though the balance between burdens and helpers differs
significantly: here, Charlotte, Sarah, Gaspard and the baby
Claude (Jacques is away at college much of the time); there
three young blind girls and Gertrude. Mlle de la M . . . has
three servants who 'help her with the greatest devotion and
save her all fatigue' (919; 58), while Amélie has to endure the

old, crotchety and none too competent Rosalie who 'invariably
wants her own way' (918; 57) – to say nothing of an irritable
husband whose idea of helping her to cope with a teething
child is to advise her to let it 'howl . . . to his heart's content
when I am not there' (918; 57). The two homes are parallel
in other respects, but his own is on all points the negative of
'La Grange'. Here the children dance gracefully (920; 59),
there they are 'horribly unruly' (918; 57). Mlle de la M. . . is
'a profoundly religious *soul who* seems hardly to belong to this
earth or to live for anything but love' (919; 58); while
'everything in Amélie's neighbourhood becomes gloomy and
morose . . . her soul gives out black rays' (917; 57). Whereas
members of his family are uninterested in spiritual matters,
poetry or reading, and offer no 'conversation . . . in which I
have any inclination to take part' (918; 58), the inhabitants
of 'La Grange' play music, charm him with their 'way of
speaking' and listen to him reading Lamartine and Hugo
(919; 59). The critique of marital relations, which as we have
seen is an important theme in the novel, here joins forces with
another key theme, that of the contrast and conflict between
the real and the ideal. The pastor visits 'La Grange' regularly,
he tells us: 'How restful, how comforting I find its warm
friendly atmosphere every time I re-enter the Grange, and
how much I miss it if I am obliged to let two or three days
pass without going there' (919; 58). Clearly, the vision of this
ideal family underlies and motivates much of the criticism the
pastor levels at his own family in the first notebook.

These details which point to the present state of the
narrator's mind as he writes are confirmed and complemented
by what we find if we examine another aspect of the narrative.
The events chronicled in the first notebook take us up to the
previous autumn when, as we have seen, Gertrude went to
live with Mlle de la M. . . . The pastor began writing on 10
February; which leaves some six months unaccounted for.
This chronological gap spans an essential period since what
immediately precedes the narration may be assumed to have
the greatest impact on how the pastor writes. Indeed, it may
explain why it was on 10 February that the pastor's diary-
narrative began, rather than in the previous autumn when
Gertrude left his house, for example. The absence in the first

notebook of any direct indication on this point was deliberately arranged by Gide when he suppressed from the beginning of the original manuscript a paragraph which would have clarified matters by alluding to the blind girl's change of accommodation before the start of her story.[85] The aim was evidently to oblige the reader to re-establish the missing details. We can do so by considering once more the start of the second notebook, where the pastor writes, 'Gertrude, as had been arranged, went to stay at Mlle Louise's, where I visited her every day' (913; 51). A few pages later he adds: 'And I have also fallen into the habit *since the* autumn – encouraged by the shortness of the days – of taking tea at Mlle de la M. . .'s whenever my rounds permit it, that is whenever I can get back early enough' (919; 58). Thus, since the previous autumn he has been a regular visitor at 'La Grange': this further confirms our interpretation of his critical comments about his own home in the first notebook. Other remarks cast additional light on matters. 'When, after a harassing day of toil – visits to the sick, the poor, the afflicted – I come in at nightfall, tired out and with a heart longing for rest, affection, warmth, it is to find, more often than not, worries, recriminations and quarrels, which I dread a thousand times more than the cold, the wind and the rain out of doors' (917–18; 57). If 'the shortness of the days' became the signal for the pastor to call in at 'La Grange', we may well imagine that Amélie would not be waiting with endearments when her husband returned to his own home after dark. Our suspicions are borne out on the following page: 'How sweet it is, when I can find the time, to linger in their company', notes the pastor a propos of Mlle de la M. . .'s lodgers (919; 59), having just stated how unbearable he finds it if he has to go two or three days without calling in on them. If the pastor complains about the reception he gets on his return home, this is hardly surprising since he has formed the habit of spending as much time away from it as he can, regularly coming in late after taking tea with Mlle de la M. . . in the company of Gertrude. This state of affairs has been going on for six months at the start of the first notebook and is to be perceived in the background throughout the pastor's narration, that is to say from 10 February to 20 May, the date when Gertrude enters hospital for the fateful operation which will restore her sight. Such then is the 'discursive situation' which precedes and accompanies the unfolding of this narrative.[86] It is crucial to appreciate this dimension of the text if we are to understand it fully. Even the opening paragraphs take on a specific sense if we read them from this angle:

> The snow has been falling continuously for the last three days and all the roads are blocked. It has been impossible for me to go to R. . .
>
> . . .
>
> I will take advantage of the leisure this enforced confinement affords me to think over the past and to set down how I came to take charge of Gertrude.

It is not for nothing that his thoughts turn to Gertrude. He is deprived of the pleasure of seeing her since, being prevented by the snow from going out on his rounds, he finds himself by the same token unable to drop in on her on his way home.[87] The second entry in his diary-narrative also begins by mentioning the snow which by this time prevents the pastor from leaving his house except by the washhouse; we may assume that at this point he will be unable to visit Gertrude even to continue with her religious education. Once more he remarks, 'I take advantage of it to go on with the tale I began yesterday' (884; 18). There are grounds for supposing, therefore, that the dates which succeed each other in the first notebook mark the stages in the writing of a narrative which the pastor pursues more or less continuously while he is housebound (he will later state that he finds his family's company so tedious that he has become accustomed to withdrawing into his study 'more and more often' (919; 58)). After 29 February he appears to set aside his notebook, which resumes on 8 March: but this is when he launches into a vigorous attack on Amélie, unjustified by anything in his narrative, whose thread he picks up again immediately afterwards.[88] We may imagine that this resumption of his writing is motivated chiefly by a dispute between the pastor and his wife some time on 8 March. Perhaps, too, a quarrel between them has revived the pastor's memory of the row precipitated by his taking Gertrude to Neuchâtel, which was the point his story had reached; he resumes his account with a half-guilty recollection which he turns into a further criticism of his wife's customary irritating behaviour:

> I must confess that I entirely forgot, that afternoon at Neuchâtel, to go and pay our haberdasher's bill and to bring her back some reels of cotton she wanted. But I was more vexed with myself for this than she could have been . . . I should even have been glad if she had reproached me with it . . . But, as often happens, the imaginary grievance outweighed the definite charge. Ah! how beautiful life would be and how bearable our wretchedness if we were content with real evils, without opening the doors to the phantoms and monsters of our imagination. (898; 34)

Whatever may be the truth of the matter, the imbrication of present and past resentment is evident in passages of this kind, underlining the need to balance the present tense of the narration against the past of the narrative.

By re-establishing the complex chronology of *La Symphonie Pastorale*, we become capable of appreciating the true value of remarks such as those the pastor makes about his children. He is pleased to evoke them in the company of Gertrude 'whom they take charge of, while she at the same time takes charge of them. (It is a pleasure for me to note that Charlotte is particularly attentive to her)' (905; 42). These present-tense remarks, written on 10 March when Gertrude is no longer living with the pastor's family, presumably reflect events on one of the Sunday outings the pastor will later allude to: 'Every Sunday she comes to lunch with us; my children are delighted to see her . . . After lunch, the whole family goes back with Gertrude to the Grange and has tea there. It is a treat for my children and Louise enjoys spoiling them and loading them with cakes and sweetmeats.' (920; 59–60). Now, according to the calendar indicated by the diary, 10 February is a Sunday, and the year in question is a Leap Year: this means that 10 March is a Monday, so it is quite plausible for the pastor to be noting the children's behaviour on the previous day's treat. Similarly, 8 March, the date of the apparently

unmotivated outburst against Amélie, is a Saturday, with a
visit from Gertrude and a trip to 'La Grange' in the offing the
following day. We later learn from the pastor that on
Gertrude's visits 'Amélie is not too irritable and we get through
the meal without a hitch' (920; 59); but it is understandable
that tension between her and her husband should mount on
these occasions – and presumably on the preceding day. This
perhaps is the specific pretext for a dispute and an explanation
for the vehemence of the pastor's remarks noted in his diary
on 8 March. Moreover, since the day when the pastor begins
his diary-narrative is also a Sunday, this would further account
for the special frustration he feels at being kept indoors by the
snow – a frustration which prompts him to write about
Gertrude as compensation for being deprived of her company.
And in this first chapter of his narrative he recalls how the
children reacted to Gertrude's first arrival among them – an
event which is bound to suggest parallels in his mind with the
customary Sunday visit which is now the only occasion when
the whole family sees her and which, as he writes, he is
experiencing the lack of. Hence his remarks about his 'chère
petite Charlotte' showing her delight at the new arrival
(880; 13) are probably not unconnected with his approving
comments on her, already quoted (905; 42). But at the end of
this first chapter, his view of his children changes brusquely:
'One thinks them tender-hearted, when really they are only
coaxing and wheedling one' (884; 18). We may speculate
that this has something to do with their behaviour on the
visits to 'La Grange' which usually conclude a Sunday, and
in the course of which they are spoilt by Mlle de la M. . . :
'It is a treat for my children and Louise enjoys spoiling them
and loading them with cakes and sweetmeats' (920; 59–60).
Moreover, in the same sentence as that in which he denounces
in general his children's shortcomings, he adduces the specific
example of 'My big boy Jacques, nowadays so distant and
reserved' (884; 18). At this point, the alert reader, practised
in the stereoscopic vision required by the text, will remember –
or anticipate – the sacrifice and quite literal distance to which
Jacques has been subjected six months before his father writes
these words.

The remarkable thoroughness and coordination with which

the text facilitates the establishment of this network of chronological interconnections shows Gide moving well beyond the
already subtle exploitation of intersecting monologues in *La
Porte Etroite*. The form of *La Symphonie Pastorale* mimics the
very texture of temporal reality, producing an effect of depth
which prompts the reader to look beyond the pastor's words,
beyond the narrative order he imposes on the events he
depicts, to re-establish a multi-dimensional version of the facts
represented. Such speculation about literary works, which are
after all only words on paper and whose characters have no
existence beyond the page, has become highly suspect in
modern times, especially since a celebrated critical polemic
denounced those whose contribution to literary appreciation
was to ask questions like 'How many children had Lady
Macbeth?'[89] But the impulse to search for such interconnections as we have highlighted is as much an effect of this
particular text as any other feature of reading; and even in
novels which seek to deny access to a consistent chronology
in the interest of subverting conventional expectations, the
very process of reading consists of responses to what linguisti-
cians call 'effects of sense' provided by the text. One of these
'effects of sense' is, precisely, the construction of a fictive
referent; in this case, the actual – though imaginary – events
the fictional pastor has lived through, is experiencing and
is retracing in his narrative. Indeed, Gide's approach to
establishing the fact that narrative is an artificial and unreliable representation of reality is, paradoxically, to enable us,
as he does in *La Symphonie Pastorale*, to grasp a fictional reality
against which we can measure the pastor's version of it. So
that we must, while bearing in mind the fictional status of
both components in the exercise, pursue events beyond the
page of the pastor's account in order to set them alongside
what he says of them. Thus equipped with an appropriate
knowledge of this extra dimension, we can appreciate the
duplicity with which the pastor claims to be digressing from
his main purpose and embarking on an anecdote of secondary
importance as he announces: 'I wish to relate a small circumstance which is connected with music' (899; 35–6). The
incident which he sets out in this casual manner to relate is
very far from being a 'small circumstance' and is only

tangentially to do with music: it concerns, in fact, his discovery of Jacques' love for Gertrude. By prefacing this incident with the remark quoted, the pastor enables us to catch him out as he distorts the facts in his narrative. What he appears to be attempting is to forestall or undo the inevitable cause and effect relation whereby the rivalry between father and son will bring about – has already brought about – disruption and disaffection within the family. This ploy may be not unconnected with the equivocation we mentioned earlier in references to the history of marriage – of the pastor's marriage in particular. Were Amélie and the pastor always thus, or did they become strangers to each other? Put another way – and this is more pertinent to the plot of the narrative, of course – was Gertrude a cause or an effect of the estrangement between the married couple? W. D. Wilson sees it as testimony to the acuteness of Gide's grasp of human psychology that we cannot decide which.[90] Psychoanalysis is indeed familiar with the phenomenon whereby a fantasy of trauma is projected into a distant childhood past to explain and justify after the event a neurosis occurring in later life: the fact that the one comes after the other in terms of narrative chronology is sufficient to confer the authority of a cause on what is to all intents and purposes an effect.[91] It is in the pastor's interest to imply that Amélie's unpleasantness drove him into the arms of Gertrude; hence the significance of his attempts to predispose the reader against her in his narrative. Hence, too, the care with which he builds up an unsympathetic portrait of her before developing the attractive features of Gertrude. The pastor is exploiting the confusion between chronology and the logic of cause and effect that occurs in narrative, suggesting that what came first – acquaintance with Amélie's character – is a *cause* of what came afterwards – infatuation with Gertrude.[92] But the reader who fully appreciates the 'backwards causality' which affects a protagonist composing a first-person explanatory account after the event may sense that in fact the implied cause and effect relationship may be reversed. There are suggestions of this in the latter part of the narrative, in particular when, contrary to almost all he has said about her up to then, the pastor writes of Amélie as 'the angel of those early times, who smiled encouragement on every high-minded

impulse of my heart, who I dreamt would be the sharer of my
every hope and fear, and whom I looked on as my guide and
leader along the path to Heaven' (918; 57–8). It is true that
he adds immediately 'or did love blind me in those days? . . .':
to which we may be tempted to respond that that is what is
happening at present, as he tries to deny that he ever really
knew Amélie.

Such are the all-pervading effects of the complex chronological interactions in *La Symphonie Pastorale* that consideration of
essential themes must take account of them too. Religious
questions, central to the narrative, require to be placed in the
correct temporal perspective. In the second notebook the
pastor says: 'Gertrude's religious instruction has led me to re-
read the Gospels with a fresh eye' (913; 52), but this religious
education has been going on from an early stage in their
relationship, though it has evidently taken a new turn since
she moved from his house to 'La Grange' (it is the pastor's
chief pretext for seeing so much of her there: 907; 44. 913;
51). Hence the six months preceding his diary, and the month
during which he writes the first notebook, are characterised
by the dubious spiritual fervour of a man who is in love with
his pupil. Consequently, the basic mental shift in relation to
religious doctrine is already well advanced as he writes the
first notebook. This can be perceived, again, in the way he
tends to drop the past tense of narrative when noting his
religious observations. On 8 March, after railing against
Amélie's limitations in a passage whose relevance to the
present in which he writes we have already discussed at length,
he expostulates, 'Ah! how beautiful life would be and how
bearable our wretchedness if we were content with real evils,
without opening the doors to the phantoms and monsters of
our imagination . . . But I am straying here into observations
that would do better as the subject of a sermon – Luke xii.
29: "Neither be ye of doubtful mind" ' (898; 34). In the French
text the pastor refers erroneously to Matthew xii. 29 whereas
the passage he has in mind is actually Matthew vi. 25; but
the verse he quotes is in fact from a corresponding section of
Luke's Gospel, as Dorothy Bussy indicates by giving the
correct reference in her English translation. What both passages have in common, however, is that they hinge on

injunctions to 'Consider the lilies of the field, how they grow':
and these words have already been the subject of at least one
lesson and a conversation with Gertrude during the previous
autumn – to which the pastor alludes in his chronicle dated
12 March (909; 46–7). They embody a key principle of the
doctrine the pastor has elaborated in the inspiring company
of Gertrude, in order to justify his brushing aside his responsi-
bilities to his family. Small wonder then that the reference
comes so readily into his mind when he has failed to carry
out a domestic errand. There is some evidence that the pastor
had a tendency to bend the scriptures for self-justification
even before undertaking Gertude's religious instruction: he
tells how he invoked the parable of the lost sheep to counter
Amélie's horrified reaction when he first brought home the
verminous foundling (881; 14) – notwithstanding his declaration that 'I never think it becoming to allege the authority
of the Holy Book as an excuse for my conduct' (882; 15). But
his later musings on this and on the parable of the prodigal
son, couched in the present tense, refer rather more obviously
to continuing friction on the subject of the pastor's responsibilit-
ies than to a specific dispute which occurred more than two
years previously: 'It has often been my experience that the
parable of the lost sheep is one of the most difficult of
acceptance for certain people' (889; 23. Cf.897; 33). Similarly,
and again running counter to the ostensibly retrospective
nature of the narrative, the pastor's criticisms of his wife's
unimaginative views on the Gospels – 'Amélie will not admit
that there can be anything unreasonable or super-reasonable
in the teaching of the Gospel' (881; 14) – manifestly derive
from recent or concurrent readings of the Gospels influenced
by his love for Gertrude.

It is sometimes asserted, chiefly in the context of an
argument seeking to establish distinctions between the tone
and characteristics of each of the pastor's two notebooks, that
in the first events are remote from him and his delusion is
largely emotional, whereas in the second notebook, as we shall
see, events are catching up on him and he becomes involved
in a series of moral or theological delusions.[93] It is true that
there is a contrast between certain aspects of the two notebooks;
but distortion of religious doctrine is present in both – the

difference lies in the nature of the factors determining each.
We have seen that in the first notebook the narrator repeatedly
invokes the parable of the lost sheep and that of the prodigal
son: both these, of course, serve to justify his comparative
neglect of his own children while he spends so much time with
Gertrude. Another recurrent and related preoccupation in the
first notebook – arising, as we have seen, both from the events
it chronicles and from the experiences the pastor is living
through as he writes it – is the evident strain on his domestic
relations brought about first by the arrival of this extra child
to feed and clothe and then by the increased importance she
assumes in the pastor's emotional life. It is plain that Amélie
is concerned about the threat to their family life presented by
this newcomer. She expresses her anxiety repeatedly, as her
husband indicates: 'Whenever I was occupied with Gertrude,
she managed to make out that I was wanted at that moment
for someone or something else, and that I was giving her time
that ought to have been given to others' (889; 23). Such
repeated remonstrations determine the pastor's portrayal of
his wife in terms of 'what the material cares of life have made
her – I was going to say the *cultivation* of the cares of life, for
Amélie certainly does cultivate them' (918; 57). Hence when
he invokes religion in the first notebook it is as a counter to
what he sees as Amélie's petty-mindedness. He is saying more
than he realises, however, when he accuses her of viewing
Christianity as 'the domestication of our instincts' (898; 34);
for indeed Amélie's interest lies in protecting her domestic
situation against the pastor's wayward instincts. But his
religion chiefly consists at this stage, as we have seen, of the
doctrine he has culled from Matthew, vi, 25–34: 'Take no
thought for your life . . . Consider the lilies of the field, how
they grow; they toil not, neither do they spin . . . Take
therefore no thought for the morrow'. Besides noting his
proposed sermon on this theme (898; 34), his narrative reports
how Gertrude quotes from the same biblical source, recalling
'You have often told me that what this world most needs is
confidence and love' (909–10; 46). He tries to persuade
Amélie to subscribe to such a belief, expressing his disappointment when she 'will have none of it', and laments
'Everything she sees causes her uneasiness and distress' (917;

56) – once again viewing as a regrettable flaw in her religious sensibilities what it is obvious to the reader is a bitter appraisal on her part of what her life has come to as a result of her husband's insouciance.

Thus we can see throughout *La Symphonie Pastorale* that the book illustrates a recurrent feature of Gide's portrayal of ideas: a moral, religious or other intellectual doctrine is a function of the conscious or unconscious needs of the individual. As such it is subject to change and is dictated by the events an individual encounters. For example, even in his carefree phase the pastor is not averse to invoking the principle of authority, calling it an appeal to conscience, when he wishes to rid himself of a rival by compelling Jacques to renounce his love for Gertrude (903–5; 40–1).[94] Hence when the pastor moves on to the theological arguments of the second notebook, the mechanism of delusion does not change; but of course the circumstances have changed.

A critical incident occurs between the first and second notebook: the pastor reads what he has written so far, and it dawns on him that he has been in love with Gertrude all along. Whether or not this belated realisation is plausible either in terms of psychological verisimilitude or chronological consistency, it might be expected to produce drastic changes in the pastor's outlook.[95] It is possible to argue, however, that it does not do so. Such modifications as may be seen to occur in his views are actually responses to provocations from outside: his family refuse to take communion, Jacques reveals that he has converted to Catholicism and criticises his father's religious principles, Doctor Martins offers the prospect of an operation which will restore Gertrude's sight, and Gertrude herself asks difficult questions about the relationship between the love they feel for each other and that which is preached in the Gospels. If we acknowledge this point, we grasp the true implications of Gide's psychological analysis. The pastor is quite clear, at the start of the second notebook, on the nature and the workings of the self-delusion which he has fallen prey to:

The fact is that I would not then allow that any love outside marriage could be permissible, nor at the same time would

I allow that there could be anything whatever forbidden in
the feeling that drew me so passionately to Gertrude . . . –
and so I made a moral obligation, a duty of what was really
a passionate inclination.   (913; 50)

Later, when commenting on Jacques' authoritarian stance, he
will attribute its emergence to the violence the young man has
had to do to his own feelings concerning Gertrude, and will
quote La Rochefoucauld to the effect that 'the mind is often
the dupe of the heart' (916; 55). What La Rochefoucauld
actually wrote is that 'l'esprit est *toujours* la dupe du coeur'
(the mind is *always* the dupe of the heart); and this is the
principle which rebounds on the pastor. For no amount of
lucidity about his own case, or intellectual insight into the
same phenomena as they affect others, can make any difference
to the instincts which drive him. Having exhaustively diag-
nosed his errors, he will proceed to compound them through
his responses to the circumstances he finds himself in.

An important element in the second notebook, highlighted
in a pioneering article by John Cruickshank, is that the time-
gap between what the pastor is writing about and the moment
at which he is writing has narrowed considerably since the
start of his account. From two and a half years, it is reduced
to a fortnight in the entry dated 25 April. It will diminish to
zero in the course of the second notebook, which thereby
acquires the characteristics of a conventional diary.[96] It does,
however, have the distinguishing feature of the exceptional
momentum which background incidents have acquired by
this time, so that as the diarist writes he is under great pressure
from events which are advancing outside his control. As we
have seen, it was an illusion to suppose that the retrospective
narration of the first notebook was an instance of discourse
setting down a pre-existing story which had already taken
place and reached a denouement. Similarly, though the second
notebook is more nearly a conventional diary, the open,
unpredictable future we normally associate with such a form
is belied in fact by the denouement rapidly closing in on the
diarist.[97] This gives a particular urgency to his reflections, and
may perhaps help explain why he does not act on his new-
found self-awareness – by this time he cannot reverse the

drama he has set in train. As a result we read a rapid
succession of rationalisations, drawing on biblical texts, for
the pastor's urge to indulge his attraction to Gertrude in the
face of rebukes from Jacques (916–7; 54–6); while at the same
time he seeks to fend off the prospect of her regaining her
sight – or even acquiring knowledge of life's bleaker aspects,
which he has kept from her – by adducing further biblical
authority for the alleged benefits of blindness ('If ye were
blind ye should have no sin', 915; 53). Another key motif in
his self-interested distortions of religion is his exploitation of
the ambiguity of biblical injunctions concerning love. From
the outset he portrays himself as bringing out of the night 'her
sweet and pious soul for no other end but adoration and love'
(877; 9). When Gertrude first says to him, 'C'est vous que
j'aime', he seeks to hide his confusion by intoning: 'It's never
in love that the wrong lies' (911; 48), thereby enlisting
Christian charity (*agape*) as a disguise for sexual attraction
(*eros*).[98] However, when on 17 May Gertrude raises the
question of the sexual nature of their attraction for each other,
this arouses in him an almost irresistible and blatantly erotic
desire: 'I felt as if the smallest pebble in the path might send
us both rolling to the ground' (923; 63).[99] He writes down his
account of this conversation on 18 May (significantly this is
the only Sunday on which he does any writing apart from the
initial occasion when he was snowed in), and on 19 May
Martins confirms the possibility of restoring Gertrude's sight
by means of surgery. At this point the pastor is on the horns
of a dilemma his resolution of which can be put very crudely,
though not inaccurately, as this: he delays telling her the news
until after he has gratified his desires, entering her bedroom
at 'La Grange' in the night of 19 May (924; 63). Thus
his theological, pedagogical and poetic pretensions stand
condemned by the explicit emergence of the underlying
impulses they have been shown to serve and by the hypocrisy
for which they were vehicles.

Gertrude's death that follows from her throwing herself into
the river marks the complete collapse of the Utopian vision
he had been constructing for them both and which had come
to supplant reality.[100] Their poetic idyll of nature – exemplified
in Gertrude's idealised description of the alpine meadows

(909–10; 46–8) – is revealed as a poor compensation for the real thing he would have denied her, 'a world more beautiful than I had ever dreamt it could be' (928–9; 69). The theology of innocence built on ignorance of sin is exploded when she reads Saint Paul (929; 69); Gertrude's moral innocence is shown to have been a sham when she sees reflected in Amélie's face the suffering and unhappiness she has caused (929; 68). Moreover, the harmony that the pastor had taught her existed between the moral and physical universes is also unmasked as an illusion when she realises that the face she loved and imagined was the pastor's actually belongs to his son. Manifold structural ironies reinforce our sense of the pastor's intellectual bankruptcy. Two *mises en abyme* and a central metaphor provide this dimension. The *Pastoral Symphony* which left Gertrude '*drowned* in ecstasy', especially the 'scene on the bank of a stream' (895; 30) finds its counterpart in their own pastoral idyll, which plays itself out to its tragic denouement with Gertrude literally drowning in the stream. Doctor Martins' reference to *The Cricket on the Hearth*, a story which in several particulars anticipates that of Gertrude, prompted the pastor to express his disapproval of a 'deception . . . thank Heaven, I shall not have to make use of . . . with Gertrude' (888; 22): nonetheless, he *has* lied to Gertrude, like Caleb Plummer to his blind daughter Bertha in the Dickens story, with disastrous consequences. And above all, of course, in this novel whose first title was *L'Aveugle* (*JI*, 300; *J1*, 26: 30 May 1910), we become aware that the spiritual blindness of the pastor has implications and consequences far more distressing than the physical blindness of his charge. This man loses both his son and his adoptive daughter, betrays his family and his cloth: there is a particularly bleak irony in the book's closing lines, which show him kneeling before Amélie while she intones 'Our Father' (930; 71).

However, just as the pastor's ideas are in a sense irrelevant to the crude facts of his behaviour, so, as Ireland puts it, the disaster that finally befalls him 'argues nothing against the values of which he is the unhappy champion'.[101] For although *La Symphonie Pastorale* operates the same ironic undermining of the narrator-protagonist as occurs in the other *récits*, we see that it is his personal shortcomings – above all his hypocrisy –

which determine the outcome; his liberal views on religion and morality, in another context, have much to commend them – particularly if we consider as alternatives authoritarian attitudes like those Jacques promotes, or sullen fastidiousness like that of Amélie. Indeed, it can be argued that Jacques, insensitively proffering comminatory scriptural texts to Gertrude when she is at her most vulnerable, and Amélie, whose surly refusal to speak her mind clearly when it would have helped, have also contributed to Gertrude's death.[102] This is a feature which distinguishes *La Symphonie Pastorale* from the earlier first-person narratives, though we have noted a development in this direction in the transition from *L'Immoraliste* to *La Porte Etroite*: interaction between characters, and the repercussions of their separate existences one upon the other, have a considerably greater bearing on the conclusion than heretofore. As Charles Du Bos pointed out, the crisis of *La Symphonie Pastorale* highlights the autonomous existence of the other characters in the drama: and this fact points to the limitations of the first-person technique for the presentation of such a narrative.[103] Moreover, the significant implication of other protagonists, as well as the melodramatic nature of the climax, give special force to the pastor's cry: 'What horrible thing can you have learnt? What did I hide from you that was so deadly?' (927; 67). Is Gertude's death a necessary consequence of the pastor's actions and attitudes? To what extent is he solely guilty, and in what proportions is blame to be allocated to each character? We are bound to ask whether the trauma Gertrude has undergone is, in fact, sufficient cause for her to commit suicide at all, and in so doing we imply that her story might have had a different ending. These questions concerning cause and consequence, and responsibility accruing from the actual playing out of events, as opposed to their distortion through retrospective and other types of first-person narration, are the stuff of another line of enquiry which Gide was simultaneously exploring through different forms of narrative.

3

Third-Person Narratives

The a priori logic of Gide's *récits* necessitates a certain outcome, in keeping with the aim of exploring an idea and pushing it to its limits. But when calamity strikes, the hero of each of these narratives asks if it had to happen. Even Jérôme, lacking in enterprise, envisages, albeit reluctantly, an alternative set of possibilities his story could have led to: 'But to have kept her, to have forced the door, to have entered by any means whatever into the house . . .' (579; 117). The pastor is taken aback by the tragic turn of events which terminates his narrative, implying that it need not have culminated in so disastrous a climax: 'What horrible thing can you have learnt? What did I hide from you that was so deadly?' (927; 67). Like Michel, as Germaine Brée describes him, each of these narrator-protagonists 'wears himself out trying to understand how a succession of apparently unimportant moments has assumed the inscrutable configuration of the ineluctable'.[104]

Narrative manipulates events systematically to produce such an effect. As Roland Barthes points out, there is an overall 'solidarity' within a text which turns chance into necessity: 'This is the narrative fabric: seemingly subject to the discontinuity of messages, each of which, when it comes into play, is received as a useless supplement (whose very gratuitousness serves to authenticate the fiction by what we have called the *reality effect*), but is in fact saturated with pseudo-logical links'.[105] Gide's *récits*, based as we have seen on an a priori logic, are particularly flagrant cases, seeming to present an autonomous character with a freely chosen pattern of behaviour in circumstances governed only by chance; whereas in reality the narrative is governed by the author's wish to construct a case-study in self-delusion. But such is the condition of all narrative. If events are to be perceived as believable, they must appear to come about by chance or by psychological motivation, without reference to any ulterior authorial purpose (and as Barthes stresses, the apparent gratuitousness of their occurrence will itself be read as realistic); yet in order that the narrative may fulfil its purpose events must in fact be determined in advance, called into being by the needs of the plot.[106] We have seen that in his *récits* Gide foregrounds the relationship between narrator and narrative, between story and teller, so that any distortions – or indeed, straightforwardly significant occurrences – can readily be interpreted as the cause or effect of emotional involvement on the part of the narrator-protagonist. But, of course, the irony in these texts stems from the presence, behind the narrator, of an implied author who sees to it that events turn out in a certain predetermined way.[107] To this extent, the unfolding of events is independent of both narrator and protagonist, and says something about the way the world works – or the way its workings are viewed by an author, real or implied.

It is a striking fact that at the very time when he was implementing the a priori aesthetic in *L'Immoraliste*, Gide was actually formulating a slightly different view, involving a shift of emphasis towards the way the world works. In a lecture prepared in 1901, he examines the relationship between the external world and the artist, which he sees expressed in the proverb, 'God proposes and man disposes'. The two halves of this proverb express two opposing heresies, argues Gide, and only by reconciling their exigencies can the true work of art emerge:

> *God proposes*: this is naturalism, objectivism, call it what you will.
> *Man disposes*: this is apriorism, idealism . . .
> *God proposes and man disposes*: this is the work of art.[108]

This period therefore sees him moving beyond the a priori principle towards an outlook which went further in the direction of accommodating objective reality. His contemporary correspondence with his friend Henri Ghéon indicates the extent to which he attributes the ironic or critical dimension of his fiction to what he calls – ruefully, it must be admitted – a dose of 'empirisme';[109] and Ghéon was no doubt echoing Gide (as he did so often) when he himself used the term in a similar way, of the Russian novel, 'with its exalted "empiricism" bursting through our poor little literary formulae'.[110] Gide was highly conscious of the fact that narrative conveys a vision of the world through its actual articulation of events. Running parallel to his *récits* in which this problem is little more than incidental, he pursued his 'empirical' interests through his efforts to formulate a type of narrative which would offer something of the true texture of reality as he perceived it.

In this connection he appears to have been especially concerned to counter narratives that tend to present human reality as predetermined or preordained. Nourished as he was on the Bible, he came to query its narrative pattern, in which references to the cross appear to presage Christ's crucifixion, so that 'It is *in order to be crucified* that Christ comes on earth, and to save us by this indispensable sacrifice toward which his whole life led him' (*JI*, 1049; *J3*, 165; 9 June 1931). On the contrary, asserts Gide, it is clear that at the time they were headed for Jerusalem, the expectations of Jesus and his disciples were of triumph and the confirmation of Christ's divine vocation; so that 'There was, in the eyes of the world at least, complete failure' (*JI*, 898–9, *J3*, 30–1: 1928). The crucifixion was in reality 'an accident' (*JI*, 1049; *J3*, 165), 'the check or rather the supreme obstacle' (*JI*, 899; *J3*, 31) to Christ's mission. Gide suggests that the Gospel references to the cross before the account of the crucifixion were interpolated to presage this latter, 'to purge the crucifixion of any appearance of accident and, incorporating it in the predestined life of the "Saviour", to base on it the significance of Christ's teaching. In this case, the cross, far from interrupting that teaching, becomes its very aim, its explanation and perfect consummation' (*JI*, 1049; *J3*, 165). Hence the Scriptures present, for Gide, an example of narrative distortion in the interests of propaganda. The Gospels transform an arbitrary (and in Gide's view, unfortunate) curtailment of what would have been a different story by shifting the emphasis of Christ's mission away from the lessons of joy and love he taught, towards suffering and death as necessary conditions of his message. 'Let us try to imagine a Christ well received by men, immediately converted to his word, a Christ *who could not succeed in getting himself crucified*,' Gide argues (*JI*, 1318; *J3*, 402: 10 September 1938). Jesus's career could have turned out otherwise: it was governed, like the rest of human affairs, by contingency and chance, but when it was put into the particular story form that came down to us it took on the appearance and significance of a destiny accomplished in torment.

It is a feature of all narrative forms that they confirm ideological presuppositions. Indeed, the reason why narrative flourished in so extraordinary a way in the nineteenth century is that its form could be readily adapted to the ideological assumptions of scientific positivism. The nineteenth-century novelist, as Michel Raimond shows, is so often a determinist in his presentation not only because he depicts the influence of the milieu on his characters, but because he presents their lives as a mechanical succession of circumstances, linked in a chain of causes and effects which are expounded in the form of a necessary logical and chronological evolution – which is itself the favoured explanatory model of positivist philosophy.[111] But Gide was seeking a form which would furnish a different vision. What impressed him about history, the dominant narrative which determines so many of the stories humans tell each other, was that it could have been different: 'The world could have had a different history. The surface of the earth might have been covered otherwise', he wrote in 1896;[112] and in his autobiography he recalls that as early as 1893, on the eve of his departure for North Africa, he was planning a book on the imaginary history of a fictitious people, with its own art, literature, revolutions, wars, and so on. 'To prove what? That mankind might have had a different history, that our manners and customs and morals might have been different, our tastes, codes and standards of beauty different'.[113] History, like the narrative of Christ's life, is not for Gide synonymous with destiny: it did not have to be that way. Throughout his life he remained fond of evoking the 'different possibilities' of a universe in which, as Pascal had suggested.

'Cleopatra's nose was shorter and the face of the world was changed' (*JI*, 1051; *J3*, 166: 16 June 1931). We shall see that Armand Vedel, in *Les Faux-Monnayeurs*, debates the question in the same terms (1162–3; 255).

As his faith in the 'Grand Narratives' of History and the Bible faded, Gide was beginning to understand the implications of a new formulation of the world's workings which was to supersede these other discourses and make possible a new approach to narrative. Gide's acquaintance with the work of Charles Darwin began at least as early as 1890, the year of *Les Cahiers d'André Walter*; the hero of this first novel writes of his intention to read *The Origin of Species* (*W*, 100; 85). A letter to Valéry in December 1893 announces that Gide is 'having fun' with Darwin;[114] in early 1894 he is reading Darwin still;[115] and in September 1894 Gide mentions Darwin once more, in a letter to Marcel Drouin.[116] Even the narrator of *Paludes* is reading Darwin (107; 37); and Henri Ghéon, who knew Gide well, mentions Darwin as one of Gide's *maîtres à penser* in an article of 1897.[117] The fascination was to continue throughout Gide's life, linking up as it did with the novelist's passion for natural history.[118] Now the impact on a writer of Darwin's theory of evolution could be considerable. Gillian Beer's book, *Darwin's Plots*,[119] provides an admirable portrayal of the way Darwin affected the literary landscape in England, and we can assume at least an equal effect on Gide. The vision that Darwinian evolution made available gives prominence to the random forces operating in history, and demonstrates that accidental deviations from the typical, not the consistent observance of a putative norm, are the creative key to evolutionary development. It denies the existence of a teleological design within nature and suggests that nature develops through the disordered exploration of multiple possibilities. Natural selection operates upon the products of contingency.

This vision will become a hallmark of Gide's fiction. In *Les Faux-Monnayeurs*, he introduces a naturalist, Vincent Molinier, who expounds his views on nature's workings: 'What . . . diversity! It seems as if Nature had essayed one after the other every possible manner of living and moving, as if she had taken advantage of every permission granted by matter and its laws' (1051; 135).[120] There are no norms to constrain the development of individuals and species; there is no grand design dictating the direction in which evolution will move. The story of nature is not unilinear, but tree-like, with innumerable branchings. No single line of evolutionary history has any claim to consideration beyond the fact that it exists; profiled behind and alongside it are the multitude of other equally viable pathways which could just as easily have come into existence – and which could yet be realised as Nature continues her exploration of the infinite possibilities of life.

Clearly, if chance was to be the only determinant then the positivist conception of the natural sciences, in which cause and effect relations have a predictive value, was called into question. Moreover, since mutation is the only way in which new variations enter the species and permit evolutionary development, then departures from the norm are the very engine of that development.[121] The appeal such a vision had for Gide was considerable. We may recall the narrator-protagonist of *Paludes*, yearning for an event or events which will break the causal chain extending forward from the already accomplished. The book's subtitle, 'A Treatise on Contingency', highlights the theme of alternative possibilities in a world where determinism gives way to random variation. Inconsistencies and unforeseen developments are of crucial importance in Gide's world-view: we have seen how Adam's longing for 'a little something unexpected' started the poetico-theologico-evolutionary process in the first place. 'It is precisely the *inconsequences* in a life which lead to the most significant consequences', Gide will write.[122] Gide's narratives, then, will become workshops in which he will experiment with alternative modes of being, trying out possibilities which may not (yet) have come to fruition in real life.

Another consequence of evolutionary theory as adumbrated by Darwin is that by highlighting the vast field of possibilities in nature, it shows up the narrowness of the range of options permitted by conventions of narrative verisimilitude. The comparison arguably generates pressure to modify the scope of the novel, particularly in regard to its attitude towards chance and contingency. It would be excessively simplistic to suggest that Darwin's influence is directly involved here; but

it is a fact that the decade or more during which Gide absorbed
the lessons of the great naturalist also saw an increase in
interest both on Gide's part and on that of the writers around
him in what is best termed the 'roman d'aventure' (novel of
adventure). The element of adventure in the novel was a
standard ingredient until, around the mid-nineteenth century,
it began to be seen as the prerogative of the inferior genre of
the newspaper serial or *feuilleton*; from which point the serious
literary novel tended to shun this sensational component of
narrative.[123] But there is plenty of evidence that in the milieux
frequented by Gide, writers were turning to this form as a
possible means of renewing the moribund novel of the 1890s.
Marcel Schwob, an admirer and acquaintance of Robert Louis
Stevenson, foresaw the potential of the *roman d'aventure*, as
exploited by Stevenson, as early as 1891.[124] Gide was reading
and re-reading *Treasure Island, Dr Jekyll and Mr Hyde*, and *The
Dynamiter* from at least 1896;[125] he writes of *The Black Arrow* in
a letter to Drouin of June 1901;[126] by 1905 he was thoroughly
familiar with the Scottish writer's work (*JI*, 173; *J1*, 147). In
one of his critical essays, collectively entitled *Letters à Angèle*,
of 1899, he tempers the expression of his admiration – probably
by way of concession to the 'high art' schools of thought – but
the points he makes about Stevenson are significant in that
they indicate the importance he attaches to features not widely
favoured or practised among aspiring novelists of the time:
'The absence of thought here is willed and charming; the
keen, subtle intelligence of Stevenson is solely devoted to the
excellence of the narrative; and what choice of details! what
tact! what superior *technique*! ... He remains correct and
discreet; always the story-teller, never the actor'.[127] Similarly,
in 1900 he reviewed Kipling's *The Light that Failed* and Wells'
The War of the Worlds, hailing them as Stevenson's heirs and
stressing the vigour of their outlook on life: evidently their
'empirical' aspects impressed him. Here, too, it is noteworthy
that Gide singles out the power of Wells' narrative gift:
'the sensations are integral to the narrative' he writes, and
comments on the novel's technique: 'The figure of the principal
hero, the one who tells the story, is deliberately kept in the
background, as befits such a novel of adventure (so that
the events remain more interesting than the reactions they

provoke)'.[128] Gide was to dedicate the next ten years to perfecting a form of first-person narration diametrically opposed to such techniques: in which 'story-teller' and 'actor' are one, in which the narrator is very far from 'kept in the background' and in which the events are *less* interesting than the reactions they provoke. None the less, it is clear that in these writers he saw a model for a contrasting type of narrative which also attracted him. We should recall that Gide was giving much thought to *Les Caves du Vatican* (*The Vatican Cellars*) in 1898[129] and that 1899 also saw the publication of *Le Prométhée Mal Enchaîné* (*Prometheus Misbound*): both these texts manifest startling experiments in the manipulation of narrative, and show that Gide had no intention of restricting himself to a single formula. Moreover, he continued to pursue his interest in techniques that ran counter to his a priori aesthetic – it is in part as a result of this interest that he frequently complained that writing *L'Immoraliste* and *La Porte Etroite* tied him to a stage in his work that he was impatient to put behind him.[130] Indeed, the evidence of Gide's attachment to the *roman d'aventure* can be seen in the debates on the subject which occurred in his immediate environment: his younger admirers and disciples were taking up the idea and formulating in polemical terms the notions Gide had discussed in conversations with them.[131] Thus, Gide congratulated Jacques Copeau on a book review in the *Nouvelle Revue Française* of May 1912, saying it 'follows on from our conversations'. The main point Copeau makes in this review is that the 'roman d'aventure' is the essential form of the novel, the chief ingredient for which is 'the aptitude for the narration at length of adventures'. Moreover, he declares: 'I shall welcome even chance in the novel', and on this basis formulates a crucial new aesthetic for the genre: 'An aesthetics of the illogical and the unconditioned', to permit a structure which is 'polymorphous and ramified'.[132] We can see Gide's views on history and evolutionary narrative bearing fruit here; the *roman d'aventure* provided a form that expressly dealt in random events, offering Gide the opportunity to explore their implications in his fiction. Another notable product of Gidean cross-fertilisation is Jacques Rivière's essay 'Le Roman d'Aventure', which appeared in instalments in the *Nouvelle Revue Française* during

May, June and July 1913. For Rivière, the *roman d'aventure* mercifully puts paid to the world-weary aesthetic of the symbolists and opens up time and space to the novelist. Familiar Gidean leitmotifs reappear: the novel is composed exclusively of events and actions; the action 'breaks out in a score of different directions at a time', unexpectedly and illogically; incidents are merely accumulated in succession, and do not grow one out of the other – 'The novel of adventures is a novel which progresses by exploiting novelty'.[133] Gide had planned his own article on the subject, but abandoned the project on reading that of Rivière, who, he notes, 'says almost what I should have liked to say in my article and much better than I could have done' (*JI*, 391; *J1*, 341: 10 July 1913). In 1912 he had referred to *Les Caves du Vatican* as 'a great novel of adventure with a large number of characters';[134] as he put the finishing touches to the novel in 1913, the theoretical ground had in fact been well prepared for some time.

Le Prométhée Mal Enchaîné (*Prometheus Misbound*)

In the summer of 1898, when he was completing *Le Prométhée Mal Enchaîné*, Gide wrote one of his 'Lettres à Angèle', critical essays taking the form of a dialogue with an imaginary correspondent. In it he speaks of Angèle's novelistic ambitions, and describes the difficulties under which aspiring novelists labour. He encourages her to think of 'the permissions granted by the whiteness of the pages' and not to allow herself to be inhibited by the 'complicated enslavements' – fear of the judgement of others, the urge to comply with critical expectations, and so on – which can stand in the way of creativity. 'Chaque sympathie, chaque théorie, chaque réprobation vous enchaîne' ('Each affinity, each theory, each act of reprobation binds you'), Gide writes. The allusion is telling, and signals *Le Prométhée Mal Enchaîné* as an attempt to break free from such influences. He next addresses himself to the anathema of the post-realists, plot in the novel: 'All around you people disapprove of plots; they dream of narratives without incidents: it's a pity; you were good at plots'.[135] This too may be taken as a mark of his own determination to defy the prevailing literary consensus and give his own talents free rein. Certainly *Le Prométhée Mal Enchaîné* is, as Helen Watson-Williams declares, 'an audacious book on all counts . . . Its plot is complicated . . . its structure is complex'.[136] The construction of a plot is the very stuff of this text; it is in fact the explicit concern of the café-waiter, a character who acts as a kind of novelist within the text. His function in life is to bring people together by seating strangers at the same table, so that they may interact with one another. He expresses his aims and activities thus:

> There's nothing so interesting as personalities, and the relations between personalities . . . I set relationships going; I listen, I scrutinize, I direct the conversation. When dinner is over I know three inner beings, three personalities! But they don't. As for me, you understand, I listen, I relate, they undergo the relationship. . . . My private hobby is to create relationships.   (305; 106–7)

We may perceive an ambiguity here, in that the waiter starts out by asserting his primary interest in personalities, adding interaction as an afterthought; but it is clear that the establishment of 'relations' precedes and indeed is essential to the emergence of an observable personality. This ambiguity is in fact inscribed in the unusual structure of *Le Prométhée Mal Enchaîné*, as W. W. Holdheim was the first to point out.[137] The text falls into three parts, and is divided throughout into *both* numbered *and* titled chapters; but the two types of chapter are not the same, and do not fit into any overall structural frame. Those with titles are interrupted by divisions corresponding to the sequence of numbered chapters; and similarly, they themselves form a sequence which cuts across the flow of the numbered chapters. In this respect as in others, this *Prométhée* is 'mal enchaîné' – that is, disjointed, as the punning title invites us to conclude. Holdheim makes the pertinent point that the sequence of numbered chapters traces and corresponds to the interplay between events and between characters, while the chapters with titles highlight the individual, subjective and essentially separate state of each character. The lack of fit between the two systems suggests a kind of incompatibility between two views on human reality, a tension between two distinct domains in which human reality is played out.

Let us consider first the question of relations and events. In this connection it is clear that Gide is exploring the possibilities offered by the *roman d'aventure*. When the three characters Damoclès, Coclès and Prométhée, seated together at the same café table, embark on their acquaintance by introducing themselves, their conversation turns on one recurring theme. It is illustrated by Damoclès' story. 'After what happened (*advenu*) to me last month, not a vestige of what I previously thought survives', he declares (308; 111), introducing the gist of his story with the remark, 'Now, what should happen (*advint*) to me one morning but a personal adventure' (308; 111). His words anticipate by some twenty-five years those of Bernard in *Les Faux-Monnayeurs*: 'Adventure! What a splendid word! *Adventitious happenings in store*' (975; 56).[138] The motif and associated vocabulary, playing on the etymology of the word 'adventure', establish the prominent role of unexpected incidents and chance occurrences in the lives of the protagonists. 'This adventure has determined my identity', Damoclès asserts (310; 113). Coclès, for his part, was actively seeking 'some external event that might *determine my life*', he tells his interlocutors (310; 115). He too has undergone an inexplicable event, involving him 'by the merest chance' (310; 114) in a set of unforeseen situations. As for Prométhée, he can only apologise: 'Please believe it was with unmixed interest that I heard each of you telling an adventure . . . But . . . There hasn't been time yet for anything to happen to me (*m'advenir*)' (313; 118). In a sense, something of the sort is happening to him as he speaks, of course, since by an effect of a 'new accident' (310; 113), he happens to be present at this chance meeting of Damoclès and Coclès, whose lives have in fact intersected earlier, albeit unbeknown to them since they were hitherto complete strangers.

What has befallen them, as the reader pieces together while digesting their separate stories, is that they have been picked out as playthings by Zeus, the 'miglionaire' banker. It is clear from the waiter's words and from what the mysterious figure himself says (305; 107. 328–30; 151–3) that Zeus is the embodiment of a superhuman power which deals in gratuitous actions. It is not correct to affirm (as some critics have) that he is God, although as he puts it, 'I have no objection to their saying so' (330; 153). It would be more accurate to say that, as his Greek name indicates, he represents the forces working in Nature – which is what the Greeks had in mind when they evoked their deities. The Christian error is to suppose that behind Nature is a power whose chief interest is in the fate of human beings. Zeus, though he may be seen as the first cause, the originating source of things, merely lets events run their course: 'Mine is, above all, the spirit of initiative. I simply launch. Then, when a business is launched, I leave it; I don't touch it again' (329; 151). As such he personifies the random influences which impinge indifferently on human beings and the rest of the universe. It is true that his depiction within *Le Prométhée Mal Enchaîné* as a 'stout, middle-aged gentleman, whose unusual corpulence was his sole remarkable feature' (303; 101) gives to his intervention the tongue-in-cheek, self-conscious air of a literary conceit based on parallels between the God of Creation on the one hand and the novelist manipulating his characters on the other.[139] But such playful analogies should not distract us from the actual nature of his intervention and the consequences it entails. These can be seen to be purely contingent – much more like the 'evolutionary' narrative than any creationist one. We learn that he has randomly selected Coclès to address an envelope to the person whose name first came into his head, and to be the recipient of a mighty slap in exchange. Damoclès in turn receives by mail a 500-franc note in the envelope Coclès addressed to him as 'a perfect stranger' (311; 115). A point to observe is that the original encounter between Zeus and Coclès occurred through the chance conjunction of Zeus' dropping a handker-chief and Coclès' being in the vicinity. Moreover, Zeus at first merely thanks Coclès 'and was about to continue his way, when, changing his mind, he leaned towards the thin person' (303; 101). He could just as easily have proceeded on his way, and none of what follows would have happened. Moreover, the motif of alternative paths for the narrative is highlighted in subsequent events. Coclès, who first incurs a vicious slap from Zeus and then loses an eye when Prometheus' eagle swoops down into the café, responds positively and actually does surprisingly well out of his misfortunes; he becomes the beneficiary of a public appeal and sets up a hostel for one-eyed people, appointing himself its director. On the other hand, the windfall which comes Damoclès' way unexpectedly provokes in him an enfeebling guilt, a sense of responsibility which prompts him to dispose of the money at the first opportunity (on a glass eye for Coclès, among other things); thereafter he succumbs to distress and remorse at the thought of the unknown person who had been deprived of the cash, and dwindles to death as a result. Not only are these two characters presented as illustrations of alternative outcomes from the same random event; we can also see that while the one could just as easily have received the banknote and the other the slap, so too extreme distress might have been more likely to flow from Coclès' mischance while great happiness could more readily be imagined to ensue from the large sum of money that falls into Damoclès' lap. The pairing of these individual stories highlights a feature of narrative and of its structure which has drawn the attention of literary theorists in recent years. Claude Bremond in particular has constructed a model of narrative structure which stresses the fact that any story consists of a series of moments at which bifurcations occur. Thus each narrative sequence starts with the possibility of a certain action or event: confronted by a closed door and no answer to our knocking, we may break the door down – or we may not.[140] The story proceeds, after posing the possibility or virtuality of an incident, via the realisation (or otherwise) of the incident, and its result. What characterises the stories of Damoclès and Coclès is that though they conform to this process, they are shadowed, as it were, by the unrealised virtualities which rather than being superseded by the actual course of events, remain in our minds because they are invested with a greater weight of plausibility. The sequence which realises itself does not conform to primary patterns of narrative verisimilitude. Indeed it ostentatiously avoids a more conventional storyline which the reader is tempted to compose in his or her own mind on the basis of the 'overcoded, ready-made paths', as Umberto Eco calls them, deriving from our past experience of the kind of thing which normally happens in stories: loss of an eye triggers misfortune while acquisition of money produces an increase in happiness.[141] This branching narrative presents its two paths as entirely contingent, governed by random circumstance, and just as likely – on balance, marginally more likely – to have produced different outcomes. It is true that in each case, the outcome is actually determined by the temperament of the individual concerned: we shall have more to say about this element later. But what is stressed by this type of narrative structure is that there is nothing determining about events themselves: losing an eye is not necessarily a bad thing, just as finding a fortune is not intrinsically good. Events and actions do not necessarily produce the results we might expect. The 'Epilogue' to the book confirms this idea through its evocation of Pasiphaë who hoped that consorting with a bull might result in her producing a child of Zeus, as happened to Leda after her adventure with the swan: instead of which she merely gave birth to a calf.

Elsewhere in the story, another pair of parallel paths emerges, linking in this case the fate of Damoclès and that of Prométhée.[142] That there is an affinity between the two is evident from the sympathy Prométhée evinces on hearing Damoclès' story (316; 125–6) and from the fact that he continues to show great concern for Damoclès as the latter's condition deteriorates: he even pleads with Zeus on the suffering human's behalf. The crucial analogy lies, however, between the remorse which is devouring Damoclès and the eagle which feeds on Prométhée's liver. The former questions the events which befall him using interrogations which the latter will repeat with reference to his eagle (309; 113. 325; 143). The significance of the parallel derives chiefly from the outcome of each story: Damoclès dies from what is eating him, while Prometheus quite literally makes a meal of his eagle, overcoming the enfeebling conscience it represents. Here too, then, the narrative presents forking paths leading from the same initial ingredients, implying that for one set of events which occurs there is an equally possible though diametrically opposed alternative. The plot of *Le Prométhée*, then, is conceived in such a way as to highlight the contingency governing human affairs. None of these things had to happen. They were largely 'adventures', in the sense of unpredictable occurrences, and therefore deny validity to positivist explanations involving necessary cause and effect connections in groups of events.

Why should Gide go to such lengths to stress chance as the chief factor in reality? He indicates the function of chance in *Le Prométhée* in a letter to Maurice Beaubourg, who had sent him an enthusiastic commentary on the work. Gide was ready to endorse most of what his correspondent said – suggesting that he would like to see his letter as a preface to the book – and made the following remark:

> There is one sentence above all that I like, which to my mind explains the whole of my book to me: 'They believe themselves responsible for chance', you say; perfect![143]

The random events which a blind fate inflicts on human beings have no moral connotations, and no codes of conduct or patterns of behaviour can be deduced from them. Nor can any pattern of significance justifiably be read into them, since, as we have seen, such events are purely contingent. To speak of Providence, or God's will, is already to impose on raw chance a *human* vision of things which is not relevant to any part of the workings of the universe at large. And yet humans do tend to react to chance with a sense of responsibility, assuming their fate as if it is theirs to justify, vindicate or expiate. This, essentially, is what Gide depicts via that other dimension inscribed in the dual structure of *Le Prométhée*. The external world has no morality, as the narrator says at the beginning of his 'Chronicle of Private Morality': 'I shall say nothing about public morality, because there's no such thing' (304; 105). None the less, subjective experience centres largely on moral questions. The correlative of cause and effect connections, in the subjective sphere, is moral interrelatedness; and the chapter headings provided in the book highlight the efforts of the protagonists to make sense in moral terms of the incidents which shape their lives. For, as the waiter points out, in the whole of nature the human being is 'the only creature that is incapable of acting gratuitously'. 'That doesn't mean that I believe in determinism' (305; 107), he adds: what denies gratuitousness to human actions is not that human *behaviour* is determined, therefore; rather, humans are in-capable of *thinking* in terms of randomness when it comes to considering the actions they perform or the incidents they undergo.[144] Thus the chief concern of Coclès and Damoclès is to establish connections between disparate elements in their experience, to make them fit a pattern and thereby confer on them some kind of meaning or justification. The waiter has preceded them in this regard: in telling Prométhée of Zeus's actions he has stressed 'the relationship': 'One gets 500 francs for a slap in the face, the other gets a slap in the face for 500 francs' (306; 108). But of course there *is* no reciprocal relation between what befell Coclès and Damoclès, so there is no possible relation of exchange based on what each receives: neither owes anything, except to an entity (Zeus) who remains beyond their sphere of influence. Consequently as the waiter continues his commentary he is led to admit that gratuitous activity subverts moral categories: 'and then it becomes too bewildering . . . one loses track. – Think of it! A gratuitous action! There's nothing more demoralizing' (306; 108). Damoclès and Coclès repeatedly squabble over the implied notion that there is a connection between the good luck of the former and the ill luck of the latter. Coclès' first impulse on hearing Damoclès' story is to slap him, though he quickly realises that this would not be appropriate (310; 114); but he cannot escape the need to blame someone for the pain he has undergone, and Damoclès, despite his protests, is the likeliest candidate: 'Do not argue the point, if you please. Between your gain and my misfortune there is a relationship; I don't know what, but the relationship exists' (312; 117). Similarly, Damoclès needs to know to whom he owes his good fortune: 'Grateful – I am only too anxious to be grateful – but I don't know to whom' (309; 113). In the absence of a benefactor to express gratitude to, he seeks to rid himself of the banknote, seizing on the pretext of the waiter's bill: 'gratuitously, fortuitously, providentially . . . slip my money into the gap between these events' (331; 155). This attempt at an *action gratuite*, disposing of the banknote as chance provides an opportunity, fails for the very reason we are discussing; Damoclès remains morally attached to the money. But now Coclès is as well, in his view; the latter's glass eye was

purchased with ill-gotten cash, so he too should feel remorse:
'But your eye is burning you, Cocles! . . . If it doesn't burn
you, then it ought to' (332; 156). Coclès and Damoclès resort
to moral blackmail of each other, to reinforce the sense of
relations in their universe. In Sartrean terms – terms of which
Gide is an important precursor – they are trying to deny
human freedom, both that of others and their own. Before
receiving the banknote, Damoclès says, he was 'commonplace
but free. Now I belong to the banknote. This adventure has
determined my identity' (310; 113). This is not so, of course;
but the mistake is instructive, the more so as he will later say,
'from that day forward . . . I felt, at one and the same time,
that my life had acquired a meaning and that I could no
longer bear to live' (331; 155). It is not so paradoxical as it
seems that a cause of suffering should bring with it a reason
for living – and dying; particularly if we consider that
Damoclès follows through his conviction to the bitter end,
dying from a sense of undischarged debt. He achieves martyr-
dom for the sake of the new-found meaning in his life.
Similarly, before his misadventure Coclès suffered from not
having 'some reason for continuing to live'. Not knowing who
his parents were, he went in search of 'some external event
that might *determine my identity*' (310; 115), ready at the drop
of a . . . handkerchief to perform an act – any act – which
might 'motivate existence' for him. 'I thought my destiny
would depend on the first thing that happened to me', he
argues (310; 115), only too willing to sacrifice his own free
will to a predetermined notion of who he is and what he
should be. The network of moral interconnections provides,
therefore, a comforting solution to the contingency of existence.
The problem is that none of these relations stands up to
scrutiny, as we have seen; attempts on the part of the two
protagonists to provide convincing theories of their moral
interconnectedness founder on the simple absence of any such
link.

'See how today everything somehow links up (*s'enchaîne*),
yet instead of explaining itself becomes still more complicated',
complains Coclès when the bare facts are initially revealed
and corroborated by their separate narratives (312; 116). This
allusion to the title of the text calls for further consideration.

What we notice in the first part of *Le Prométhée Mal Enchaîné* is that the protagonists offer projections of their experience in the form of narratives: each contribution is headed 'The Story of . . .'. Again, this is to be expected, given that moral interrelatedness and cause and effect connections are homologous constructs conventionally placed upon experience through the medium of narrative. If we can tell how things happened we can apportion blame. But narrative cannot accommodate the chance interaction which characterises a large part of this experience: as we have seen, its structure transforms gratuitousness into necessity; so neither singly nor together – after four different versions of the salient events – can the various narrators provide a satisfactory account of what has happened to them. Such specious connections as they can suggest by means of narrative merely complicate matters rather than explaining their situation. The whole sequence, the entire 'chronique', remains *mal enchaîné*.

A noticeable exception to the pattern in part one is the fact that Prométhée's contribution is not announced as 'Histoire de . . .', but simply with the words, 'Prometheus Speaks' (313; 118). We may (facetiously?) suppose that he has no (hi)story because he does not exist in the same contingent world as the others, being a mythological stereotype who has merely strayed into Paris from the Caucasus of legend; or alternatively, that he has had no 'adventures' in the short time he has been there. (The dramatic incidents his eagle precipitates suffice for it to have an 'histoire'.) More to the point, perhaps, anything he has to contribute has 'so little *connection*' (313; 118), and therefore would not fit into the system of relations the others are seeking to construct out of their experiences. Prométhée's more relevant contribution will come later; and it is significant that even then he continues to avoid narrative, but adopts a different form of discourse, that of the public lecture. This represents a variant on the preoccupation we have been examining; it is another attempt to come up with an explanatory discourse aimed at integrating subjective experience and the external world.

Prométhée's speech is about eagles, and to understand its implications we need to clarify what the eagle signifies. We know from the reactions of Parisians in the vicinity when

Prométhée's eagle arrives that everyone has one, but that it
is frowned upon to display it. His is unprepossessing at this
stage, 'a conscience, at the very most' (314; 121). But by
feeding it on his own substance during this period of enforced
introspection (he is denounced by the waiter and imprisoned
for selling matches without a licence), Prométhée develops it
into a sleek and beautiful creature with the power to fly. It
can tell him nothing about the details of the outside world
and other people, however, since it soars at such a great height
above them. It would appear that the eagle represents the
moral faculty of the human being. At one level it is the
conscience, which in its banal form provokes inhibition and
hypocrisy; but in other guises, as Prométhée's imprisonment
shows, it can enable man, albeit at some cost to his material
being and to his awareness of the everyday world, to transcend
the narrow constraints of bodily existence, just as Prométhée
escapes his prison, borne off by his eagle. This is the faculty
that Prométhée seeks to promote in his lecture. He tells how
it was born in him when he began to concern himself with
human beings (323; 138). He provoked its growth in humans
when, not content with giving them 'conscience d'être',
consciousness, he induced in them 'raison d'être' (a reason
for existing) (324; 141). The eagle here is defined therefore as
'belief in progress', that which devours humans, drives them
on to better things, denies them satisfaction in the status quo,
renders them incapable of accepting reality as it is (324; 141).
The problem arises when Prométhée touches on 'the most
serious question: – why the eagle!' (325; 142) and seeks to
justify the eagle's existence. In full view of his audience he
questions it; but it does not reply. 'Must I then leave this
earth without knowing why I loved you?' he cries (326; 143).
The answer, though not stated, is clearly, Yes. We learn later,
along with Prométhée, that the eagle is another of Zeus's gifts
to humanity (330; 153). It takes its place, therefore, alongside
undeserved slaps and unsolicited banknotes as one of the
gratuitous, contingent ingredients of human reality. Prométhée
has been speaking about Coclès' and Damoclès' experience
as well as his own; indeed, he advises them to dedicate
themselves each to their obligation as he proposes to devote
himself to his eagle (327; 145).

Prométhée's lecture highlights once more, with particular force, the problems involved in speaking about the contingent quality of human reality. He singles out the inevitability of the *petitio principii* (begging the question) in moral discourses. In seeking to make sense in human terms of the reality we inhabit, we assume at the outset that reality conforms to human models of intelligibility: which is a circular argument. Prométhée's particular case turns on the argument, 'Everyone should have an eagle', when it is clear that humans have one anyway. He turns into a moral imperative what is a contingent state of affairs: the very foundation of morality is shown to be the circular argument, 'la pétition de principes' (322; 134–5). Only Zeus is able to act, as he himself puts it, 'on principle' (306; 108), being himself the originating principle of the universe. Humans are condemned to gratuitousness and the *petitio principii*, since what pass for principles in human affairs are nothing more than arbitrary assertions. Moreover, as Prométhée further points out, 'Begging the question is always an assertion of temperament; for, where principles are lacking, assertion of temperament steps in' (322; 136). Consequently, when he declares, 'Gentlemen, we must devote ourselves to our eagle' (327; 145), his stance is as ill-founded as those of Coclès and Damoclès making determining principles out of fortuitous events in their lives. All such convictions are the product of a particular temperament; the reason why Coclès and Damoclès respond differently to the accident that befalls them is that their temperamental disposition differs.

In the absence of a principle in which to ground moral discourses, Prométhée's lecture exhibits features of another type of coherence, complementing those patterns of narrative coherence we have already seen discredited: here logical connections take over from cause and effect connections. They are no more effective, as we have already seen; in fact Prométhée's lecture stands as a satire of rational approaches to contingency. He invokes the standard methods of classical rhetoric in support of his case:

My lecture, gentlemen, has three points; (I felt there was no need to reject this style of construction, which suits my classical turn of mind.) – And with this as an exordium, I will now announce, in advance and without meretricious disguise, the first two points of my discourse . . . (321; 135)

His rhetorical questions, apostrophes, and rhythmic sentence-structures all stem from the same source.[145] Their comic futility is underlined by Prométhée's recourse to fireworks and obscene photographs, which he circulates at moments when his audience is losing interest; and by tricks the eagle performs as diversions 'after every tedious portion' (321; 134).

By the conclusion of Prométhée's lecture, therefore, we have been presented with two critiques: one concerns human responses to gratuitousness, the other concerns the discourses employed to speak of gratuitousness. What *Le Prométhée Mal Enchaîné* suggests of human responses to gratuitousness clearly points forward to the a priori logic which will dictate the narratives of *L'Immoraliste* and *La Porte Etroite*. These books demonstrate the way a particular temperament determines a particular line of moral conduct, the *petitio principii* at the source of each character's rationalisations revealing the mark of an arbitrary predisposition. Indeed the twin-like relationship between these two texts mirrors the parallel structure of Coclès' and Damoclès' stories.[146] But the end of Prométhée's lecture is not the end of his story; and this text has more to say on the matters it has raised. The third part of *Le Prométhée Mal Enchaîné* recounts the illness and death of Damoclès, who is in effect annihilated by the particular eagle Zeus has bestowed on him. These events have a considerable impact on Prométhée, the more so as in his meeting with Zeus, who resists his entreaties to offer comfort to Damoclès, he comes to understand more about the workings of the universe and its indifference to human fate. The death of Damoclès, which was in part due to the influence of Prométhée's own lecture, alters Prométhée's perceptions: not that he would have expressed himself differently had he known Damoclès was to die; he remains convinced of the validity of what he was trying to convey, but remarks that 'Damocles was all too convinced' (334; 161). This suggestion that Damoclès went to excessive lengths in his devotion to his eagle evokes once more that notion of 'the delicate moment when thought breaks down' we have had cause to refer to previously.

A transformed Prométhée appears at the funeral of Damoclès. 'Since the death of Damocles, I have discovered the secret of laughter', he declares (340; 171). He has arrived at the conception of irony which lies behind Gide's own exposition of his protagonists' stories: he invites the reader to see their point of view, but only up to a point, since beyond that point their devotion to their ideal – their eagle – becomes absurd. So with Prométhée; and his transformation is an effect of his having meditated on the case of Damoclès, as we readers might ruminate on Michel or Alissa. He reveals, to the surprise of all, that he has killed his eagle – this, indeed, is why he can laugh today – and invites his acquaintances to feast upon it. They find it delicious, and Prométhée concludes, 'If it had made me suffer less, it would have been less plump; if it had been less plump, it would have been less delectable' (341; 173). The eagle has not proved useless, therefore; the secret lies in knowing when to cease feeding it and instead to nourish oneself on what it has become. In the final analysis, an eagle bestowed gratuitously by fate can be made to serve human ends, given the right proportions of application on the one hand and of detached humour on the other.

Furthermore, Prométhée presents at the funeral an oration which appears to exemplify a discourse suited to engage with gratuitousness. It is an 'Histoire', but its form is that of narrative fiction. It does not recapitulate the lives of the protagonists, but transposes their concerns into a narrative structure which is symbolic, rather than referential. It concerns Tityre, the erstwhile protagonist of the fiction-within-the-fiction of *Paludes*, who devotes himself to an idea sown, in the form of a seed in the midst of his marshlands, by Ménalque. The seed grows into a tree which dries out the marshes, making them suitable for cultivation and bringing an ever-increasing burden of obligations for Tityre as he takes on a work-force, administers the resulting population, supervises the local economy, appoints office staff, a judiciary and so on. Finally, the commitment becomes too much for him and, prompted by his wife Angèle, he breaks the ties that bind him to his tree and heads for Paris. There Angèle in turn is

captivated by the pastoral pipes of the naked Moelibée (like
Tityrus and Menalcas a character from Virgil's *Bucolics*) and
leaves for Rome, disappearing arm in arm with him into the
sunset. The story is judged highly amusing and is enjoyed by
all the listeners, although Coclès remarks: 'Your story was
charming, and you amused us extremely . . . but I didn't
quite grasp *the connection*' (340; 171). '*If there had been more of a
connection*, you wouldn't have laughed so much', Prométhée
replies: but in Coclès's question is a crucial reference to links,
connections and relationships, which as we have seen run like
a motif through the text as a whole. Narrative discourses
reconstitute history in cause and effect sequences which do
not explain reality; rhetoric and logic encapsulate moral
questions within the articulations of circular arguments;
does Prométhée's fictional narrative offer a more appropriate
'enchaînement' of the text's elements? The first thing to note
is that the 'Histoire de Tityre' is a *mise en abyme*; it relates to
the main narrative via structural parallels and metaphorical
cross-references rather than in any linear or logical way. It
has characteristics of the Biblical parable, an impression
reinforced by the cadences of its opening lines: 'And this Idea
was the seed, and this seed was the Idea' (335; 164).
Consequently, it makes its point by indirection, rather than
through a logical or rational demonstration.[147] At the same
time, passing motifs echo allusions encountered earlier in *Le
Prométhée*: the seed parallels the slap, banknote and eagle;
Tityre's obligations resemble Prométhée's earlier ones in that
'if they increase I decrease'.[148] Tityre breaks free of 'scrupules'
as did Prométhée (337; 168. 304; 105), and like him enters
Paris along 'the boulevard which leads from the Madeleine
to the Opéra' (338; 168. 304; 105). The public's sudden
perception that Moelibée is naked (338; 178) repeats
Prométhée's awareness of his own nakedness that accompanied
his moral awakening (323; 138). Such cross-references mark
the establishment of sense via associative networks, and
ground the *mal enchaîné* text in which it is embedded in a
homogeneous composition. So much so, suggests Helen
Watson-Williams, that the incoherence which is the raison
d'être of the overall work is almost invalidated: 'The effect of
Gide's transposition is so to reduce the dispersed and appar-

ently digressive story of Prometheus to its main outline that it tends to stand out from the whole and by its very economy and condensation satisfy the reader's need to an extent that endangers the total effect.'[149] Be that as it may, the relationship between this story and the text in which it figures offers a model for that between the fiction and the reality it articulates. In terms borrowed from linguistic theory, the relationship is paradigmatic, rather than syntagmatic; metaphorical rather than metonymic.[150] Above all, the fiction is itself gratuitous; it represents, therefore, humanity's appropriate response to the contingency of the universe. Prométhée both prefaces and follows his story with the words: 'Let's forget all I have just said' (335; 163. 339; 171). He could just as easily not have said anything. He has produced a discourse which does not give a false impression of logical or mechanical necessity to the world it portrays.

Prométhée declares after the company have eaten the eagle that he has kept all its feathers; and the narrator, in the final lines of the narrative, announces: 'It is with a pen made from one of them that I have written this little book' (341; 173). The remark extends the scope of the debate about the eagle and its uses beyond the world of the diegesis, and prompts us to consider the relationship of the author to the fiction. This relationship is, of course, already inherent in the portrayal of Prométhée's development into a story-teller; but in *Le Prométhée Mal Enchaîné* can be seen clear indications of Gide's own developing aesthetic of the novel.[151] It is worthy of note that Gide called *Le Prométhée Mal Enchaîné* a novel both on its publication in 1899 and again in 1903.[152] It is clear, however, that it is a highly self-conscious example of the genre, setting out to question novelistic conventions through its form as well as its content. Great liberties are taken with the depiction of time and place, a staple ingredient of realism: Prométhée arrives in Paris 'between four and five o'clock *in the autumn*' (304; 105), and at the end of his first day's adventures there is shown 'slowly wend[ing] his way back to the Caucasus' (315; 122) – which still mysteriously seems to fall within the jurisdiction of the Paris police, since he is jailed a few days later (316; 125). The levels of reality of the characters depicted also defy traditional conventions: Zeus becomes a corpulent, middle-aged banker, a bourgeois gentleman strolling along the Paris boulevards, while Prometheus, bringer of fire, is locked up as an unlicensed match-seller. Moreover, on the same Paris boulevard which saw the arrival of Prometheus and Zeus, a naked, flute-playing shepherd from Virgil addresses Angèle in Latin. Gods, myths and men mingle in defiance of chronology and topography. Transitions in the story are handled with a cavalier disregard for coherence and consistency, as we have seen in connection with the two contradictory systems of chapter divisions. The leitmotif 'while we're on the subject, here is an anecdote' marks transitions which highlight the actual lack of connection between the elements thus linked;[153] and when the same phrase is uttered by characters within the story after initially being established as an instrument of the narrator (304; 105. 305; 107. 335; 163) it provokes a subtle kind of disjunction since the overlap between the language of the narrator and that of the characters suggests a narrative metalepsis, or blurring of levels in the narrative hierarchy, which flies in the face of conventional consistency of technique. In fact, of course, at various moments the narrator's function is taken over by the protagonists as each in turn intervenes with a contribution. Elsewhere the narrator breaks into the fabric of his fiction with remarks which draw our attention to the fact that it is an artificial construction: 'The reader will allow us . . . to pay no further attention for the present to a person of whom he will see quite enough in the sequel' (303; 102) he says in conclusion to the opening sequence. Later, he brings an episode to a close with the remark: 'The end of this chapter can present only a much inferior interest to the reader' (315; 122); and one chapter heading actually reads: 'A Chapter to Keep the Reader Waiting for the Next' (319; 131). Elsewhere the narrator admits he is not omniscient and introduces a new chapter with the words: 'Not having known him personally, we have promised ourselves to speak only briefly of Zeus . . . Let us report simply these few phrases' (328; 151). Similarly, the chapter titles interrupt the flow of the narrative – reinforcing the impression of a narrative which is *mal enchaîné* – to tell us what is coming while paradoxically postponing its arrival:

Damocles said:

THE STORY OF DAMOCLES

'Sir . . .   (308; 110–11)

All these devices are typical of a certain kind of self-conscious fiction, drawing on eighteenth-century models such as Diderot's *Jacques le fataliste*, Sterne's *Tristram Shandy* or Fielding's *Tom Jones*, which has become an important strand in the evolution of the twentieth-century novel. Gide's most significant contribution to the trend is generally held to be *Les Faux-Monnayeurs*, but *Le Prométhée Mal Enchaîné* can be seen to anticipate the techniques of the later text by a quarter of a century. Even the device of multiple points of view, so important in *Les Faux-Monnayeurs*, is foreshadowed here in the fact that the initial encounter between Zeus and Coclès is told and retold five times in all, so that we view it as an incident with as many dimensions as it has ramifications for the group of people it impinges upon.[154] Narrative as an element in everyday intercourse is highlighted by the way Coclès, whose special aptitude is for making deals, insists that Prométhée must tell his story if he is to be accepted as a member of the group.[155] The interactive aspects of the form are foregrounded, held up for scrutiny: 'Gentlemen, I see, from the absence of your amazement, that I am telling my story badly', says Damoclès (308–9; 112), and the phatic elements of narrative – those essential ingredients that serve to maintain the reader's attention – are satirised in the fireworks and photographs which Prométhée distributes during his lecture.

In fact, however, Prométhée's lecture represents a different genre within the work, and it says something satirical for the character of the novel that when Prométhée feels his impassioned rhetoric is failing to hold his audience's attention or compel their assent, he resorts to the tactics of a novelist: 'Gentlemen! Don't get up now: I'm going to bring personalities in' (327; 145). The work as a whole makes striking use of such juxtapositions of contrasting discourses, some of which have been touched on already. It begins with the appearance of a chronicle, a factual record or *fait divers* susceptible of corroboration by a number of witnesses who were present:

but the reference to 'Zeus, the banker' (303; 102) shows this to be a parody. Elaine Cancalon catalogues other discursive genres which make their appearances: the lecture/sermon, the parable, the myth, an interview between Zeus, Prométhée and the waiter; choral voices of the bystanders commenting on Prométhée's eagle and his lecture, or Moelibée's appearance on the boulevard.[156] To these we could add the publicity poster, reproduced in the text (320; 113), as is a line from Virgil's *Bucolics* (339; 170) and biblical quotations and allusions in large numbers, such as the pastiche of John 1 with 'in the beginning was Tityrus' (335; 164).[157] The communicative power of journalism is satirised as the Parisians mob the news-stands to learn from the press that 'this Meliboeus was someone without any clothes who was going to Italy' (339; 171). Similarly the fact that the slap dealt out by Zeus to Coclès 'was not reported in any of the newspapers' (303; 101) is noted as a double-edged testimony to the status of what we are reading – more real than the news? Or unreal, since unreported by the press? Hence *Le Prométhée Mal Enchaîné* can be seen to be flamboyantly self-conscious, flaunting its own devices to keep the reader aware of what goes to make up a novel. It highlights in its burlesque way the interpenetration of forms and structures which are used conventionally to create an impression of a seamless reality. Here the resolutely disjoined – *mal enchaîné* – structure through which they are presented serves to blur the very distinction between reality and fiction. *Le Prométhée Mal Enchaîné* is therefore a forerunner of those modern texts of which Jonathan Culler has written: 'In place of the novel as mimesis we have the novel as a structure which plays with different modes of ordering and enables the reader to understand how he makes sense of the world'.[158]

Les Caves du Vatican (The Vatican Cellars)

Gide worked intermittently on *Les Caves du Vatican* for some fifteen years before seriously putting pen to paper. The idea for the book dates from 1893,[159] and in 1898 he was gathering newspaper cuttings on the Vatican swindle which inspired it;[160] but the earliest manuscript draft of an introductory passage appears to have been written in 1909.[161] The work was not completed until mid-1913.[162] Hence, many of the intellectual preoccupations we have referred to earlier fed into this text. In particular, it is clear that the state of the natural sciences is of considerable interest to the author since Anthime Armand-Dubois, whose activities furnish the narrative impetus in the first part of *Les Caves*, is the personification of a certain type of experimental scientist. It is through his story, indeed, that Gide establishes much of the novel's thematic underpinning. Gide's own concern with natural history acquired a particular intensity when, some time before 1908, he embarked on *Corydon*,[163] which was to be a justification of homosexuality using arguments drawn from as wide a range of human activities as possible, embracing literature, history and the law as well as the sciences. This book was obviously controversial, and Gide was wary of releasing it. He published a version consisting of the first two chapters and the first third of chapter three in 1911, in an edition amounting to only twelve copies; and he continued working on it while writing *Les Caves du Vatican* and subsequent books, up to the date of publication of the complete text in 1920.[164] It entailed wide research, particularly in the natural sciences; and throughout the first decade of the century, Gide pursued a systematic study of Darwin, evolutionary theory and related scientific topics. We have previously indicated the extent of his interest in Darwin; already by 1900 he had been seeking to reconcile, as he put it, Darwinism and creationism.[165] His diary shows him reading Darwin's *Diary* in February 1906; *Voyage of the Beagle* in May 1906; his autobiographical writings in June 1910; *The Origin of Species* in 1911. He read Bergson's *L'Evolution créatrice* in 1908 and polemics against Darwin by the entomologist J.-H. Fabre in 1910. It is significant, therefore, that the first section of *Les Caves du Vatican*, 'Anthime Armand-Dubois', was written in 1911, the very year which saw the completion and publication of the first section of *Corydon* which sets out, as Painter puts it, 'a Darwinian theory of the evolutionary necessity of homosexuality'.[166] Daniel Moutote, who has examined the background to *Corydon*, picks out *L'Evolution créatrice* in particular as an important source of inspiration for Gide at this time.[167] In fact, when Gide read this work in 1908 he noted the 'Capital importance of this book, through which philosophy can again escape' (*JI*, 269; *J1*, 233; 28 July 1908). The full relevance of this remark strikes home when we consider that Lafcadio, the hero of *Les Caves du Vatican*, is lodged at the start of his story at an address in the 'Impasse Claude-Bernard' (708; 36). His adventures will illustrate the liberating influence of a revolution in scientific and philosophical thought which permits an escape from the dead end of mechanical positivism. Anthime Armand-Dubois epitomises the narrow approach to science with his ambition relentlessly to pin down, measure and quantify natural processes. Specifically, his scientific reputation has been built on his achievements in attempting to 'reduce all the animal activities he had under observation, to . . . "tropisms"' (683; 5). The narrator of the novel comments on the tremendous vogue the concept acquired almost immediately it was coined. Just as a sunflower turns in response to the sunlight, so any organism's movements can be explained in terms of a reflex response to an external stimulus, 'a fact which is easily to be explained by a few simple laws of physics and thermochemistry' (683; 5). The satirical tone with which these theories are presented, the ironic cry 'Tropisms! A sudden flood of light emanated from these syllables!' leads to the debunking 'The order of the universe could at last be hailed as reassuringly benign'. The crudely deterministic, cause-and-effect interpretation of life's processes is indeed comforting to some; and despite Gide's mocking stance, it is a fact that such theories were extremely influential around the turn of the century. The most celebrated proponent of the theory of animal tropisms, Jacques Loeb, attained great fame and worldly success for works such as *The Mechanistic Conception of Life* (1912) in which he expounded his views on how simple physico-chemical mechanisms accounted for the most complex biological phenomena.[168] Both he and his disciples Bohn and Weiler are said in an early manuscript of *Les Caves du Vatican* to be collaborators of Armand-Dubois,[169] and they are also referred to in *Corydon* (57–8; 34) as having reduced instincts to the status of 'un mécanisme'. How, then, was Gide in a position to counter the prestige their theories commanded?

The authority with which he dismisses the tropistic school of scientific thought apparently derives from a note he read in Bergson's *L'Evolution créatrice*, which states that 'A very penetrating critique of the idea of tropisms has recently been carried out by Jennings (*Contribution to the study of the behaviour of lower organisms*, Washington, 1904)'.[170] Bergson himself underlines the impossibility of applying 'a physico-chemical explanation' to the movements of living organisms, thus providing Gide with just the ammunition he needed and confirming him in his opposition to the mechanistic universe exemplified in the theories of Anthime Armand-Dubois.

This example demonstrates the extent of the genuine scientific curiosity and detailed knowledge which inform *Les Caves du Vatican*. Arising from the same source, and developing themes we have already seen in Gide's narratives, are numerous other features of the work. Several incidents and aspects of the novel's plot can be related to Gide's continuing preoccupation with evolutionary theory. One of the reasons he was impressed by *L'Evolution créatrice*, for example, was that Bergson was striving above all to break the connections which persisted between evolutionary theory and 'the mechanistic conception of life'.[171] Most notably the philosopher tackles an important aspect of Darwinian evolution which had proved unacceptable to Gide. For all the far-reaching implications of Darwinism, his insistence that the random processes in nature operate through gradual transformations and minute variations left his theories tied, in significant respects, to a notion of linear, unbroken causality. Gide had certainly experienced this as a limitation on the theory's potential for reshaping the contemporary world-view. In his own attempts to reconcile Darwinism and creationism[172] Gide was in practice joining the ranks of the so-called 'saltationists' who sought to modify Darwin's theories by insisting on the feasibility of the sudden appearance of complex organs or organisms manifesting a break in the chain of gradual evolutionary progression.[173] No really radical breaks or novel departures in the evolutionary sequence are possible in Darwin's formulation. Indeed the naturalist was concerned to stipulate this as a principle, invoking what he calls 'that old canon in natural history of "Natura non facit saltum". . . . Natural selection can act only by taking advantage of slight successive variations; she can never take a leap, but must advance by the shortest and slowest steps'.[174] Gide will return to this stumbling-block more than once. Armand Vedel in *Les Faux-Monnayeurs* declares sceptically, ' "Natura non fecit saltus", What absurd rubbish!' (1163; 255), and in a letter dating from 1932, Gide remarks:

> There is no adage more fiercely opposed nowadays by naturalists themselves than the one which not long ago was considered an unimpeachable truth: 'Nature does not proceed by leaps' – Natura non fecit saltus . . . it is indeed on this point . . . that Darwin's theories, when put into practice, showed themselves to be most vulnerable.[175]

These later declarations simply state the position Gide had reached much earlier, partly at least through his reading of *L'Evolution créatrice*. Bergson devotes a section of his essay to 'la variation insensible' and 'la variation brusque' in which he points out that experiments performed by the Dutch botanist Hugo de Vries have shown that Darwin was wrong, and that previously unknown species *can* come into being through the sudden appearance of new characteristics.[176] Gide obviously registered these observations, since he read de Vries' work on mutations, finding that it further increased his own mistrust of the gradualist principles of transformism.[177] In fact, he alludes tellingly to de Vries in that first version of *Corydon* which was contemporary with *Les Caves du Vatican*. 'Today it may seem to us that the whole of Darwin's theory is tottering *upon its very foundation*', he writes, referring to de Vries as the cause of this uncertainty.[178]

These considerations are crucial to an appreciation of *Les Caves du Vatican*, since the book takes up and gives new impetus to Gide's long-standing concern with sudden departures from the norm and with unforeseen occurrences. As we have observed, since *Le Traité du Narcisse* and *Paludes*, Gide's protagonists have demonstrated their desire for 'the unforeseen' as a means of breaking out of determinism and stagnation.[179] By the time he wrote *Les Caves du Vatican*, Gide was equipped with a scientific vindication of the theme confirming that there was apparently no restriction on the creative potential of the random forces operating in the world. The idea therefore recurs with new force, chiefly through the character of Lafcadio, who is another character in search of 'the unforeseen', seeing it as incompatible with scientific theories of cause and effect which tend to imply that events can be predicted. As Lafcadio puts it: 'One imagines *what would happen if*, but there's always a little hiatus through which the unexpected creeps in' (823; 184). The important point is that scientific explanations do not exhaust the possibilities of what might happen, since reality has a capacity for sudden jumps and discontinuities which defy our predictions. Furthermore, the very secret of development, in the evolutionary perspective, is variation and diversification, rather than truth to type and the faithful replication of pre-existing patterns. Lafcadio himself is 'a creature of inconsequence' (744; 83), an exception to, and indeed a critic of, those views on personality, held by such as Julius de Baraglioul, which see consistency, continuity and logic as the hallmark of human psychology. There is even a suggestion that Lafcadio represents an evolutionary mutation; being illegitimate, he came into being, as Protos/Defouqueblize puts it 'owing to an erratic impulse – to a crook in the straight line' (854; 225), and certainly in him the genes of Juste-Agénor de Baraglioul prove capable of considerable variations from their respectable lineage. Moreover, Lafcadio himself briefly considers a journey of exploration to Borneo, in search of 'a belated anthropopithex', the paleontologists' missing link which would highlight the potential alternatives inherent in evolution, 'the chances of a future race of mankind' (823; 184). The mysterious Protos is mutation personified: only once may we be said to see him as he really is, since throughout the novel he exercises his faculty, exemplified in his name, for sudden, unexpected changes of identity. In the person of Defouqueblize, indeed, he sets out a theory of mutations, arguing that 'an honest man' can be transformed into 'a rogue' by the effect of 'a cessation of continuity – a simple interruption of the current' (854; 225).

The possibilities contained in humanity, underscored by evolutionary theory and hinted at in the motifs we have mentioned, express themselves in a burlesque way in *Les Caves du Vatican* through the surprising mutations undergone by Anthime Armand-Dubois and by his brother-in-law, the novelist Julius de Baraglioul.[180] It is after all Julius himself who flies in the face of the science Gide had been exploring by declaring: 'There is no such thing as inconsequence – in psychology any more than in physics' (744; 84). In spite of the gulf which separates the respectable Catholic de Baraglioul from the atheist Freemason Armand-Dubois, at bottom they share the same conservative world-view, which serves to transform reality into something 'reassuringly benign' (683; 5). All is predictable, consistent and explicable in positivist, rational or commonsense terms. Both characters have a horror, expressed by Anthime Armand-Dubois, of all that threatens 'the established order – the natural order – the venerable order of cause and effect' (696; 21) – and it is significant, of course, that their two discourses, which differ in other respects, have in common the notion of order.[181] Both these characters will become victims of transformations which ironically disprove their orderly views on nature and society. It represents a striking comeuppance, for example, that with scientific theories such as he holds, Anthime Armand-Dubois should be subject both to a 'miraculous' cure which rids him of his rheumatic disability and to a dramatic conversion which transforms him overnight from an atheistic, free-thinking materialist to a pious and devout Christian. There is an obvious irony in having the scientist's own life contradict the views he propounds as he passes by a sudden mutation from one extreme to another. Similarly, Julius de Baraglioul, the embodiment of all that is respectable, distinguished and restrained, finds himself embarked on a train of thought and obsessed by a set of notions that change him into the wild-eyed, excitable character whom his other brother-in-law, Amédée Fleurissoire, barely recognises beneath the transformation (811, 815, 817; 169, 174–5, 177). The full extent of these two mutations is underlined by the way in which Gide shows each to have moved to his opponent's initial position and become the mirror-image of what he was originally. Anthime, the erstwhile materialist, scientist and rejecter of all that is spiritual, when converted so develops his pious lack of regard for material matters that it is Julius himself who by reaction becomes the materialist, concerned with possessions and financial well-being and even hinting at the shortcomings of the Church, whereas earlier such questions could hardly have been further from his mind: 'Yes, but those worldly goods were yours by rights. It's all very well that the Church should teach you to despise them, but not that she should cheat you of them' (771; 118).[182] A parallel though no less astonishing mutation brought about by this turn of events is undergone by Mme Armand-Dubois, whose initial disposition of 'smiling unruffled smoothness' (698; 24) is brusquely replaced by acrimonious irritation (722; 119) when she has to live on the limited means at her newly pious husband's disposal. At the same time, from resistance to Lafcadio's views upon life and literature, Julius is completely converted, to the extent of planning a novel on precisely the theme he had dismissed as impossible: 'a creature of inconsequence' (813; 171).

Julius has an afterthought on inconsistency: 'No doubt this apparent inconsequence hides what is, in reality, a subtler and more recondite sequence' (813; 171). While this may be taken as an indication of Julius's reluctance to take the idea too far and thus as a presage of his subsequent conversion back to respectability, none the less it does place limits on Gide's apparent portrayal of random mutations in human nature. For while on the one hand the occurrence of such mutations confirms that nature and human nature are much more complex and richer in possibilities than bourgeois forms of science, psychology and morality will admit, on the other, Gide is concerned to indicate by a further set of ironies that some element of choice, and therefore of will, enters into these conversions. The motif of choice figures most noticeably – and most significantly – in the epigraphs to the books that introduce Anthime and Julius. At the start of the novel, a quotation from Georges Palante is used, as emerges with hindsight, to satirise the idea of choice: 'For my part, my choice is made. I have opted for social atheism' (680).[183] The pompous, definitive tone suggests someone for whom choice is rather a rejection of alternative possibilities, a retreat from life's complexities. This is certainly the case where Anthime is concerned; he is determined to banish nuances and uncertainty through his scientific work, and will not admit of anything inexplicable in life, 'for he was bold enough to aim at storming God in His most secret strongholds' (684; 6). Moreover, Gide takes care to indicate here as he does in the case of Michel or Alissa that psychological or temperamental determinants give to Anthime's views a 'vérité psychologique' which is more important than any putative general validity they are unlikely in any case to have. The remarks of Julius in the opening paragraphs of the book suggest a possible connection between Anthime's unnaturally stiff body and his rigid convictions; and the narrator intervenes at some length to reinforce the link, adding to the rheumatic affliction Anthime's wen:

> And, indeed, who could affirm that this wen had no share, no weight, in the decisions of what Anthime called his *free* thought? He was more willing to overlook his sciatica; but this *mean trick* was a thing for which he could not forgive God.   (686; 8)

Perhaps, then, Anthime's atheism and his scientific research merely serve to express his resentment of God for the undeserved afflictions he has had to bear. His need to offend believers actually indicates an attachment, though hostile, to what they hold dear. His sacrilegious act, damaging the statue of the Virgin, constitutes a kind of recognition of Her importance to him. Similarly, his association with the Freemasons and the Lodge can easily be seen as a substitute for a relationship with the institutions of religion. In fact the way in which announcements of his conversion are used as ammunition in the continuing war between the Church and the Masons (703–6; 31–4) shows up the similarities between both sides: each represents a form of orthodoxy, so that as Anthime passes from one to the other little has actually changed.

This becomes all the more clear if we study his subsequent behaviour. 'From that day onwards, Anthime, absorbed by more elevated preoccupations, scarcely noticed the noise that was made about his name', we learn (705; 35). He is financially ruined as his former sources of income, from articles in radical newspapers, dry up, but he 'accepted these blows with that serenity of countenance which *the truly devout soul affects*' (705;

34). The suggestion of deliberate role-playing here casts doubt on his good faith. Subsequently, his stubborn refusal to seek redress for the wrongs done him by the Church hierarchy which lets him down after promising material assistance on his conversion shows him adhering to principles which are every bit as fixed and unyielding as those he formerly upheld. Before his conversion, too, 'Anthime professed great contempt for the advantages of rank, fortune and looks' (690; 14).[184] His lack of concern for what he now calls 'worldly goods' (771; 119) is therefore nothing new. His previous main characteristic was his 'obstinacy' (681; 2); that he has changed little since his conversion is evident in the way his wife berates him for being 'like [that] the whole time' (771; 118). When he and Julius meet again at the funeral of Amédée Fleurissoire, Anthime is still set in his ways, still resolutely resigned and pious in the face of continuing misfortune and neglect by the Church; and Julius accuses him of betraying 'pride rather than sanctity' and of adopting a posture 'savouring more of rebellion than of true piety' (862; 235). Thus, when Julius reveals his apparent discovery that the Pope is an impostor, Anthime experiences little difficulty in reverting to his earlier stance – evincing indignation, notwithstanding his erstwhile lack of concern, at the fortune and position he had sacrificed for what now appears a bogus ideal – and resumes his vendetta against the universe in its earlier guise (863–4; 238–9). Even his physical disability reasserts itself. If he cannot be sure of the Church and the certainties it offers, he will go back to his scientific convictions.

What are we to make of this paradoxical saga? First, that Anthime remains constant beneath an appearance of evolution; his hypocrisy, conscious or unconscious, remains his chief characteristic, along with his need for convictions. In his case, no real change has occurred. And yet he has undergone shifts in his point of view, and he has undergone unaccountable physiological transformations: so Gide does not seem to be suggesting that he is entirely trapped within the determinations of his condition.[185] The point is that the changes he undergoes are not experienced as true freedom of choice; he chooses to change from atheism to belief and back again, but does not realise that in so choosing he demonstrates his potential to opt to remain free of all fixed views and pre-ordained beliefs. He is not willing or able to choose to live with uncertainties; change in him is merely a change from one set of fixed values to a substitute set which is little different in character or function: such sets of convictions serve indifferently as alibis for the indulgence of basic needs and instincts.

Julius's mutations reinforce this motif of choices which leave essential issues untouched. The epigraph with which he is introduced announces that 'one should never deny anyone a change of heart' (707; 35), a precept borne out by what we have seen of Anthime's boomerang-like itinerary. Julius will follow an identical pattern. His fundamental characteristic might be summed up by saying that he makes a virtue of what comes easiest to him. We learn that he lives in accordance with Descartes' rule of a 'provisional moral law' – giving to the regime an indefinite extension which spares him the trouble of considering morality more closely. In the meantime, remaining respectable imposes no hardship on him: 'Julius's temperament was not so intractable nor his intellect so commanding as to have given him hitherto much trouble in conforming to the proprieties. On the whole, all that he demanded of life was his comfort' (731; 66–7), says the narrator with heavy irony. Julius is in fact the embodiment of an ideal which Protos/Defouqueblize evokes, tongue in cheek, as the aim of all who seek social approval: 'Respectable! yes – and it mustn't look as if it were forced . . . One must not only never *do* anything out of the way, one must persuade other people that one *couldn't* do anything out of the way, even with all the licence in the world – that there's nothing whatever out of the way in one, wanting to come out' (853; 224). However, Julius's comfortable existence is slightly unsettled when his edifying novel based on the life of his father fails to win him the recognition he had hoped for, either from his father or from the Académie Française, where his chances of admission appear to be slim. 'For the first time in his life awful questionings beset him. He . . . felt rising within him a doubt . . . as to the genuineness of his life' (710; 39). His meetings with Lafcadio, who calls into question his art and lifestyle, further trouble him, as does the Church's neglect of

Anthime following his much publicised conversion. Before
long he is alluding to 'the strange preoccupations' (773; 120)
which are disturbing him. Thus he is gradually weaned away
from his former comfortable assumptions and habits of mind.
Here too, then, a sequence can be seen to underlie the
apparently inconsequential shift in his outlook.[186] When in
Rome, he seeks an audience with the Pope in an attempt to
bring to his attention the distress of his brother-in-law; but
by this time he has all but broken free from his former
attachments under the influence of the unconventional ideas
Lafcadio has inspired in him. He is, in fact, planning a
subversive novel which will feature 'inconsequences' and
gratuitous actions – a radical departure from his previous
works. This is what accounts for the transformation Amédée
notices when he comes across him by chance in Rome. Amédée
has become convinced that the Pope has been kidnapped and,
fearing for his own life, vouchsafes to Julius a revelation that
the Pope he has seen is an impostor. The latter's reaction, a
refusal to believe rather than an inability to believe, is
surprising but revealing:

> Not that! Good God! No! Not that! . . . What! I succeed –
> with great difficulty – in clearing my mind of the whole
> thing; I convince myself that there's nothing to be expected –
> nothing to be hoped for – nothing to be admitted; . . .
> *Dammit, I break free; and no sooner have I reconciled myself to this*
> *state of affairs than* up you come and say: 'Hold hard! There's
> been a mistake – a misdeal – we must begin again.' Oh, no!
> Not a bit of it! Never in the world! I shan't budge. If he
> isn't the real one, so much the worse. (815; 174)

Julius is put out at the prospect of having to liberate himself
all over again. But, in fact, in liberating himself from the
Church he was merely accomplishing the least demanding
solution to the problem he had been faced with. This problem
essentially lay in a contradiction: between on the one hand a
belief in the Catholic Church which cares for all its members
irrespective of social hierarchies, and on the other hand the
evidence that the Church has not come to the assistance of
Anthime and Véronique. If now he has to attribute this neglect

to the fact that the Church is in the control of unscrupulous con-men, then he will be faced with the need to reconstitute his relationship to the 'real' Church and his problem will require yet another solution. (We see the same reflex later when he avoids facing up to the implications of Lafcadio's admission that he has murdered Amédée.) So he chooses, quite deliberately, not to believe Amédée: at the moment his 'radical' new outlook paradoxically keeps his life simple and commits him to nothing other than writing a book. What he says to Lafcadio about his present state of mind is highly significant: 'Now I feel in myself the strangest possibilities. And as it's only on paper, I shall boldly let myself go' (837; 202). Like Lafcadio, like Gide himself, Julius perceives the potential for variation and evolution in his nature; but literature serves him as an alibi, providing a fictional outlet which carries no practical consequences for him. It is true that the murder of Amédée provides him with just the real-life incident he needs for his projected novel about the *acte gratuit* ('gratuitous action'); but he resolves to use this example only because he has decided that in reality Amédée was killed for money (839; 208). That is after all the simplest explanation for the sad event. But when Lafcadio points out that the murderer did *not* rob Amédée of the money he was carrying, this means the incident confirms all Julius's theories about unmotivated crimes: whereupon real life threatens to become complex and unsettling again. Faced with an explanation of such far-reaching subversive significance, Julius turns to that theory he had previously rejected as uncomfortable – but which now looks like the lesser of two evils: Amédée was killed because he had found out about the kidnapping of the Pope (841–2; 208–9). 'There's no such thing as a crime without a motive' (842; 209) he says, with the same peremptory conviction with which he had earlier denied the possibility of *inconséquence* in nature. With his choice of the least difficult of these two options available to him, Julius is back to square one after a number of shifts and choices each of which asserts his capacity for intellectual and imaginative freedom, but all of which show him actually refusing freedom and the uncertainty and discomfort it brings in its wake. Descartes' 'provisional moral law' is not at all to his taste, in fact: when

under pressure, he wants ready-made frames of reference set
out in clear conventional terms – and which he can substitute
one for the other as circumstances require – rather than
provisional views, always liable to revision, that call for
creative moral effort and commitment on his part. Through
never sticking his neck out he has never denied himself 'a
change of heart', as his epigraph puts it; and in the end, with
his election to the Académie Française, he can congratulate
himself on the constancy he has shown throughout:

> 'Faithful . . . to my opinions, to my principles . . .' . . . He
> was filled with admiration for the subtle consistency which
> his mind had shown in its temporary deviation. It was not
> *he* who had changed – it was the Pope!
>
> (861; 234. Italics in original)

Anthime bitterly indicates the most consistent fact about
Julius's behaviour, addressing him as 'You who profit by
everything – true or false' (864; 238). Julius adopts the belief
which best serves his own conventionally defined view of what
constitutes his interest, and will always find a moral principle
that permits him to do what he wants. (An example would
be the manner in which he gives way to his curiosity about
the contents of an unlocked drawer in Lafcadio's room, telling
himself that 'in obedience to his father's command' it is his
duty to find out all he can (716; 46).)

Another striking thesis illustrated by the stories of Anthime
and Julius is that it is above all imaginary constructions of
the world which are the foundation for the ethical codes people
maintain. *Les Caves du Vatican* might thus be said to anticipate
by over half a century those theorists who have used the term
'ideology' to denote the workings of the imaginary relationship
through which individuals live out the real conditions of their
existence.[187] Both Anthime and Julius make sense of the
universe they inhabit by accepting the proposition that the
Pope has been incarcerated and replaced at the head of the
Church by a criminal substitute. The fact that such a state of
affairs constitutes a moral scandal as well as an outrage against
common sense is immaterial to them; to preserve their
psychological and moral equilibrium they will subscribe to

any cockeyed theory. Plausibility or verisimilitude, as Barthes has argued, is very much a matter of consensus:[188] for Anthime, Julius and Amédée, not to mention Arnica Fleurissoire and the comtesse de Saint-Prix, the fictional invention conforms to the reality they experience – or vice versa. The politics of the situation alone are enough to require an explanation in these terms for conventional believers, as the scoundrel Protos indicates when pointing to historical reality as proof of the cock-and-bull tale he has recounted to the countess. Pope Leo XIII, who had issued an encyclical letter in 1892 exhorting the faithful of France to rally to the support of the Republic, was in effect going against everything that French Catholicism, traditionally monarchist and anti-republican, had stood for for over a century. Protos' chief gambit is to suggest that this incredible document has been written by an impostor; and where reality itself defies belief, fiction gains enthusiastic adherents.[189]

Amédée Fleurissoire, setting out on a solo crusade to rescue the Pope, will find himself enmeshed in just such an insubstantial labyrinth where reality and plausible possibility overlap. He learns that objectively the false Pope is serving the interests of the Jesuits with his outlandish encyclicals: 'Perhaps they are not aware that the Pope who promulgated them is not the *real* one; but they would be heart-broken if he were changed' (803; 159). At a clandestine rendezvous Amédée is obliged to carouse for security's sake with the two con-men passing themselves off as priests who in turn have had to disguise themselves as ordinary mortals: this does not prevent him from seeing, beneath the jovial air of the man he has been introduced to, 'a discreet touch of cardinalesque unction' (800; 155). Reality, in this perspective, is what the individual has been conditioned to see. But as a result of the dizzying play of perspectives to which he is exposed, Amédée has his eyes opened to another, more authentic and disturbing reality, the kind from which he and his family have instinctively averted their gaze. 'I see something disquieting in the appearance of everyone I pass in the street . . . I didn't realise till today how rarely people's presence in the street is justifiable' (795–6; 149). Antoine Roquentin in Sartre's *La Nausée* comes to a similar perception: it concerns the contingency of existence, the sense that there is nothing necessary or fixed about the forms which furnish the world.[190] In this perspective, reality *is* the absence of explanation or justification for what is simply there; uncertainty is the closest human beings can get to an authentic perception of the real. Reality is what is left when ideological constructions – authorised and unauthorised – cease to compel credence. Thus, though he is utterly taken in by the 'Millipede', Fleurissoire proceeds through the whirligig of delusion and illusion to confront a problem none of his fellow-protagonists has dared face up to. As he is presented with a real newspaper article warning against fraudsters and sees in it confirmation of the truth of the story the crooks are telling him, we read: ' "*So* what is one to do?" *groaned (gémit)* Fleurissoire' (804–5; 161). 'I can approve only of those who seek while groaning *(en gémissant)*', is the Pascalian epigraph to this book which depicts the hapless Fleurissoire ensnared by the 'Millipede' (774; 121); and for all the burlesque or grotesque aspects of the tale, there is at the core of this narrative a serious exploration of existential uncertainty. Truth, falsehood and the distinction between them are functions of belief, convention, or imagination. When the central convictions upholding the meaning systems we inhabit – God, the Pope, the gold in Fort Knox, the value of sterling or whatever – cease to command assent, then the individual is reduced to the state of Amédée: 'He walked as though in a dream, doubting the solidity of the ground, of the walls – doubting the actual existence of the people he passed – doubting, above all, his own presence in Rome . . .' (809; 167). He will later attribute his state to having contracted a fever: 'A fever that cannot – that *must* not be cured; a fever . . . which I hoped – yes, I own it – you too would catch from me . . . I see only too clearly now that the path I follow – the dark and dangerous path I am called upon to follow – must needs be solitary' (818; 177–8). Far from the ordered, reassuringly benign cosmos inhabited by Anthime and Julius, Amédée finds himself in a menacing universe filled with doubt and insecurity. Fleurissoire may be a pathetic figure, but he is none the less exemplary as he struggles to find his way in a world in which the hierarchy of meanings and values has evaporated.

As the normal distinction between reality and imagined world-views ceases to be operable, so the possibilities open to the imagination impose themselves with renewed force. Similarly, as contingency is seen to be the chief characteristic of existence, then the fact that existence could have been, could be, different demands to be considered. These ideas are again inherent in Darwinian theories of evolution, and they have far-reaching implications for the construction of narrative and plot in the novel. As formulated by Bergson, natural evolution is a narrative whose plot defies the application of 'both mechanistic and finalistic conceptions of development'.[191] Gide glosses this view at length in the second chapter of *Corydon*, bringing out the analogy with the two types of causality, 'backward' and 'forward', we have seen working in narrative and remarking that it is impossible to decide which way to 'read' Nature, 'and if the whole book of nature, to be properly understood, should not be read backwards – in other words, if the last page is not the explanation of the first'.[192] Science explains phenomena after the event, and always in terms of 'already conceived, already known', says Bergson.[193] Consequently it cannot account for, still less predict, true novelty brought into being by a random event. Narrative too, as Barthes demonstrates, is dependent for its intelligibility on patterns provided by the 'already-written, already-read, already-seen, already-done'.[194] However, the workings of nature and the world are governed by chance, which defeats the intellectual categories through which we attempt to think it: 'The mind . . . when it tries to define chance . . . hovers, unable to settle, between the idea of the absence of a final cause and that of the absence of an efficient cause, each of these two definitions sending one back to the other', argues Bergson.[195] Similarly, as we have remarked earlier, the nature of narrative militates against attempts to portray chance since all its constituents are fitted into a structure which, by making a place for them, renders them necessary. Thus the fortuitous in a novel produces, in Barthes' term which restates Bergson's philosophical aporia, an effect of 'undecidability'.[196] The narrative which is informed by the spirit of evolutionary theory, as *Les Caves du Vatican* undoubtedly is, must therefore find ways of coping with the incompatibility between its form and the desired content.

Les Caves du Vatican engages most significantly with this problem through the motif of the *acte gratuit*. We have seen from our discussion of *Le Prométhée Mal Enchaîné* that in its pseudo-divine manifestation, as performed by Zeus, the *acte gratuit* marks the injection of chance into the world. Now chance, as defined by the philosopher Hegel, 'is a reality which is simultaneously nothing other than a possible for which another or the opposite exists just as much':[197] which is to say that when a chance event occurs we are made aware that something entirely different might just as easily have happened, and that chance therefore brings in its wake, and establishes a place within reality for, the notion of alternative possibilities. Chance and contingency are essential ingredients in evolutionary theory, as Bergson points out; he also links them to the living organism in an illuminating way. 'A living being . . . represents a certain sum of contingency introducing itself into the world, that is to say a certain quantity of possible action', he writes.[198] Much discussion of the *acte gratuit* has centred on plausible mechanistic interpretations of its motivation, prompted no doubt by the untenability of Julius's suggestion that it would in fact be unmotived, disinterested, and therefore unattributable to any specific individual (818; 178).[199] Gide himself later felt obliged to refute the more extreme implications of this thesis: 'Certainly, no gesture is really unmotivated; no act 'gratuitous' except in appearance'.[200] What he did suggest was that actions which are apparently unmotivated are so because they cannot be explained in terms of received psychological notions; thus the *acte gratuit* offers the possibility of exploring hitherto uncharted regions of the psyche from whence it erupts.[201] Yvonne Davet maintains plausibly that Lafcadio's action in pushing Amédée out of a moving train is nothing of the sort, but merely a caricature or parody of it.[202] The misunderstandings which occur in discussions of the *acte gratuit* stem from a failure to link it properly to its antecedent in Zeus' actions and to stress the random or contingent character of Lafcadio's behaviour.[203]

We get a hint of what Gide had in mind in recounting

Lafcadio's adventures from a note in his diary for 1909. Here
he discusses 'La Partie de Tric-Trac' ('The Backgammon
Game'), a story by Mérimée in which the hero cheats in a
dice game, wins a fortune and provokes the suicide of his
opponent, a Dutchman. Gide was profoundly dissatisfied with
the way Mérimée works out the plot, and set about positing
a different version in which an alternative set of events
develops out of the initial premiss: 'But what would he have
done if the Dutchman hadn't killed himself? What would he
have done if he had won only a little? *That is what interests me.*
. . . He would have cheated again. And that would have been
very *poignant*'. Gide links this version of the story to the
transformation of an 'honest man' into a 'rogue' which he will
have Protos/Defouqueblize expatiate upon in *Les Caves du
Vatican* (854; 225); and he concludes his ruminations with the
remark: 'This is the story of Lafcadio' (*JI*, 277; *J1*, 241: 3
December 1909). In fact, the only material detail Lafcadio's
story acquires from this passage is 'one of a pair of *backgammon*
dice' (831; 195), a present from his uncle Baldi though
clearly deriving from Mérimée, which he has carried around
everywhere for years, and which does play a crucial role in
his narrative, as we shall show. The more general interest of
the text lies in the way Gide adumbrates a mode of reading
between the lines of a narrative, bringing out a range of
possibilities which tell a different story. The implications of
contingency – the fact that events originating in chance
occurrences come shadowed by equally plausible alternative
versions of reality – alter the way in which causality, both in
reality and in narrative, is envisaged. Thus Lafcadio thinks
about the old woman whose bag he carried up the hill for her:
'I could just as easily have throttled her', he muses, wondering
'what the old woman would have said if I had begun to
squeeze' (823; 183–4). He is fascinated by all the possibilities
that accompany what actually occurs; the actual course of
events does not exhaust the potential of a given situation. He
is constantly curious about 'what would happen if', just as
Gide was in relation to 'La Partie de Tric-Trac'; and behind
what he does subsists a kind of shadow-plot, charting these
alternatives. 'One does so little!', he exclaims, and wishes he
could bring into being all that the narrow dimensions of a

single human existence cannot accommodate: ' "Let all that can be, be!" That's my explanation of the Creation. . . . In love with what might be' (823; 184). It is this vision which is served in *Les Caves du Vatican* by Gide's use of the *acte gratuit*.[204] Gide is concerned first to avoid constructing a mechanistic sequence of events and second to evolve a mode of narrative which does not lose sight of alternative pathways leading simultaneously from any given situation. He achieves his aim by having his hero, like Zeus, inject chance into the plot. It is true that part of the appeal for Lafcadio of committing his *acte gratuit* is that he would have 'no more right to take back one's move than at chess' (829; 192): but chess is after all a game which permits repetition with variation of strategies, and which has the potential to produce many different outcomes from the same initial ingredients. Hence the story of Lafcadio shows him choosing certain actions, but at each stage we are made aware that another path lies open to him.[205]

'Certain critics of no little discernment have considered that fiction is history which *might* have taken place', says the narrator of *Les Caves du Vatican*, declining to acknowledge his source in the *Journal* of the Goncourt brothers (24 November 1861). More importantly, the remark links up with the Gidean theme of alternative histories (748; 88). Indeed, Gide's exploitation of the latent possibilities of history is at its most evident in the use to which he puts material deriving from the scandals involved in the alleged kidnapping of the Pope in the 1890s.[206] Protos in turn, in his disguise as the chanoine de Virmontal, will enlist the similarly scandalous historical enigma of the Mayerling affair of January 1889 to add plausibility to his affabulation (753; 94–5). These are telling examples of the hypothetical variants which make up the stuff of so-called real life. Something of the theoretical relationship of the novel (and other fictions) to history is reproduced in the analogous relationship, within *Les Caves du Vatican*, between on the one hand the narrative line and on the other what Umberto Eco calls 'inferential walks', narrative possibilities which the reader is induced to envisage by the way in which certain turning-points in the plot are presented.[207] An appeal to chance is the device Gide most typically uses in this respect. Lafcadio creates in himself a state of *disponibilité* ('availability') and makes himself available for whatever chance brings along: 'From whatever quarter the wind blows now it will be the right one' (745; 84). He explicitly trusts to random combinations of events to determine his most important actions: 'If I can count up to twelve, without hurrying, before I see a light in the countryside, the dromedary is saved' (829; 192). He and Amédée might just as easily journey on together to Naples. Once the murder is committed, however, and Lafcadio's hat – potentially incriminating evidence – has fallen from the train along with Fleurissoire, the reader conditioned by detective fiction or the *roman d'aventure* begins to speculate with some urgency as to whether or how he will avoid being caught.[208] The best thing would be to get off at the next station and go back to retrieve the hat. This is where the die comes in, to renew the recourse to chance: ' "If I throw six," he said to himself as he took it out, "I'll get *off*" ' (831; 195). The systematic refusal of a psychologically or generically determined course of action – not just at the moment of the *acte gratuit* but repeatedly thereafter – provokes within the reader an urge to follow precisely these 'overcoded, ready-made paths for inferential walks', to quote Eco's expression,[209] which arguably in this case have greater verisimilitude than what the novel actually narrates.[210] Gide deliberately plays on this response. Lafcadio throws a five, declares 'I shall get *off* all the same', but when he returns to his compartment to get his suitcase he finds it has gone, then sees it being carried along the platform by a receding figure; whereupon, instead of chasing after the man, he decides to stay on the train after all. Random conjunctions of circumstance dictate Lafcadio's behaviour and we are kept aware of divergent possibilities.[211]

In a sense, of course, all this is elementary narrative manipulation; but harnessed as it is to the quasi-philosophical notion of the *acte gratuit* and its consequences, it might repay further probing. It has been argued that a serious moral lesson can be derived from the fact that Lafcadio's action leads to his being drawn into a social context that threatens henceforth to determine his behaviour.[212] But this threat is only experienced as a *possibility*; for, in fact, the narrative traces the most elaborate path actually to prevent such a possibility from coming to pass. It is inferences drawn from clichés of the *roman-feuilleton* which activate the so-called moral lesson. Lafcadio first plans to 'sail as soon as possible', this being the most prudent course; then, with the discovery of the extraordinary coincidence that his victim is actually related to his half-brother Julius, he opts to return to Rome, which will be 'a good deal less wise, but perhaps a little more amusing' (832–3; 196–7). From this point on, he takes care to keep his trunk with him, because 'travellers without luggage are looked at askance'; and he contemplates buying a gun. Fillaudeau, pointing out that this latter plan does not come to fruition in any way, wonders whether it is to Gide or to Lafcadio that we are to attribute the oversight.[213] This misses the point: the effect of the reference, as of other similar ones, is to provoke speculation on the part of the reader – who readily embroiders on the detail left hanging in the air. Lafcadio's gratuitous activity, far from breaking with the established order, prompts a heightened awareness of such conservative patterns which here work chiefly through the reader's own conditioned responses, eliciting the spectre of Lafcadio's being tracked down. The press report of the discovery of one of Carola's cufflinks in the railway compartment opens further possibilities of detection and arrest, for example (834; 199). Shortly thereafter Lafcadio finds himself once more in a train, in conversation with a 'professor . . . of comparative criminology', when he is suddenly confronted with the missing cufflink which appears on his plate from nowhere. His instinctive reaction – to grab and hide it – reveals his guilt, and the episode prompts in him a paranoid sense of 'the police . . . *who doubtless have him under observation, are lying in wait for him*' (851; 222). From a mysterious, inexplicable convergence of chance events we are emboldened to make guesses as to what will follow. Clearly we can predict nothing in a world governed by random processes, but positivist reflexes die hard, especially in the reading process.

Notwithstanding the aura of possible apprehension by the police that accompanies Lafcadio's story, the real threat to him emerges from another quarter, since it is Protos who has Lafcadio in his power by virtue of the incriminating evidence he has accumulated. His plan to blackmail Lafcadio represents in fact the only serious consequence for the latter that his gratuitous act entails. It is interesting to note what Goulet has to say, from his scrutiny of the manuscripts, about the scene in which these threats are made. The plan of 1911–12 actually ends with this encounter; and the subsequent development evident in the manuscripts shows Gide working deliberately to circumvent Protos' plans. This he does by adding a dimension to the character of Carola Venitequa, making her fall in love with Amédée, so that when she learns of his death she will denounce Protos to the police.[214] In the finished version it takes Gide little more than a page to dispatch the two of them; we are told in three lines that she hates him because she is sure he killed Amédée, and that he strangles her, 'exasperated at learning that she had betrayed him' (866; 240). They are not given the time to realise Carola's mistake, and when the label from Lafcadio's hat is found in Protos's pocket, that clinches it for the authorities. The solution is nothing if not contrived.

Just as the *acte gratuit* may or may not have happened, so the events that follow from it plot a line which, at each 'disjunction of probabilities', to borrow another phrase from Eco,[215] leaves the reader contemplating an entirely different outcome, usually more plausible than the one the text makes explicit. The intrusive narrator's frequent allusions to the difficulty of reconciling his story-line with narrative verisimilitude (685–7, 748, 760, 831; 8, 88, 104, 195) further condition the reader to assess or recompose events in the light of a more likely set of consequences. At the decisive points in a narrative sequence, says Barthes, there are 'moments of risk . . . at every one of these points, an alternative – and hence a freedom of meaning – is possible'.[216] The extent to which *Les Caves* exploits this risk and hands to the reader this 'freedom of meaning' is evident when, for example, Lafcadio chooses to defy Protos' threats and declares: 'Excuse me if I prefer the police. Go and inform them. *I'll be waiting*' (859; 232). Lafcadio is a 'creature of inconsequence', and the fact that he so often makes the unlikely choice, taking the course of action that exposes himself to the greatest risk, invites comparison with the pusillanimous options selected by Anthime and Julius. It also enhances the effect of arbitrariness in the narrative line. But a similar effect is generated when the narrative itself, in the face of overwhelming odds in favour of Lafcadio's incurring some form of retribution, selects the least plausible outcome: that he will get off scot-free. Protos has conveniently removed from the scene of the crime the chief clue which could lead the police to Lafcadio; and when he in turn reveals himself as the major danger to the hero, the aforementioned unlikely conjunctions of circumstance dispose of him with ironic neatness. Even when Lafcadio denounces himself to Julius the reaction is the most improbable one (though in keeping with Julius's temperament, as we have remarked earlier), grotesquely highlighted by the depiction of Julius as more concerned about his broken finger-nail than about Lafcadio's criminality (867–8, 242–5). The fact that readers tend to draw the sort of moral lessons they do from *Les Caves du Vatican* has to do with the way in which the novel's hero emerges unscathed from a succession of notably contingent events: things could have – more likely would have – turned out less innocuously for him. Not for nothing does George Painter, drawing on the Dostoevskian model which *Les Caves* also evokes in order to subvert, entitle his chapter on the novel 'Crime without Punishment'.[217] Gide seems to be marking a disjunction between normal expectations to which moral judgements relate and the limitless possibilities thrown up by the random creativity of reality.[218]

The traditional narrative, say that of a Balzac novel, points a moral by conforming to what one critic has called 'the "law" of diminishing possibilities'; after an initial choice of action, the character 'will find it progressively more difficult to explore other behavioural possibilities . . . there is a reduction in the courses of action open to the individual'.[219] Similarly, Peter Brooks speaks of plot 'diminishing as it realises itself'.[220] In the case of Lafcadio's story the opposite occurs. The narrative line multiplies the possibilities as it proceeds, stressing the openings available to Lafcadio – keeping avenues open even when he defies fate by attempting to plunge into an impasse. While the story thus steers a course which renders Lafcadio ever freer to do as he wishes, the reader constructs, on the basis of narrative possibilities the text ostentatiously shuns, an imaginary version of events which can be seen informing many critical conclusions about the novel. At the same time, all around Lafcadio the characters are jumping to conclusions, and the net closes upon his crime leaving Lafcadio himself entirely out of account. Having elaborated a 'ridiculous fancy' which happens to follow the line of Lafcadio's adventures, Julius promptly abandons it and prefers to believe Amédée was murdered by the non-existent organisation which has supposedly kidnapped the Pope; first Carola, then the world at large, make sense of the incident in the best way they can; and these imaginary constructions supplant the reality of Lafcadio's conduct. That 'freedom of meaning' which is made available proves in practice to be tightly circumscribed by the criteria of verisimilitude, those 'over-coded, ready-made paths' along which credibility is customarily pursued. As Paul Valéry emphasised, chance brings into being the *possible*, not the *vraisemblable*.[221] By implication the real – construed as contingent possibilities – remains beyond the reach of these fossilised patterns which operate a kind of 'unnatural selection' on the manifold branching paths of the evolutionary-style narrative. Again a comparison with traditional realism is illuminating. According to Bersani, the nineteenth-century novel's concern with human possibilities is strictly subordinated to a 'forme signifiante' which actually neutralises them, bringing them within the compass of narrative patterns which are all-embracing.[222] *Les Caves du Vatican* appears to distance itself from this tradition by producing a skewed parody of a narrative resolution. Conventional morality is first left to the conventionally conditioned imagination of the reader and then gratified through a derisory caricature. The family networks are re-established – but the principal protagonist is overlooked, indeed dismissed in Julius's final comments to him (868–9; 243–5). The logic which requires a punishment to fit each crime and a reassertion of the moral unity the crime has temporarily disrupted has been followed through – but has missed the mark. The moral vision of the denouement is off-centre: Lafcadio has been marginalised, but since he is still centre stage at the end, the 'real-seeming world' – the moral universe of convention – has been banished into the wings, in favour of this alternative enterprise, these other possibilities, embodied in Lafcadio. The gratuitous act and its contingent aftermath remain – as indeed they were from the outset, having emerged at least in part from the alternative possibilities neglected by the more conventional story of 'La Partie de Tric-Trac' – the stuff of multiple narrative elaborations.

At the end of the novel, the narrator asks somewhat incredulously: 'Does he still think of giving himself up?' (873; 250). It is as if the crime never really happened. This impression is reinforced by inferences we may derive from recurring motifs in the text. When Lafcadio reads in the newspaper that the all-important cufflink is missing from the cuff of the dead man, and that the manufacturer's address has been cut from the hat he clutched in his hand, he deduces correctly that 'his crime had been . . . *retouched*' (840; 206). This immediately tends to remove us from real life, which we have earlier learned from Lafcadio does not offer '*scope for retouching*' (736; 72). The narrative shifts into the realm of fiction, characterised by '*corrections*, scratchings out and touchings up' (736; 72). Protos will later confirm our suspicions when he tells Lafcadio: 'Your handiwork . . . was sadly in need of touching up' (856; 227). Protos is therefore a surrogate novelist, tying up loose ends for the hero. We are precisely in the domain, as Julius puts it, of 'the strangest possibilities . . . as it's only on paper, [we] shall boldly let [ourselves] go' (837; 202). By means of the *mise en abyme* mechanism, narrative fact – what Lafcadio actually does, since the parallel is quite plain between this and Julius's projected novel – is deprived of substance, as if it were fanciful hypothesis; and this even when the possibilities raised in the narrative – arrest or ensnarement – become increasingly actual. It would be an exercise of great philosophical subtlety to speculate about the ontological status of possibilities which remain unrealised in a text, as opposed to those which 'actually' happen;[223] but it is worth pointing out that the motif of the dream accompanies, paradoxically, all that one might be tempted to describe as the most authentic features of the narrative. Amédée's encounter with the contingent nature of reality is experienced by him 'as though in a dream' (809, 817; 167, 177), and similar sensations are evoked in connection with everything that befalls Lafcadio from the *acte gratuit* onwards. His meeting with Amédée is immediately preceded – that is, foreshadowed – by his reminiscence of a nocturnal adventure with his uncle

Wladimir – a midnight ritual which left the boy wondering
the next day 'whether the whole thing wasn't a dream' (827;
189). He first sees his victim between half-closed eyelids as he
pretends to sleep, and the entire murder is imbued with oneiric
qualities, in the same way that its aftermath is punctuated by
remarks such as: 'could he be dreaming? ... The whole
thing was becoming a nightmare' (850; 221). When Lafcadio
witnesses the emergence from behind the Defouqueblize disguise of 'a bigger, taller, *enlarged* Protos, who gave an impression
of formidable power' (855; 266) it is difficult not to draw
parallels with that night when he 'is aroused from a deep
sleep to see Uncle Wladimir – or is it a dream? – standing by
his bedside, looking more gigantic even than usual – a very
nightmare' (825; 187). Lafcadio will later declare: 'I killed in
a dream – a nightmare, in which I have been struggling ever
since ... What is the use of waking me?' (871; 248); and the
narrator approaches the novel's conclusion with a related
reference to the effects of desire: 'At your touch the phantoms
of my brain grow dim and vanish' (873; 250).[224] The entire
novel appears to have been little more than a disjunction of
probabilities, an offshoot from reality that generates its own
possible worlds: Anthime's conversion to religion; Julius's
dalliance with the *acte gratuit*; Lafcadio's crime which to all
intents and purposes might never have happened. The novel
thus blurs the distinction between the real and the merely
possible, in a movement anticipating that *gommage* ('erasure')
which will become a characteristic technique of Robbe-Grillet
and other *nouveaux romanciers*, building up texts by proposing
certain narrative developments and then retracting them.

   Through another set of structural associations, *Les Caves du
Vatican* highlights the experimental nature of its project. A
remarkable feature of Protos' organisation, the 'Mille-Pattes',
is that it has representatives everywhere they are needed to
forestall and manipulate the victims of its machinations. As
Amédée gets off the train in Rome, he happens to be intercepted
by Baptistin, a representative of the 'Mille-Pattes'; and when
Amédée indicates where he wishes to seek accommodation for
his stay, 'by a providential coincidence, that was the very
place where Baptistin proposed to take him' (780; 130). The
local post-office also numbers among its staff one of Protos'

accomplices, 'as was to be expected' (788; 140), so Fleurissoire's mail can be monitored. When Amédée is at his most
confused, he happens to bump into Julius de Baraglioul, who
by chance has come to Rome at the same time, though on a
different errand. In the middle of their conversation, however,
Amédée is handed a note which shows a fantastic inside
knowledge of Julius and his movements, and advises Amédée
to seek his help in cashing the cheque he has been entrusted
with. Such penetration of and intervention in the affairs of the
characters goes well beyond the resources of even the most
sophisticated criminal organisation. Protos happens to be on
the same train from which Lafcadio ejects Amédée: 'It was
lucky I happened to turn up the other day, eh? . . . Not
altogether by accident, maybe' (855–6; 227), he says. All these
coincidences defy belief, and point to an organisation of which
'Le Mille-Pattes' is in fact a metaphorical projection: Protos'
plot is a microcosm, a *mise en abyme* of the novelistic plot,
which manipulates the characters to make them meet its own
ends. Thus Julius judges it 'a providential stroke' (839; 205)
that he should encounter in the newspaper the story of
Fleurissoire's murder just as he was in need of such an incident
for the plot of his novel. Lafcadio for his part is amazed to
discover that his victim was travelling on a ticket bearing the
name of his own half-brother de Baraglioul (832; 196); and,
moreover, that his cufflinks were the very ones he, Lafcadio,
gave to Carola Venitequa: 'The old boy is a regular public
meeting-place' (834; 199). The complex but conveniently
convergent ramifications of the plot foreground the internal
logic of narrative, the fact that chance occurrences actually
conform to a pre-arranged plan in novels.[225]

Such self-conscious exploitation of narrative techniques in
turn shows up as a formal contrivance what in the conventional
realist novel seeks to pass itself off as natural. The amused
suspicion this flaunting of techniques may provoke in the
reader is accompanied, and mirrored, by a burlesque form of
paranoia which afflicts the characters as they begin to suspect,
or are told by Protos and his accomplices, that they are
being scrutinised by some agency which is tracking their
movements.[226] The protagonists' experience frequently involves allusions to labyrinthine complications, as if they are

being induced to follow, without knowing where they lead, complex interweaving pathways from which they cannot escape: and, as Christopher Bettinson has shown in detail,[227] such allusions have their origin in and relate back to Armand-Dubois' scientific experiments using 'a complicated system of boxes – boxes with passages, boxes with trap-doors, boxes with labyrinths, boxes with compartments' (683; 5) designed to test the conditioned reflexes of his rats. It has also been argued that these six rats – 'two of them were blind, two were one-eyed, and two could see' (686; 6) – parallel the characters who are compelled to go through various programmed itineraries to demonstrate their characteristics.[228] Rome as the centre of the contrivance is the focus of stimuli which draw the characters passively to it: the verb 'appeler' and variants recur systematically, in phrases which echo each other, to highlight the arranged nature of incidents which await the characters there.[229] The irony is, of course, that Anthime's experiments are designed to extract from the victim 'the acknowledgement (*l'aveu*) of its own simplicity'; his theories of tropistic, conditioned reflexes are built on the model of stimulus determining response: 'In all the motions of life, however surprising, a perfect obedience to the agent could be universally recognised' (683; 5). Does the novel as a whole confirm the satirical treatment meted out to Anthime's theories? Certainly he and Julius change in surprising, unforeseeable ways in response to the stimuli they receive; their reactions can be reduced to mechanical – even tropistic – patterns, but the fact that these reactions are at bottom chosen signals the presence of a factor Anthime's theories overlook. Here the satire is at the expense of the characters, whose behaviour, in spite of their possessing free will, confirms the reductionist scientific theories. Their cases may be compared to observations concerning Lafcadio, the epitome of freedom and unpredictability. In the train with Protos disguised as Defouqueblize, he is indeed duped and produces the unthinking conditioned reflex when, having first been distracted by the red stocking and shapely ankle of an attractive widow (who turns out to be an accomplice of Protos), he discovers on his plate the incriminating cufflink. Snatching it up without thinking, he immediately realises that he has given himself away:

What an admission (*aveu*) is implied by this instinctive and absurd action – what a recognition! How he has given himself away to the people – whoever they may be – who *doubtless have him under observation* (*l'observe*), who are watching him – the police perhaps! He has walked straight into their booby trap like a fool. (851–2; 222)

The language of Lafcadio's repentance is the language we have seen associated with the motifs of experimentation in the text. He is immediately ashamed of having provided an 'aveu', through his instinctive reaction confirming the simplistic hypothesis on human nature which inspired whoever set up the 'booby trap' (*piège grossier*). Later, Protos emerges from his disguise to underline the extent to which he has manipulated Lafcadio, and to make his principles explicit: 'I don't act (*agis*) on my own – I cause others to act (*agir*)' (858; 231). He is therefore the 'agent' who provides the stimulus to provoke the desired response; and what he wants from Lafcadio is 'obedience' (857; 229). He points out that this is precisely what he has already obtained from the young man in acting upon him in such a way as to provoke the mechanical reflex whereby Lafcadio grabbed the cufflink: 'Do you think it wasn't out of obedience and just because I willed it, that you picked up Mademoiselle Venitequa's sleeve-link off your plate at dinner? (858; 231). It is no accident that the scene originally formed the conclusion of the narrative and the pendant to the opening section on Anthime's scientific theories. This crucial confrontation, recalling the very terms (*aveu, observe, obéissance, agent*) which have been used in the exposition of Anthime's experimental practices, draws on that debate between determinism and unpredictability in the behaviour of living organisms which forms the thematic framework of the text. Protos, clearly subscribing to the former view for all his own mutability, thinks he has pinned down Lafcadio's nature, but is not certain of the particular motive which accounts for his behaviour. He insinuates a pedophilic relation with Julius, alluding to the way Lafcadio's 'connexion with Count Julius has become . . . exceedingly intimate' (859; 231); he is clearly unable to account for a pattern of behaviour which as we have seen is determined by chance and therefore eludes positivist explanation. Moreover, in the face of the villain's pseudo-scientific attempt to coax a pre-arranged response from Lafcadio by appealing to his self-interest and compelling him to blackmail Julius on pain of denunciation to the police, Lafcadio disproves the mechanical theory of human behaviour by choosing quite deliberately, and against his own immediate material interest, not to comply. Coclès and Damoclès in *Le Prométhée Mal Enchaîné* revealed surprising divergences, attributable to temperamental differences, in their responses to Zeus's action upon them. Lafcadio's case demonstrates that when a human's freedom of choice is added to the picture, it is even less possible to predict the result a given set of circumstances will produce: which represents a further rebuttal of Anthime's kind of science. His choice proves the hero's capacity to escape determinism and to assert free will against compulsion. It marks, however, one of those points where the reader's own conditioned reflexes are mobilised. As we respond to Lafcadio's behaviour with the conventional expectations born of reading (or nowadays, viewing) thrillers, adventure stories or detective fiction, we are drawn into a game which challenges us to free our imaginations by recognising the influence upon ourselves of inferences deriving from previous intertextual experience. Thus, the experiment which constitutes *Les Caves du Vatican* also has the reader as subject. We are manipulated, it is true – and necessarily so – by the techniques the novelist employs. But by foregrounding its own mechanisms and departing from conventional expectations the novel highlights that special kind of debate between the creative freedom of the reader and that of the writer, each of which operates by limiting the other, but both of which tend to refute the deterministic science of Anthime Armand-Dubois and the equally deterministic plotting of the string-pulling 'novelist' Protos.

Les Faux-Monnayeurs (The Counterfeiters)

Gide was disappointed by what he had produced in *Les Caves du Vatican*. The 'grand roman d'aventures' he had spoken about to Du Bos in 1912 turned out to be what Hytier has

called a 'parodie . . . du roman d'aventures'.[230] It is true that
Gide had realised he was producing something other than
what may have been expected: 'These *Caves* . . . can't be and
mustn't be a "masterpiece" – but rather a bewildering book,
full of holes and gaps, but also full of amusement, strangeness
and partial successes'.[231] He was splitting the seamless fabric
of traditional aesthetic theory, offering a text which did not
present itself as complete and conventionally structured, but
which questioned expectations and forced the reader to
participate in making sense of it. Such qualities have become
the criteria of value for post-structuralist critics, and for this
reason Gide deserves a place as a pioneer in deconstruction.
But in producing a critique of the novel, Gide was aware that
he had in some sense failed actually to write a novel, and
had therefore not succeeded in realising his long-standing
ambition.[232] Already around 1911, after writing the first-
person narrative *Isabelle*, he had adjusted his aesthetic sights
in order that such works should not be taken as indications
of his true ideal: he published *Isabelle* as a *récit*, and in a sketch
for a preface wrote, 'Why did I take care to entitle this little
book a *récit*? Simply because it does not correspond to my idea
of a novel; no more than did *Strait is the Gate* or *The Immoralist*;
and because I did not want people to be misled'.[233] His
dissatisfaction following *Les Caves* prompted him once more
to reconsider the nature of his achievement thus far, and led
him to reclassify his works, referring again to the first-person
narratives as *récits*, and baptising *Les Caves* a *sotie*, a term
borrowed from a burlesque satirical form of medieval drama
which he also applied retrospectively to *Paludes* and *Le Prométhée
Mal Enchaîné*. He explains himself in a preface to *Les Caves du
Vatican*: 'Why do I call this book a *Sotie*? Why *récits* the three
preceding ones? In order to demonstrate that they are not
novels, properly speaking. . . . Récits, soties . . . it seems to me
that up to now I have only written *ironic* (or if you prefer,
critical) books, of which this is doubtless the last'.[234] Gide
suddenly became aware that the qualities of irony which
typified his work meant that he had thus far presented only
the obverse of his world-view; and repeatedly during this
period he expresses the feeling that his work up to this point
misrepresents him and that he has much more – indeed, the

essential – still to say. 'If I were to die right now, I should
leave only a one-eyed image of myself, or an eyeless one', he
writes. 'I think of the importance of what I have to say . . .
of my novel'.[235] It was to the novel – now defined largely
negatively as a genre at which he had not yet exercised
himself – that he turned once more, this time as a vehicle for
an affirmative statement of his views.

Les Faux-Monnayeurs, which Gide was to call his 'premier
roman', was the product of such efforts, though it did not
actually come to fruition until 1926; its gestation spanned a
period which saw the writing of *La Symphonie Pastorale*, the
autobiography *Si le Grain ne Meurt*, and the expanded version
of *Corydon*, among other texts. Gide's work on this book also
spawned the *Journal des Faux-Monnayeurs*, in which can be found
traces of the aesthetic and moral musings which contributed
to the finished novel, as well as newspaper cuttings which
provided part of the inspiration for the narrative.

Les Faux-Monnayeurs does present, however, Gide's first
systematic analysis of human consciousness and of those
mechanisms which can be seen at work in the delusion and
self-delusion which the narrator-protagonists of the *récits* fall
prey to. What this novel reveals is that Gide has moved
beyond the terms of the conflict he evoked as a young man
between 'être moral' and 'être sincère', a dilemma he had
then resolved by rejecting preconceived morality in favour of
the search for sincerity.[236] But by now sincerity itself, as we
have seen in the cases of Michel, Alissa and the pastor,
generates new uncertainties. Edouard, the novelist-character
in *Les Faux-Monnayeurs*, declares: '*Sincerity!* . . . I cease to
understand its meaning. I am never anything but what I think
myself – and this varies so incessantly, that often, if I were
not there to make them acquainted, my morning's self would
not recognize my evening's. Nothing could be more different
from me than myself' (987; 68). The difficulty in being sincere
stems from the essential instability of the self, so that it is
impossible to know what one is to be sincere *about*, particularly
since the self may be only a projection of the imagination –
'what I think myself'. This is compounded by the split within
the self which is the very condition of conscious existence:

I am constantly getting outside myself, and as I watch myself act I cannot understand how *the person I see acting can be* the same as the person who is watching him act, and who *is struck with astonishment, and doubts whether* he can be actor and watcher at the same moment.   (988; 68)

Armand Vedel suffers similarly from this perceived fissure in consciousness, and comes to the same conclusion about its effect:

Whatever I say or do, there's always one part of myself which stays behind, and watches the other part compromise itself, which laughs at and hisses it, or applauds it. When one is divided in that way, how is it possible to be sincere? I have got to the point of ceasing to understand what the word means.   (1229; 325)

Gide here presents an analysis of the mind which anticipates Sartre's notion of the *pour-soi*, consciousness as that which is forever defeated in its efforts to grasp itself and constitute itself as an unchanging essence. In Sartre's striking formulation, consciousness is what it is not and is not what it is. The consequence of this state of affairs is that human beings are virtually condemned to bad faith or hypocrisy, as Sartre puts it: 'The essential structure of sincerity does not differ from that of bad faith since the sincere man constitutes himself as what he is *in order not to be it*. This explains the truth recognised by all that one can fall into bad faith through being sincere.'[237] In the *Journal des Faux-Monnayeurs* Gide also stresses the falsification of motives which can occur in the case of 'un esprit faux', which he defines as 'the person who finds it necessary to convince himself he has a *reason* for committing every act he wants to commit, the person who enslaves his reason to his instincts, to his interests (and this is worse), or to his temperament'.[238]

In the realm of human feelings, a consequential indeterminacy prevails. When Olivier Molinier accuses Armand Vedel of assuming a pose in his extreme cynicism, the latter replies: 'As if we weren't all playing parts more or less sincerely and

consciously. Life, my dear fellow, is nothing but a comedy'
(1229; 325). If the essence of the self is unstable and ungraspable, then actions cannot be said to spring from a temperament,
mood, or some other motivating factor, and can only be
arbitrary gestures: pretence lies at the heart of human behaviour. Thus, as Edouard notes, psychological analysis becomes
untenable: 'Psychological analysis lost all interest for me from
the moment that I became aware that men feel what they
imagine they feel. From that to thinking that they imagine
they feel what they feel was a very short step . . . In the
domain of feeling, what is real is indistinguishable from what
is imaginary' (988; 68–9). Hence actions may be motivated
by groundless emotional states. Moreover, since the emotional
response which mediates the perception of the real can itself
be the product of the imagination, through autosuggestion a
human being can construct an imaginary world to supplant
the one which is the case. Such phenomena are very much in
evidence in *Les Caves du Vatican* and *La Symphonie Pastorale*, as
we have seen: and the theme is crystallised in *Les Faux-
Monnayeurs* by Edouard's declaration that his planned *Faux-
Monnayeurs*, the novel-within-the-novel, will take as its 'deep-
lying subject . . . the rivalry between the real world and the
representation of it which we make to ourselves' (1096; 183).

Hence Gide formulates in *Les Faux-Monnayeurs* a complex of
ideas which effectively undermines the entire notion of character as it is understood and illustrated in the traditional novel.
Moreover, another feature of, say, a Balzacian character, the
single-minded and sustained motivation seen in its extreme
form in the monomanias of Old Goriot or Cousin Bette, is
also jettisoned in Gide's aesthetic – at least, as Edouard
expresses it:

Inconsistency (*Inconséquence*). Characters in a novel or play
who act all the way through exactly as one expects them
to. . . . This consistency of theirs, which is held up to our
admiration, is on the contrary the very thing which makes
us recognize that they are artifically composed . . . as a rule,
such consecutiveness is obtained only by vain and obstinate
perseverance, and at the expense of all naturalness.

(1201–2; 295)[239]

These remarks clearly echo the reproaches levelled by Lafcadio, that 'être d'inconséquence' ('creature of inconsequence'), against the conventional characterisation practised
by Julius de Baraglioul. And once again they reveal Gide
basing his novel on a rejection of customary constituents of
the novel.

In practice, what this means is that the characters in *Les
Faux-Monnayeurs* can be seen as challenges to traditional
character-analysis. La Pérouse, for example, has spent his life
devoted to an ideal of self-denial: 'When I was young, I led a
very austere life; I used to congratulate myself on my force of
character every time I refused a solicitation in the street'. But
he has lately realised with some bitterness that in all this he
was entirely deluded, since in essence he was indulging his
pride through choosing difficult options, much as we have
seen Alissa do:

> 'I didn't understand, that when I thought I was freeing
> myself, in reality I was becoming more and more the slave
> of my own pride. Every one of these triumphs over myself
> was another turn of the key in the door of my prison. . . .
> God has fooled me. He made me take my pride for virtue'.
> (1027; 110)

Vincent Molinier is presented as a case-study in the process
whereby the individual with a highly developed moral conscience is duped by the devil (as Gide chooses to name that
combination of instincts and intellect which produces the
'esprit faux') who provides 'reasons for self-approval' and
thereby succeeds in 'presenting us our defeats as if they were
victories' (1045–6; 129–30). Another illustration is Edouard,
who makes the disastrous decision to bring the vulnerable
young Boris back to Paris ostensibly on the grounds that it
will be good for the boy, whereas he is really indulging his
novelist's curiosity to see what will happen – a fact for which
the narrator criticises him severely (1109; 195). Ultimately all
the characters are deluded in similar ways. The narrator
declares, 'I do not deny that there are actions in the world
that are noble, generous and even disinterested; I only say
that there often lies hidden behind the good motive a devil

who is clever enough to find his profit in the very thing one thought one was wresting from him' (1109; 195–6). Such distrust about a character's declared motives, coupled with uncertainty about the real reasons for a person's behaviour, makes of characterisation in the novel a subject for extensive speculation rather than precise analysis. Douviers, having discovered that his wife Laura has been unfaithful to him, is at first relatively unperturbed; but he produces reactions of jealousy out of complex indirect responses, as Edouard perceives:

> When a Douviers becomes jealous it can only be because he imagines he ought to be. And no doubt he nurses this passion from a secret need to give body to his somewhat insubstantial personage. Happiness would be natural to him; but he has to admire himself and he esteems only what is acquired, not what is natural.   (1201; 295)

'Men feel what they imagine they feel': so Douviers feels as jealous as the next man. It is difficult to assess the degree of personal responsibility attaching to an individual's actions when both intellect and emotions are prone to such sinuous distortions.

Similarly, the self-consciousness we have seen at the core of human existence actually diminishes the motive force of passions and emotional upheavals, since even the most intensely disturbed individual is, as we have seen, at once protagonist and spectator in his drama. At the start of the novel, Bernard has just discovered evidence of his mother's extra-marital affair and proof that he is not Profitendieu's son: but even this excitement does not override the detached irony which operates at his own expense, inducing him to see himself as the hero of a cliché situation from melodrama. The opening line has him thinking, 'The time has now come for me to hear a step in the passage'; and as a drop of perspiration caused by the summer heat falls on the incriminating letter he reflects, 'Pretending to be a tear' (933; 11). He will suffer from this inner division throughout his story (in fact when he thinks it has ceased he is deluding himself under the influence of his infatuation for Laura, pp. 1094; 181. 1150; 241). The exception to this rule is perhaps the crisis he undergoes when he first confronts Laura and breaks down in a fit of uncontrollable sobbing: 'What! is he sobbing? is it possible? . . . He, Bernard!' (1034; 117) exclaims the narrator in surprise. This rare case when the individual coincides with himself is reserved for a select few. Armand is similarly overcome by 'an unspeakable emotion' on witnessing Bernard and his sister Sarah asleep together (1177; 270); Profitendieu momentarily forgets his professional demeanour and cannot prevent himself from sobbing when he evokes Bernard (1204–5; 299–300). Edouard is subject to the same sensation, which he discusses with Bernard, referring to it as 'the lyrical spirit', or 'the state of the man who consents to be vanquished by God'.[240] However, though it seems clear that the experience of 'lyrisme' is the mark of a profound and authentic humanity – it is not vouchsafed to Passavant, for example, a fact which is offered as proof of 'a certain poverty of temperament' on his part (1192; 285) – it does at the same time occur always as an unpredictable interruption in the expected course of psychological and other developments. Hence it underscores that instability of character which is the hallmark of *Les Faux-Monnayeurs*; the characters in this novel do not conform to expectations, and we cannot plot a preordained story for them. Bernard exemplifies the 'être d'inconséquence', starting out as anarchic and rebellious, but later becoming conservative in outlook, prepared to dedicate himself to Laura and viewing his earlier behaviour as that of 'a dreadful person' (1091; 177). His problem, which is the problem of all Gide's characters, is how to come to terms with the contradictory personalities which inhabit him. Gide notes in his *Journal des Faux-Monnayeurs*: 'Will he know enough to rise to the point of accepting and assuming all the contradictions of his too rich nature? To the point of seeking not to resolve them but to feed them' (82; 48: 3 January 1925). That mutability of character depicted schematically in *Les Caves du Vatican* is here grounded in a systematic analysis of the conditions of consciousness. The 'very essence of a man's being' (1030; 113) which Edouard wishes to place at the centre of his novel is, in fact, the contingency of the human personality. This is not the stuff of which traditional novels are made.

The same goes for other time-honoured ingredients of narrative. Description is dismissed by Edouard as being irrelevant to the novel, as is dialogue; 'outward events, accidents, traumatisms' are the prerogative of cinema, and should be left to it (990; 70–1). In the *Journal des Faux-Monnayeurs*, Gide expresses his wish to 'purge the novel of all elements that do not belong specifically to the novel' (57; 31), just as he has Edouard do (989–90; 70–1). But, as Gide was to realise with hindsight, his difficulty arose from the fact that the very essentials of narrative were uncongenial to him. Most of the elements he resists incorporating in *Les Faux-Monnayeurs* are indispensable constituents of the genre. 'The novel requires a certain slowness of progress that allows the reader to live with the characters and become accustomed to them', he later wrote (*JI*, 1050; *J3*, 165: 12 June 1931). Creating the impression of time passing much as it does in real life requires precisely a mixture of description, dialogue and incident, the writing of which calls for what Gide termed 'a large proportion of adipose tissue',[241] the retailing of banal padding merely for the sake of making reading time approximate to living time. 'What a success I could have had with my *Faux-Monnayeurs* if I had been willing to *lay out* my picture somewhat *more*', he commented. 'This stretching of the story allows the reader to keep contact with the characters over a greater surface' (*JI*, 991–2; *J3*, 113–14: 23 June 1930). What Gide notes here coincides with a comment by Barthes on the function of the secondary elements in a narrative structure which he calls 'catalysers'. Their role is a phatic one: they maintain the contact between the narrator and the addressee.[242] The seamless continuity of a text composed in this way draws the reader along with it; but Gide had a horror of the encumbrances such a text is charged with, and refused to clutter up his narrative with inert, 'adipose' tissue. He was quite clear about his aim, discussing his novel in these terms as early as 1919: 'I would like the reader to have the feeling that it is coming into being before him; I would like to cut out the inert sections in a novel'.[243] Looking back later, he saw the risks he had taken, but did not retreat from his position: 'I recognize that those neutral passages are the very ones that rest, reassure and win over the reader . . . What is easier than to write a novel like others! I am loath to do so, that's all, and no more than Valéry can I resign myself to writing 'The Marquise went out at five o'clock' (*JI*, 1068; *J3*, 181: 1 August 1931). The fact is that the notion of reality as a chronological continuum, which the traditional narrative techniques tend to articulate and reinforce, ran counter to Gide's views on the discontinuous manner in which significant events actually occur. The author who prizes 'inconséquence' and 'imprévu' above all, as we have seen, is bound to have problems when operating with a literary form whose readers are conditioned to expect continuity. Like Edouard, Gide is caught between 'two incompatible requirements' (1083; 169): the ways in which he copes with such contradictions are one source of the richness of *Les Faux-Monnayeurs*.

The salient features of Gide's text have been greatly illuminated by critics such as Michel Raimond[244] and more recently, by David Keypour and Michael Tilby. There is general agreement as to the 'extreme briskness in the development of the narrative';[245] and Tilby in particular analyses the means by which the action is presented as non-sequential, lived by the characters as a succession of present moments and perceived by the reader in such a way that the past and present of the story are continually confused.[246] There is, in fact, very little of the explicitly retrospective in this narrative; background is not construed as such, but is filled in via letters, diaries, dialogues, in which the information comes across with the same air of immediacy as in the novel's opening paragraphs. The multiplicity of narrative viewpoints, one of the constants in Gide's definition of the novel (and which we have seen him experimenting with as early as *Le Prométhée Mal Enchaîné*), is used by him in such a way as to fragment the diegesis: elements of the story are communicated piecemeal as they crop up seemingly by chance in the conversation or correspondence of characters who are themselves engaged upon unrelated narrative lines. Hence the story of Bernard's illegitimate origins emerges from ten retellings in the course of the narrative; and the details of the affair between Laura and Vincent are sketched in cumulatively over a similar number of disparate allusions.[247] At the same time, the text as a whole performs repeated rapid leaps from one set of characters to another. 'On all sides life offers us many beginnings of drama but only rarely do these continue and take shape as the novelist is accustomed to spin them out', Gide writes in the *Journal des Faux-Monnayeurs* (80; 47). A somewhat neglected commentator, André Julien, writing in 1951, brings out forcefully the key aspects of the presentation Gide devises as a means of remaining faithful to the true nature of reality, and reminds us at the same time of the model of the *roman d'aventure* which has played so important a part in enabling Gide to break away from conventional patterns of narrative: 'Fragment the action into adventures and write everything in the present' is his summary of Gide's method.[248] But given that the action is broken up in this manner, the question of transitions necessarily arises. We know that Gide was preoccupied with the work of 'jointoiement' ('grouting', 'smoothing over the joins') between scenes, episodes and characters,[249] and part of the attraction of the novel stems from the devices he hits on to accomplish this without having recourse to 'adipose tissue'. Indeed he attached great artistic importance to success in this domain, being inclined as he put it 'to devote the most care to just what most discourages me: the transitions, the welding of joints, everything in which Flaubert recognized the master writer' (*JI*, 920; *J3*, 49: 10 April 1929).

From the end of one chapter to the beginning of the next, and sometimes in the middle of chapters, we are pulled along by a variety of more or less ostentatious methods, such as in the statement: 'No, it was not to see his mistress that Vincent Molinier went out' (959; 39). This declaration, which forces us to acknowledge that we had taken Olivier's story at face value – whether we had or not – is an example of the strategies whereby a text presents or points to possible readings of itself.[250] Transitions like this serve to foreground the narrator's voice; but, equally important, they serve to construct a narratee[251] who is very much at the narrator's beck and call. What might be termed the 'co-optive *nous*' is strongly in evidence, from 'Let us follow him' (959; 39) and 'Let us leave them' (950; 28. 1145; 235) to 'Let us make use of this . . . season' (1109; 196) and 'Bernard's father (we need not concern ourselves with him)' (950; 29). 'Let us follow him' and 'Let us leave them' blur the distinction between the represented world and the world of the reading experience, just as the transitions involving 'It is at this same hour . . . It is time to return to Bernard' (974–5; 54–5), for example, cause representations of chronology to dissolve into reading time. The narrator constructs an intermediate zone, somewhere between the 'real' world and that represented by the text, where a conversation-cum-commentary on events takes place between himself and the narratee. This latter is told he is moving from one element to another, but that does not make the shift more intelligible: if anything it heightens the impression of a random succession of items.[252]

But if the narrator browbeats the narratee in order to maintain cohesion in the narration, the remarkably fluid forms of free indirect speech and dramatic monologue which have increasingly commanded critics' attention[253] also reveal him to be in the habit of exploiting metalepsis and taking liberties with different levels of the narrative. Gide's brand of *style indirect libre* in the present tense[254] effectively runs together the narrator's voice and that of the character: 'Heavens! How hot he is! Where shall he go now? . . . What shall he do with it [the suitcase]? . . . No! No! Certainly not! He will not break open the lock; what the devil, he isn't a thief! . . . And now that he has the wherewithal – quick! a hotel' (996; 78–9).

This serves as another means of moving the text along between episodes. It is used frequently with Bernard, but also with M. Profitendieu (944–5; 23–4. 948; 27), Olivier (1141; 231), Vincent (1045–6; 129–30) and Edouard (991; 72. 1191; 284). The device has two significant effects. First it confuses the locus of the narrative: are we in the world of Bernard or in the world of the narrator recreating Bernard's words and actions? Second, it confers on the narrator something of the prestige and status of a protagonist. In a sense the novel is performed before our eyes by this narrator-showman; he might be said to absorb rather than describe his characters. When he does not actually imitate their way of speaking but presents their words in more conventional forms, his presiding presence is none the less evident in the ironic intrusions and the framing devices used. These implicitly include epigraphs, chapter headings, editorial comments ('We have already seen the first

pages; this is what followed' (997; 79)), dates and phrases
such as 'Ce même soir' in Edouard's diary.[255] But above all,
in this text in which quotation is far from being an innocuous
mimetic device, the narrator's appropriation of the words of
his characters is marked by the ubiquitous quotation marks,
which have an overdetermined ironic impact.[256] They are
especially noticeable around the extracts from Edouard's
diary, which have – not entirely convincingly, perhaps – been
taken by some critics to constitute a competing focus of
narration.[257] One has only to look at a page of this diary in
the French text to see how firmly it is subsumed under the
category of secondary material and subordinated to the
narrator's discourse by the insistent quotation marks at the
start of each indented line. This is essentially a one-man
show. Thus the disquisitions on characters and events, the
disruptions of the narrative fabric, the nudges and winks
aimed at the reader, the general ironic chattiness of the text
have the effect, not primarily of distancing the reader from
the story, but rather of involving him or her in the narration.
They are bids to establish a form of collusion between the
reader and the narrator. In other words, the obtrusive
discourse of the narrator has a phatic function:[258] it bears the
hallmarks of language used to keep in contact with the
addressee. It is Gide's answer to the problem of maintaining
the reader's attention without providing a uniform diegetic
world in which the reader can immerse himself or herself. The
technique of the playful narrator does not fracture the text; it
permits a certain discontinuity at the level of the action but
re-establishes contact, maintains continuity, at the level of
reading.

Viewed from this angle, the text encourages a purely
'superficial' reading. The narrator's elegant patter and the
fluency of his technique tend to elide questions of representation, of narrative chronology and causation. The position
constructed for the reader is reminiscent of La Fontaine's lines
about the 'Papillon du Parnasse' of which Olivier offers an
idiosyncratic gloss when he discusses them after Bernard's
baccalauréat exam: 'The artist . . . the man who consents to
take merely the outside of things, their surface, their bloom'
(1142; 232). We slide off into the pleasures of parody and the

ironic intricacies of a citational text[259] as illustrated, for example, in the opening paragraph of Chapter 3, Part II: 'Notwithstanding first appearances, and although each of them, *as they say*, *'did his best'*, Uncle Edouard and Bernard were only getting on together fairly well' (1076; 163). Here the text makes a spectacular display of its polyphonic characteristics – 'as they say', unattributable quotation marks, 'Uncle Edouard' evoking yet another voice. The focus is clearly less on events than on the imbricated discourses which seek to speak about them: ' "Benefits", *says Tacitus, through the mouth of Montaigne*, "are only agreeable as long as one can repay them" ', the paragraph continues (1076–7; 162: my italics). The characters' as well as the narrator's language constantly overflows into, or is invaded by, other forms of discourse. Laura's 'J'ai un amant' (955; 34–5. 972; 51) echoes Emma Bovary; Bernard parodies Rastignac in *Le Père Goriot* with his 'Maintenant, valise, à nous deux' (997; 79) and repeatedly finds his impulse to self-expression embarrassed by the clutter of quotations to which he is reduced (1088; 175). All this calls into question the very power of language to do anything other than engage in a dialogue with other texts.[260] In this sense the wide range of quoted discourse and the high proportion of dialogue – 'There are nothing but conversations', Gide remarked to Dorothy Bussy about the novel[261] – are merely the most explicit manifestations of the text's essentially dialogic character: in the final analysis discourse itself is posited as the object of representation. *Les Faux-Monnayeurs* is also rich in puns, which render explicit the interplay between signifiers and signifieds, thereby short-circuiting the arbitrary link between sign and referent and disrupting the referential function of language which is crucial to realistic texts. Instead of pointing towards elements of a putative reality beyond the text, the words interact with each other in such a way as to highlight the relational structure of language in general and its 'signifying rather than indexical character'.[262] Apart from the word-play in the novel's title, pride of place is given to a number of key puns which generate the ethical basis of the entire work. Thus the family, the basic 'cell' of society, is seen as a prison cell (1021; 104) from whose injurious influence only the 'enfant naturel' – 'How full of meaning is the

expression "a natural child!" ' (1022; 105) says Edouard –
remains free to follow his 'inclination' – in either direction,
but preferably upwards (1204; 298: 'a slippery slope' would
better convey what is rendered as 'a downhill course'. 1215;
310). The moral decadence into which the adolescent is in
danger of sliding is in turn highlighted through the punning
on the Biblical image of salt which groups Passavant and his
ilk among the 'dessalés' (literally 'unsalted', but with the slang
connotation of 'wised-up') (1031; 113. 1052–3; 136–7). The
novel presents itself therefore as an assemblage of signifiers
whose meaning is intrinsic to the structures in which they are
incorporated, rather than dependent on and determined
by the normal referential use of language characteristic of
narrative. There are passages where the text appears quite
deliberately to follow the momentum of the writing alone. An
elaborate semantic and phonetic game concerning Edouard's
case generates repetitions and variations of the words *clef*,
serrure, *faix*, *porte*, *portefeuille*, *portefaix*, etc., and play around
images of closure and containment: the hotel room containing
the case containing the wallet which formerly contained the
banknotes (996; 79). Similarly, in the proliferating parenthesis
on the chair in Laura's hotel room (1035; 117–18) the
transition ceases to be a mere accessory and acquires primary
status.

The work on transitions produces, then, a text in which the
signifier has a certain autonomy, a text which points towards
the non-mimetic relations within language. These ludic elements furnish an entertaining continuity of surface texture,
divorced in many respects from events in the story. The
narrator's manipulation of language, like the conjuror's patter,
actually distracts us from the implications of what is happening
elsewhere none the less: 'it won't be of any consequence' (cf.
970; 50) is the general impression. 'The kaleidoscopic flux has
something irremediably inconsequential,' Holdheim says.[263]

But things are happening elsewhere, and there are, in the
course of the text, indications that it can be read in other
ways – as indeed can the lines from La Fontaine, Olivier's
interpretation of which so incenses Bernard (1142–3; 232–3).
The incident of Olivier's essay is obviously intended to raise
the possibility of the alternative readings to which a text like

Les Faux-Monnayeurs can be subjected. Gerald Prince has shown that reading is a significant motif throughout the novel,[264] but two examples in particular merit further analysis. Bernard, when he leaves home, writes a letter to Profitendieu explaining his action. Profitendieu reads it once – with the reader of *Les Faux-Monnayeurs* looking over his shoulder – and is distressed; reads it again and sees in it the qualities that endeared Bernard to him; and when his wife arrives, he shows it to her. She reads it and says, 'Oh! why did you tell him?', whereupon Profitendieu replies, 'But you can see for yourself that I never told him anything. Read his letter more carefully' (948; 26). It would be a curious reader who did not turn back at least once in the course of these four readings to peruse Bernard's letter again in the light of subsequent comments on it. The text virtually urges us to interrupt our linear reading and interpolate an earlier section. Here it is calling for a reader other than the narratee invoked elsewhere: it elicits a different reader, for a different reading.[265]

A related phenomenon occurs, with more far-reaching effects, in connection with the letter to Edouard in which Laura appeals for his help. This we first hear of as Edouard rereads it 'on the deck of the ship which is bringing him back to France' (974–5; 54); we do not have the opportunity to read it ourselves until Edouard rereads it again on the train (984–5; 65–6). At this stage it comes as the culmination and confirmation of a series of fragmentary narratives whereby we have learned of Laura's affair with Vincent and her ensuing pregnancy. We are told that 'The place for this letter is not among coats and shirts . . . Laura's letter will find its proper place' between those pages of Edouard's diary written the previous year (986; 66). This we can take as a signal to the reader. However, we read the diary only after the letter, which means we see things in the wrong order. The letter is read again, by Bernard, but after he has read at one sitting – unlike us – 'the notebook into which Edouard had slipped Laura's melancholy letter' (997; 79). Some fifty pages after we first read it, we learn that 'the truth flashed upon' Bernard after finding it in Edouard's diary (1032; 115). This is the moment when Bernard is alone in seeing the connection between the Molinier side of events, which he has heard about from Olivier, and that concerning the *pension Vedel-Azaïs*, as set out in Edouard's diary. But for the reader who follows up the thrice-repeated hint to reread Laura's letter in its appropriate position in Edouard's diary, its significance is transformed as we see in it, not so much an immediate consequence of Laura's seduction by Vincent, as a long-term repercussion of events in the previous autumn when Edouard contrived to wriggle out of his relationship with Laura by urging her to marry Douviers. Laura's distress which at first sight had appeared to be a contributory factor in Edouard's return to France actually emerges as a consequence of his leaving for England in the first place. As in the case of *La Symphonie Pastorale*, the text is constructed in such a way as to encourage us to embark on a mimetic reading and reconstitute the reality of events behind the printed page. Discontinuities introduced into our reading of the novel prompt questions, therefore, about the causal links between otherwise disparate incidents: and in particular the example of Laura's letter points to the fact that causality is established retrospectively, after we have read all the relevant material. This, of course, is the pattern that governs the entire novel, for nothing illustrates the principle more clearly than the death of Boris. The random, disjointed succession of adventures, each of which seemed less consequential or even less significant than the narrator's discourse which knitted them into his act, suddenly emerges, in the light of Boris's enforced suicide, as an ineluctable progression whereby each unthinking or deluded gesture contributes to the catastrophe.[266]

At this point, moreover, we see that the phatic continuity established by the narrator's self-flaunting discourse is actually a deception, a sleight of hand whose effect is to conceal the proper dynamic of events in the story.[267] This aspect of the novel's duality, not to say duplicity, is hinted at in the final chapter of Part II, when the narrator 'wonders with some anxiety where his tale will take him' (1108; 195) and suggests that things are getting out of hand. But even taking this into account, it seems reasonable to argue that another function of the playful narrator-figure was precisely to keep these ominous developments out of sight as far as possible, so that Boris's death, occurring in dramatic contrast to the inconsequential tone, should trigger all the more effectively certain reflections on its causation.

When we seek to establish retrospectively the causality behind Boris's suicide, our chief concern is to discover what exactly it is that links the actions of each character with his death. In so far as connections of whatever kind can be made, then it is possible to speak of collective responsibility for the tragedy, as Philip Thody has done.[268] But a sense of moral responsibility is not the same thing as an understanding of cause and effect connections, as we have seen in our discussion of *Le Prométhée Mal Enchaîné*: though the former can render more urgent a consideration of the latter. Such is the effect of Boris's death and the backward-reaching ramifications it precipitates. On the one hand, *Les Faux-Monnayeurs* reiterates the lesson of Gide's previous narratives: contingency character-ises human affairs, the consequences of actions and events cannot be predicted as they happen, and therefore it is misguided for human beings to feel responsible for chance as the protagonists of *Le Prométhée Mal Enchaîné* did. On the other hand, the novel's very structure demonstrates how, objectively speaking, a wide range of individuals contribute to the death of a young innocent. The dialogue between these theses is woven into the fabric of *Les Faux-Monnayeurs*. Claude-Edmonde Magny refers to the connections between the different lives and the poignant death as 'the merciless picture of novelistic causality'. She says: 'Because Bernard, in order to repair a clock, has lifted up the top of a chest of drawers . . . little Boris will commit suicide at the end of the novel.'[269] But clearly this is no mechanical cause and effect connection, and equally clearly something else is involved in the discrepancy of scale and significance between the two events; between, for that matter, the death of Boris and any other sin of omission or commission with which it might, with hindsight, be linked. Germaine Brée seems to come closer to the crux of the matter when she proposes the model 'If Bernard had been more conscious of his responsibility towards Boris, if La Pérouse . . . had not loaded the pistol. . .'.[270] The nature of this view of causation, and the leap from the trivial to the tragic plane which it entails, are illuminated by the conversation which Olivier has with Armand in the latter's room – a room which in this respect as in several others is the locus of a *mise en abyme*.[271]

Armand, as we have previously indicated, is obsessed by a theory of what he calls the *point-limite* in any progression: the point at which an entity comes into being or at which one state changes into another. He speaks of 'that dividing line between existence and non-existence. . . . A tiny bit less – non-existence. God would not have created the world. Nothing would have been. "The face of the world would have been changed," says Pascal' (1162–3; 254–5).[272] It can be argued that this generates a conception of cause and consequence upon which the novel is based. What happens was not bound to happen: the effects of contingency and chance, which Gide has been at pains to illustrate in his earlier fiction, make it clear that events could have turned out differently. Mechanistic causality, in any case more properly considered as a trope constructed a posteriori,[273] gives way to a non-deterministic vision, like that informing Lafcadio's adventures in *Les Caves du Vatican*, which plots events as emerging from a range of possibilities. This is what makes Brée's rendering of the plot particularly pertinent. The conditional note is repeatedly sounded in the text: in declarations such as Bernard's 'If I hadn't read the letters, I should have had to go on living in ignorance' (977; 58), or the narrator's 'We should have nothing to deplore of all that happened later if only . . .' (991; 73), or again: 'Why did he not simply return home? He would have found his Uncle Edouard' (1153; 243); and elsewhere: 'If he had understood what was going on, he would certainly have been able to prevent it' (1244; 340). Boris's death is, in essence, only one possibility among many equally plausible alternatives.[274] Perhaps this is why Gide was so keen to make his own a quotation from the critic Thibaudet: 'The genius of the novel makes the possible come to life; it does not revive the real'.[275] By stressing the contingency of the events depicted, Gide is, in one sense, further championing the right of fictional causality to be read as hypothetical, as he had done in *Les Caves*.[276] One has only to recall the comical effects that ensue when a character like Pangloss in Voltaire's *Candide* mistakes the gratuitous determinants of fiction for the laws of physics or the dictates of Providence. But at the same time, by substituting indeterminate possibilities for the mechanistic one-dimensional laws of cause and effect in the world the novel constructs, Gide remains faithful to the Darwinian evolutionary narrative and moves in the direction in which physics itself developed with the elaboration of quantum theory at the beginning of the twentieth century. Replacing determinism or fate with uncertainty and chance relaxes the rigour of the otherwise bleakly pessimistic depiction of human affairs which the novel appears to present. As in the world of sub-atomic physics, the transitions between states are governed by the statistics of random processes.[277] Things could have been otherwise.

But Boris *does* die, and matters *do* develop to a tragic outcome. It is not enough, as Armand says, to declare like Pascal ' "If Cleopatra's nose had been shorter." ' He goes further: 'I ask: shorter, by how much?' For it is clear that other possibilities are open only up to a point; beyond that point it is too late, a development becomes irreversible. In this sense *Les Faux-Monnayeurs* goes beyond *Les Caves du Vatican*, which, celebrating the gratuitous act, revelled in the possibilities available to the characters, proposed and retracted hypotheses for actions and consequences, and left the future open for Lafcadio at the end of the novel. In the later work, the strategic placing of Boris's death at the conclusion of the narrative sends the reader with renewed urgency to a consideration of questions the *sotie* deliberately left out of account. Armand uses the example of a man who was electrocuted because of the film of perspiration that enveloped his body. 'If his body had been drier, the accident wouldn't have taken place. But now let's imagine the perspiration added drop by drop'. He sums up: 'Gradation; gradation; and then a sudden leap. . . . *natura non fecit saltus*. What absurd rubbish!' (1162–3; 254–5). This, as we have seen, is the issue on which Gide parts company with Darwin.[278] Through Armand he asserts his belief in the discontinuity of phenomena in the natural world, and rallies to a principle which the theories of quantum physics were to confirm. For it is precisely the kind of jump envisaged by Armand, a quantum jump from the miniscule to the momentous, that allows Boris's death to arise from an accumulation of banal misadventures and misdemeanours. As Vincent reflects on the situation which is the outcome of his affair with Laura, he is led to conclude: 'It very often suffices to add together a quantity of little facts which, taken separately, are very simple and very natural, to arrive at a sum which is monstrous' (960; 40). This is an observation which may be applied to many of the developments in the story.

The novel illustrates several ways in which the humdrum course of human affairs gives rise to the perception of a discontinuity marking a dramatic change: its concern with 'les âges de la vie'[279] is an obvious example. The general view of personality which emerges from the text suggests that the characters are not individuals existing continuously through time, so much as aggregates of successive states. Bernard's development proceeds less through an accumulation of experience than through a discontinuous series of emotional and intellectual postures from which he successively detaches himself: 'Strange to himself . . . he glides into another day' (1178; 270) is a typical evocation of such mutations. As for the 'gradation' that culminates in the quantum leap, the text alludes frequently to this issue. Profitendieu, aware that if his investigation goes ahead he risks revealing more than he wishes to know, fears the irreversible consequences of excessive zeal: 'After a certain point a case escapes our control, so to speak; that is to say we cannot go back on the police court proceedings' (1204; 298). Similarly, Pauline Molinier is afraid it may be 'too late' for two of her sons to be redeemed (1155; 246. Cf. 1222; 318); and Vincent has already discovered, through Laura's reply to his offer of money, that it is 'too late' (1049; 132) in that direction. Armand, for his part, derives a perverse pleasure from the prospect of being able to say that it is 'too late' for him to be cured (1232; 328). These examples are, arguably, fairly banal – even redolent of mere melodrama – but the fact that such patterns are fundamental to the conception of the novel is illustrated by the epigraph to Part III: a quotation from a book by Lucien Febvre entitled, appropriately enough, *La Terre et l'Evolution Humaine*: 'When we are in possession of a few more . . . monographs – then, and only then . . . we shall be able to reconsider the subject as a whole, and take a new and decisive step forward' (1112; 199).

All this evades a crucial issue, of course: what is this *point-limite* beyond which a phenomenon is qualitatively different? And in particular, what is the point beyond which Boris's fate is irreversible? The answer is, presumably, that we see it only when it has occurred, when it is too late; and on this score Gide may perhaps be excused for not being more precise, since in physics too the quantum calculations only map a field of probabilities for the electron's behaviour – no particular path can be predicted.[280] For the novelist the real problem lies elsewhere. It may be perceived in Bernard's ruminations after his night with Sarah. This 'unprecedented night' will *not*, we are told, 'find [a] place in the body of the book – a book where the story of his life will continue, surely, will take up the thread again, as if nothing had happened' (1178; 271). Narrative is by its nature continuous: how then can it be prevented from merely bridging discontinuities, inducing the reader to cover over blanks and fill in gaps? Gide touches on this difficulty in the *Journal des Faux-Monnayeurs* when he considers the shortcomings of plot, which is the only available mode for articulating events in a novel: 'I have felt more urgently the need of establishing a relationship between the scattered elements. Yet I should like to avoid the artificiality of a "plot" ... Perhaps with the form I adopt I can find a way to have all that criticized indirectly' (18, 25; 6, 11). Nevertheless, critics have been at a loss to justify the means he uses to connect Boris's death with events that contribute to it. Surely this is a plot as conventionally conceived, the vehicle for representing a purely mechanistic version of cause and effect?[281] And if it is, doesn't this mark most emphatically the failure of Gide's ambition to go beyond such devices and find a construction to accommodate a more radical view of causality?

What does seem clear is that the impression of immediacy created through the device of the playful narrator stresses the random, aimless, discontinuous way the characters live, and the ingenuous narratee reads, events.[282] At the same time every detail is shaped to fit into an overall continuous sequence.

What we have here is a marked, indeed arguably self-conscious, example of the two contradictory kinds of causality inherent in narrative: the teleology or retrospective logic of plot, and the 'backward causality' of character motivation and the momentum of events in the story.[283] They both share a tendency to set up patterns of continuity, but Gide puts them to work against each other in order to prevent this. In *Les Faux-Monnayeurs* the story is dragooned into the service of the plot rather more noticeably than verisimilitude should allow. The mark of this untoward manipulation is coincidence: and on this score *Les Faux-Monnayeurs* has drawn the fire of more than one critic.[284] Overall, novelistic credibility is strained by the interconnection of so many characters and events alleged to have a bearing on Boris's fate. But in the course of a page-by-page reading, the coincidences abound: Bernard happens to be on the scene as Edouard distractedly throws away his left-luggage ticket (995; 77); he happens to find a coin in his pocket when he needs one, although he had spent the last of his money earlier (996; 78). Of all the shores he could have been washed up on, Vincent happens to be shipwrecked in Alexandre Vedel's vicinity (1233–4; 329–30). There are negative coincidences too: Olivier happens to stay out looking for Edouard when Edouard decides to call at the Molinier home to see him – on *two* separate occasions . . . (1040; 123. 1153; 243). Bernard happens to be preoccupied in wrestling with his angel on the night when Boris has heard of Bronja's death and is in particular need of comfort (1212; 307). Perhaps each coincidence contains or marks one of the *points-limite* at which events take a decisive turn: certainly they are the points at which we are inclined to say – assuming we take them seriously – 'if only . . .'. Indeed the narrator sometimes says this for us, as has been indicated above. And ultimately Boris's death, the most dramatic *point-limite*, is brought about by an appropriately calamitous accumulation of coincidences. But such a proliferation of coincidences can hardly be a . . . coincidence.

The fact is that this structure provides Gide with precisely the kind of parodic critique of conventional plots he sought. The systematic foregrounding of coincidence splits the seams of the narrative. It shows up the tension between story and plot, the conventional way in which the teleology of form masquerades as psychological motivation, fate, and so on. As Jonathan Culler has shown, the perception of such features as coincidence in a narrative lays bare 'the rigorous deployment of two logics, each of which works by excluding the other'.[285] It unsettles the priority habitually accorded to story over plot. Clearly the story is not pre-formed, waiting for the narration to set it down as it happened, since it is compelled to satisfy the requirements of a plot by coming to a significant conclusion. At the same time we are made aware of the contradiction, inherent in some of the narrator's paradoxical assertions, that while characters may be pronounced autonomous and free, their behaviour is constrained by foreordained patterns beyond their control.[286] Furthermore, by highlighting the contrived nature of the encounters (or failed encounters) in which the story abounds, this device underlines the contingent nature of fictional causation.

In terms of narrative structure, then, as a technical device that is part of the novelist's stock in trade, coincidence serves to signal more or less self-conscious contrivance. However, in discourses of life, real or depicted, coincidence confirms the contrary view: it exemplifies the authentically random character of day-to-day events. In this perspective, coincidence is an instrument for breaking the chains of mechanical determinism; it injects Gide's cherished 'unforeseen' into the succession of events.

Each coincidence therefore marks the point at which the narrative advances via an articulation which is essentially selfcontradictory, being so obviously unforeseeable as an event, so flagrantly purposive as a structuring device. This doubleedged quality is illustrated when Edouard discovers that the boy he has spotted stealing a book is actually his nephew Georges whom he has not met before. He acknowledges that such an event, though true, would be difficult to justify in a novel (1001–2; 80–4). It is in a case like this that we are made aware of the two incompatible domains the realist novel seeks to run together: the *vrai* and the *vraisemblable*, the authentic and the conventional.[287] Thus it is very much in keeping with the spirit of *Les Faux-Monnayeurs*, positing as it does 'the rivalry between the real world and the representation of it which we make to ourselves' (1096; 183), that the novel's very structure should hinge on a phenomenon whose implications are mutually contradictory when viewed from each of these angles. Borrowing our terminology from Barthes, we could say that the text mobilises two kinds of necessity in a conflict which is undecidable: and 'good narrative writing is of this very undecidability'.[288] In essence what this novel does is deconstruct the opposition between life and art by offering itself as a third, undecidable term, what Barthes calls 'a third term which however is not a term of synthesis, but an eccentric, extraordinary term'.[289]

The important point about Gide's use of coincidence is that it is an appropriate response to the problems of reconciling chance and contingency in life with the deliberate contrivance inherent in any narrative that seeks to depict them. Coincidence signals that essential disjunction at the heart of narrative between the mutually exclusive types of logic of which it is constituted. For this narrative to produce its meaning, the story must lead to Boris's death; but none of the events in the story is bound to happen; it is only by chance that they occur.[290] Thus the plot of the novel connects all the characters with the death of Boris via a network of coincidences, establishing a pattern of collective responsibility; but the story, proceeding through the same coincidences but construing them as random occurrences, denies that pattern. It may well happen in real life that accidental, random events lead up to a tragedy for which large numbers of people can therefore be held responsible: the problem is that a novel cannot depict such patterns without infringing the very codes upon which a mimetic or realistic narrative is predicated. The use of coincidences introduces a fissure into the novel by making it impossible to decide which way it should be read. We are offered two incompatible readings depending on whether we consider the text as self-reflexive, foregrounding its own structures, playing with language and with narrative conventions, or whether on the other hand we see it as an account of chance happenings leading up to a tragic death. This novel is theoretically impossible, since it cannot do and be all these things at once: but it does, and is.

Society's Narratives

After the death of Boris in *Les Faux-Monnayeurs*, Edouard, who earlier had expressed his ambition to put into *his Faux-Monnayeurs* whatever reality dictated to him, declares that he will not use the child's suicide. 'I *should* not like to put forward any fact which was not accounted for by a sufficiency of motive' (1246; 343), he writes. He finds this incident incomprehensible, classifying it among the ' "faits divers" ', which have about them 'something peremptory, irrefutable, brutal, outrageously real'. We recognise here the same retreat before fact as he has shown when Bernard confronted him with an actual counterfeit coin, saying, ' "I'm sorry that the reality doesn't interest you." "Yes, it does," said Edouard, "but it disturbs me too" ' (1086; 173). However open-minded Edouard may claim to be, he nevertheless has certain preconceptions – if only about the relationship between facts and their transposition in fiction – which are highlighted at such moments. The narrator in *Les Caves du Vatican*, apparently so unsure about these matters that he includes a lengthy description of Anthime's wen for fear of omitting a detail which might subsequently prove significant (685–6; 8), has no such hesitation when Lafcadio sets out to rescue the family trapped in a fire: 'Lafcadio, mon ami, vous donnez dans un fait divers et ma plume vous abandonne' (Lafcadio, my friend, here you require the pen of a newspaper reporter – mine abandons you!) (723; 56). Both texts, then, articulate reservations about the *fait divers*, suggesting there is no place for it within the work of art. To understand the implications of this stance, we need to understand what is designated by the term.

The label *fait divers* is used in the world of French journalism to denote a certain type of news story. Often it arises out of court proceedings. But it need not be restricted to judicial matters: the *Petit Robert* dictionary defines such phenomena as 'nouvelles peu importantes d'un journal' (unimportant news items in a paper), while the *Petit Larousse* resorts to the phrase 'événement sans portée générale qui appartient à la vie quotidienne' (an event without any general implications pertaining to everyday life). There is a measure of agreement,

then, on the notion of triviality which attaches to the *fait divers*.
On occasion Gide himself used the term in this sense, to
condemn the banality of Mérimée's *La Partie de Tric-trac*,
for example (*JI*, 277; *JI*, 241: 3 December 1909). As the
embodiment of all that is insignificant, it was frequently a
point of reference for those *fin-de-siècle* writers who were at
pains to denounce the literary ambitions of the realists
and naturalists: by transcribing raw fact, these latter were
demonstrating themselves to be not artists, but mere *fait-
diversiers*.[291] On the other hand, however, incidents which occur
in the byways of everyday life and do not find their way into
the mainstream of public affairs may owe their marginal status
not to any intrinsic triviality, but to the fact that the dominant
ideology in a society cannot accommodate them properly. The
faits divers fall outside the central concerns of a society; but
precisely because they are located on the margins of the social
consensus they may point to, or illustrate, realities that the
conventional wisdom leaves out of account. Thus the rubric
of the *fait divers* has a dual function: on the one hand, by
reporting odd or bizarre items, it seeks to translate them into
the language of common concerns; but because of its secondary
status, it marginalises such items, keeps them at a safe remove
from the centre of society. The *fait-diversier* thus lays claim to
the off-beat or grotesque on behalf of bourgeois humanism or
conventional society. 'Nil humanum me alienum puto' –
'Nothing human is alien to me' – the watchword of Renaissance
humanism, translates into modern journalistic parlance as
'All human life is here'. But at the same time, such a reporter
holds these items at arm's length, labels them marginal or
odd in order to fend off any disturbing implications they may
have for conventional wisdom. Thus, in a very real sense, the
faits divers might be said to map the sensitive outer edges of
public opinion. This accounts for other features which they
frequently embody. A story may be horrific, challenging our
sense of what is the norm; or it may hinge on an enigma,
highlighting phenomena for which we have no ready
explanation; or – as is frequently the case – it may arise from
judicial proceedings, and involve accounts of incidents which
pose a threat to customary behaviour or conventional patterns
of thinking as codified in the law. In this guise, the *fait divers*

is traditionally, and still today, presented in highly coloured language that resorts to sensationalism, eliciting and articulating standard reactions of horror, indignation or mystification. It might be viewed as a therapeutic exercise, society letting off steam at the excesses within it – and thereby containing these excesses within manageable bounds.[292]

From a literary point of view, then, the *fait divers* is an ambiguous entity. Its substance may be, as Edouard says, brutal raw reality: and in this sense it offers a challenge to the writer, moralist or psychologist to provide an account of what society has chosen to dismiss either by explaining it away or by labelling it inexplicable and circumscribing it within the stereotyped responses we have discussed. On the other hand, the fact that it is presented in such a way as to limit reflection and substitute emotional orgies for rational analysis means that its form is also likely to provoke a critical reaction from the artist. For satirical reasons, Gide has the narrator of *Les Caves* and the novelist in *Les Faux-Monnayeurs* turn up their noses at the *fait divers*: but in reality, Gide took a great interest in the phenomenon. In this he may be seen to be following in the footsteps of illustrious predecessors. Stendhal, for example, took a *fait divers* reporting the trial and execution of one Antoine Berthet, and wrote it up as *Le Rouge et le Noir*.[293] And as Gide himself relished pointing out, a propos of Dostoevsky's *Brothers Karamazov*, 'It is well known that a vulgar news item (*fait divers*), a mysterious "case", which the subtle shrewdness of the psychologist set out to explain, served as the first pretext for this book'.[294] Gide himself had friends and acquaintances track down press cuttings for him on the swindle which inspired *Les Caves du Vatican*;[295] and *Les Faux-Monnayeurs* arose directly from newspaper reports in 1909 of a schoolboy named Nény who committed suicide in his school in Clermont-Ferrand in circumstances which the story of Boris replicates.[296] Moreover, the counterfeiting ring is based on a case reported as a *fait divers* in 1906: Gide actually reproduces the relevant press cuttings in *Le Journal des Faux-Monnayeurs* (91–4; 55–7).

Gide's fiction is nourished in a number of ways by his long study of *faits divers* and related phenomena. In 1912, he interrupted his work on *Les Caves du Vatican* to serve for two weeks as a juror at the Assize Court in Rouen. His reflections on the cases he heard were published in 1914 as *Souvenirs de la Cour d'Assises*. In 1920, when he was working on *Les Faux-Monnayeurs*, he was granted special permission to use the library of the Paris Law Courts to pursue his investigations into reports of criminal and other *faits divers*.[297] Immediately after completing his novel, he initiated a rubric in the *Nouvelle Revue Française*, in which, from 1926 to 1928, he regularly published newspaper accounts of *faits divers* sent in by readers or discovered by himself. 1930 saw the publication of two books recounting particularly telling cases: *L'Affaire Redureau* and *La Séquestrée de Poitiers*. The essential unity of this corpus of publications is undeniable: its impact on the narrative fiction is very real. Two circumstantial connections are striking. In *Souvenirs de la Cour d'Assises*, Gide tells how he is haunted by the story of the survivors of the *Bourgogne* – a reminiscence which he will put into the mouth of Lilian Griffith in *Les Faux-Monnayeurs* (980–1; 61–2: *NJP*, 71); and as an epigraph to *La Séquestrée de Poitiers* he quotes from the same novel the passage we have already highlighted in which Vincent wonders how an accumulation of trivial details can produce 'a sum which is monstrous' (960; 40: *NJP*, 200).

His interest in the way the press deals with such matters is reflected within the fictional texts themselves. *Le Prométhée Mal Enchaîné* pokes fun at the public flocking to buy newspapers so as to read reports made up of banal unenlightening information they are probably already familiar with, as if they consider nothing real until they have seen it in print: 'This Meliboeus was someone without any clothes who was going to Italy' (339; 171). *Les Caves du Vatican* recounts the stuff of a *fait divers* in the murder of Fleurissoire by Lafcadio; subsequently the text enables us to read, over the shoulders of Lafcadio and Julius de Baraglioul, examples of what the newspaper makes of the incident. The interpretative force of the word 'crime' he expects to see used by the press unnerves Lafcadio, precisely because for him his action falls outside the bounds of the conventional meanings reporters are accustomed to reading into events. Moreover, the main text of the two reports we read from highlights the effort to make sense of bizarre facts, while simultaneously generating an air of mystery, which characterises the *fait divers*:

> . . . no doubt the unfortunate owner of the coat that was found last night . . . No papers were on him which could give any clue to his identity . . . Death must have been caused by the fall, as the body bears no trace of other injuries . . . which seems to prove the crime was premeditated . . . the motive of the crime, therefore, does not appear to be robbery. (839–41; 205–8)

The underlying purpose of this speculative tone – typical of the press reports it pastiches – is to offer the facts reported as fragments of a narrative that, if all the details could be retrieved and assembled in order, would explain the events in question, fitting them into recognisable patterns of causality and motivation. At the same time, and with a self-consciousness which is typically Gidean, *Les Caves du Vatican* presents, in Julius, a novelist who has hit upon the idea of using this *fait divers* as an element in the novel he is planning. His superior theory of the *acte gratuit*, with its departure from stereotyped psychology, will enable him to 'explain' the bizarre facts of Amédée's death, in a transposed fictional version. But when, prompted by Lafcadio, he realises that the *reality* confirms his theory, he retreats into customary modes of explanation and the conventional mystification of the plot to kidnap the Pope. Both these instances show humans resorting to conventional narrative modes as a refuge from a disturbing reality.

The issues raised by the *fait divers* therefore tend to subvert customary certainties. In *Les Faux-Monnayeurs* Armand's unsettling theory of the 'point-limite' and the contingency of the real world is illustrated by the story of a workman who was electrocuted – a *fait divers* he has read in the newspapers (1162; 254). But the transposition of the young Nény's death which produces the account of Boris's suicide also highlights the inadequacy of the language which is available to report these events. We read that one of the schoolboy witnesses 'told Séraphine afterwards that Boris was frightfully pale; but that is what is always said on these occasions' (1244; 340). Clichés and stereotypes, which falsify reality, are inherent in the modes of expression humanity at large is condemned to use. We have seen how *Les Faux-Monnayeurs* highlights this problem, as indeed do *Le Prométhée Mal Enchaîné* and *Les Caves du Vatican*; at the time when he was editing his *fait divers* rubric, Gide recalled in his diary another memorable instance from his own experience during World War I. As a non-combatant, having been restricted to newspaper reports of what was going on at the Front, he and others like him were anxious to question the injured men who had just come back: 'I remember our amazement on hearing those soldiers – from whom we were expecting at last a truthful account – naïvely recite the same sentences that could be read every day in the papers, sentences they had obviously read themselves and which they now put to use'. Gide's point is not merely that the language of news reports distorts the expression of experience: he is convinced that such stereotyped phraseology actually dictates stereotyped experience: 'Even their sensations, their emotions . . . submitted to it . . . It was according to [these formulas] that they had seen, felt, experienced. . . . Not one among them had been capable of providing the slightest original reaction' (*JI*, 913–14; *J3*, 43–4: 10 February 1929). In these remarks, Gide is anticipating crucial aspects of a debate about the relationship between subjectivity and language which has been important in critical theory over the last thirty years. As Volosinov (a pseudonym of Bakhtin) puts it: 'It is not experience that organizes expression, but the other way round – *expression organizes experience*. Expression is what first gives experience its forms and specificity of direction'.[298] Thus the exploration of forms – linguistic and narrative – which is one of the hallmarks of Gide's work, is not mere literary acrobatics. The forms according to which we order our representations of reality actually determine the imaginary relationship – the ideology – through which we live our real relationship with the world.[299]

This gives Gide his reasons for concern over the forms newspapers use to report *fait divers*. 'In the form in which the newspapers present them, at least, they are more often than not so insignificant' (*NJP*, 140), he wrote in 1928. He quotes one case in which a paper, having received a report from an agency, printed the text received but with the addition of the phrase 'animée d'un sentiment de méchanceté' (driven by a feeling of wickedness) as 'the only plausible explanation' as to why a girl of twelve pushed a three-year-old child down a well, killing her (*NJP*, 141–2). Treating *faits divers* in this way, argues Gide, keeps readers in a state of ignorance about the true depths of human psychology and responsibility by rushing to confirm them in comfortable conventional views on human nature which in fact explain nothing. For Gide the real value of a *fait divers* is that it 'disturbs certain notions we too readily accept, and forces us to reflect' (*NJP*, 146). But in order that it may do so, those whose job it is to record these phenomena must be prepared to avoid the easy path of resorting to the picturesque, the macabre, or the sensational (*NJP*, 145). His readers in *La Nouvelle Revue Française* assumed he was looking for evidence of the *acte gratuit* in everyday life. In reply he was induced to repudiate the concept, arguing that every act has some kind of motivation, however unfathomable; but it is in providing evidence of deviations from easily understood motivation that the interest of the *fait divers* lies (*NJP*, 143). Gide adduces a case he had heard as a juror some sixteen years earlier and recounted in *Souvenirs de la Cour d'Assises*: an arsonist who actually set fire to his own family's property among others, and who in court was utterly incapable of explaining why he had done it, despite the judge's persistent questions. Such instances, argues Gide, are better considered by doctors: but even doctors were compelled to admit defeat in the *Affaire Redureau*, concerning a boy of fifteen, well-behaved, docile, healthy in mind and body, brought up by normal, respectable parents, who hacked to death his employer and his employer's wife, mother and housemaid, plus three small children (*NJP*, 143–4, 99–136). Gide inaugurated with an account of this latter case the publication of a series of volumes collectively entitled 'Ne Jugez pas' ('Judge not'); and in a preface he announces it will be a forum for cases which 'are exceptions to the rules of traditional psychology, and confound human justice'. The traditional legal axiom *Is fecit cui prodest*, earlier called into question by Julius de Baraglioul in *Les Caves du Vatican* during his phase of toying with the *acte gratuit* (818; 178), can lead into serious errors in legal proceedings, Gide points out – once again indicating the intimate connection between the preoccupations which inform his fictional narratives and those which draw him to the *fait divers* and legal procedure. He asserts that we must be prepared to accept that there are some phenomena we cannot explain, still less explain away (*NJP*, 97–8).

This stance raises major difficulties of a practical and aesthetic nature. How can such incidents be adjudicated in a court of law? How can anyone, novelist or journalist, render an intelligible account of them while remaining faithful to their essential mystery? Barthes, in his essay on the *fait divers*, concludes that the genre produces narratives which by their nature cannot be integrated within existing systems of meaning. He argues that the *fait divers* functions as a sign which gestures towards a meaning while rendering that meaning uncertain: it calls for an explanation, but its very nature suggests that an explanation will not be forthcoming.[300] In this sense as well as in others we have mentioned, it can be argued that Gide's first major *récit*, *L'Immoraliste*, is informed by the spirit of the *fait divers*. What we read in this text is essentially the testimony of a defendant in a potentially criminal case. Is Michel guilty of contributing to his wife's death? Is he guilty of any other crimes? The frame narrative itself mimics the situation of a jury listening to Michel's deposition and submitting their views to 'Monsieur D. R., Président du Conseil' (The Prime Minister, Mr D. R.) for a final judgement. An essential feature of Michel's narrative, however, is that it undermines any sense of moral security in his listeners, calling into question the mechanism of judgement and drawing attention to the difficulty of integrating the deviant within the institutions of society that lies at the heart of the legal system: 'In what way can Michel serve society?' (369; ix). Similar concerns, though less urgently felt perhaps, can be detected in the 'testimony' of the first-person narratives *La Porte Etroite* and *La Symphonie Pastorale*, in which excess or transgression claim a place within the established order. We have seen how *Les Caves du Vatican* parodies the detective novel and mocks a system of justice which jumps to facile conclusions owing to the inadequacies of its logic. Similarly, it is notable that *Les Faux-Monnayeurs* features as significant characters Monsieur Profitendieu, the examining magistrate, and Monsieur Molinier, the presiding magistrate. At the start of the narrative this latter is prodigal in his advice on how his colleague should deal with the scandal involving children of respectable families who have taken to frequenting a brothel: wait till the school holidays when the children are away, pounce on the brothel and prosecute the prostitutes, and 'hush the matter up with *the phrase "acting without cognizance" (ayant agi sans discernement)*' (940; 18) – a legal term which in this case conveniently reconciles the obligation to proceed with the judiciary's wish not to expose bourgeois families to public opprobrium.[301] The conclusion of the novel similarly hinges on the way in which the forces of order cope with more schoolboy behaviour which departs horrifyingly from social norms. In this case the crumpled note on which Phiphi had written a message to Ghéridanisol is discovered after the event and provides, in the eyes of the authorities, proof that this is merely one more boyish prank which went wrong. Conventional prejudices prevail again: and in the misreading of this text that causes the police to overlook Ghéridanisol's guilt, may be discerned an echo of that misreading of the earlier 'text', the label from Lafcadio's hat, which enabled him to elude retribution too. In both fictional narratives, such misreadings, associated with codes of verisimilitude which cause people to come to mistaken conclusions about the *faits divers* in question, are shown to contribute to miscarriages of justice.

Conversely, these issues emerge as important features of the legal proceedings Gide documents. Again and again, in the course of cases at which he was a juror, Gide notes details illustrating the extent to which legal procedure is fundamentally bound up with the mechanisms of narrative. 'How rarely does a case present itself from the beginning and straightforwardly' (*NJP*, 48), he remarks; and it can be a painful process to 'recompose' (*NJP*, 13) a coherent story from jumbled, disjointed, often incomplete or unreliable information. A trial consists, in fact, of the construction of two stories, one for the defence and one for the prosecution; and the verdict will go in favour of the one which is the more convincing. Gide points out how frequently the prosecution's representation of the facts is an artificial simplification (*NJP*, 48). Occasionally the defendant manifests a certain unease when he senses that 'the reconstruction of his crime was not perfectly accurate' – the more so when he can neither correct the inaccuracies nor exploit them to his own advantage (*NJP*, 28). For the courtroom is the arena for a contest between different narratives, and weaknesses in one side's account will be denounced by the other. Inconsistencies render a narrative particularly vulnerable to criticism: two or more different or contradictory explanations of a single action within the same account generate suspicion (*NJP*, 52, 57); and the appeal to fortuitous conjunctions of circumstance, which will be dismissed as mere coincidence, is singularly unconvincing (*NJP*, 17). Underpinning these considerations is a constant concern for verisimilitude, essentially a convention enabling us to assess propositions about reality rather than to grasp reality itself. Hence what is at issue is an appearance of truth, rather than actual truth; so the criteria which operate in the courtroom are the same as those by which we judge fiction. The juror's only guide is plausibility, which, as we have seen Barthes remark, is largely a matter of opinion (*NJP*, 15, 68). Narrative technique also involves phatic aspects, of course; the rhetorical ability to sense or anticipate the addressee's reaction can be a first step in bidding for credence, as the example of Prométhée's speech illustrates. Hence Gide observes with sympathy the defendant who cannot get his story across (*NJP*, 16) or 'the poor wretch who realises, but only as he begins to set it out, that his defence is inadequate. His clumsy attempts to give it more substance' (*NJP*, 44). He points out, however, that when it comes to convincing the audience with a story, 'the simplest version is always the one most likely to prevail; but it is also the least likely to be accurate' (*NJP*, 44).

All these points have become commonplaces of modern fiction, at least in novels such as *Thérèse Desqueyroux* (itself inspired by a *fait divers*), *L'Etranger*, *The Trial* and *Le Voyeur*. Christopher Prendergast has argued with considerable justification that the prosecutor in Camus's novel seeks to interpret Meursault's crime in terms of narrative conventions, and

'Meursault's stubborn resistance to those interpretative moves is a resistance to the forms of explanation endorsed by the traditions of the genre'.[302] Mauriac writes of his heroine Thérèse Desqueyroux having secured an acquittal by means of a cosmetic story composed 'for the benefit of the judge, a simple story, with a strong connecting thread, capable of satisfying such a logician'. What is similarly indicated in *Le Voyeur* is the fact that the man guiltily seeking to elaborate a convincing alibi mirrors the novelist trying to ensure that his narrative is coherent. The *cas limite* of the *fait divers* tests the models of narrative convention at the same time as they come into conflict with the discourses of traditional psychology and criminology, as Barthes points out in his essays on two notorious trials of the 1950s, in *Mythologies*.[303] The important role of language emerges in *Souvenirs de la Cour d'Assises* no less than it does in *L'Etranger*. Just as Camus satirises the sanctimonious banalities of the prosecuting counsel by having Meursault report them via a corrosive mixture of direct and indirect quotation, so, for example, Gide highlights the trivial sensationalism and crude ungrammatical style of the newspaper *fait divers* by contrasting it with the facts as they emerge at the trial: 'Let us move on to the account of "the scene of the acts of violence with [sic] which these individuals are implicated", as the *Journal de Rouen* puts it'.[304] The dangerous contagion of journalistic cliché is illustrated in the example of the defendant, trying to win the jury's sympathy with an emotional outburst and a ringing turn of phrase, who mechanically lets slip the expression 'fou de colère' ('mad with rage'), which the prosecution pounces on to clinch its case (*NJP*, 48–9). Time and again Gide denounces the way in which newspaper reports on the trials he is involved in falsify the facts and sway the jury: 'Who can tell the power of persuasion – or intimidation – of the printed page on minds ill-equipped for criticism' (*NJP*, 61), he declares.

This leads us on to the aesthetic questions faced by the novelist who seeks to preserve the authentic effect of the *fait divers* in his narratives, who wishes to produce a 'printed page' which will avoid forcing them into reductive conventional models of intelligibility. What emerges from a reading of *Souvenirs de la Cour d'Assises* is Gide's concern for the process

whereby a story is established as much as for the story
itself. He repeatedly expresses doubts as to whether the
reconstruction on which the verdict was based is in fact true.
(Equally often he notes that the jury is obliged to vote against
what they consider the truth in order to secure justice, or vice
versa.) What the juror is faced with is a number of different –
often mutually contradictory – versions of events, in the
testimony of the defendants and witnesses, which he or she is
left to collate. At the end of the hearing the juror may be
merely perplexed by details which do not fit any overall
pattern, by events which defy verisimilitude, by unexplained
but irrefutable contradictions between corroborative depositions. The courtroom has been the scene of a narrative process:
the product is what the listener makes of it. The judicial
procedure embodies that presentation of a multiplicity of
points of view which Gide had only recently, in 1910, declared
the hallmark of the novel as he saw it.[305] Indeed, after
L'Immoraliste which presents a kind of statement by the
defendant, and the model of two parallel testimonies in *La
Porte Etroite* of 1909, his comments of 1910 suggest that he was
on course to arrive at just the model of narrative presentation
for which he found confirmation in the courtroom.[306] Instead of
offering his narrative material as one homogeneous structure,
Gide preserves the essential character of reality by stressing
the observer's contribution to any observation. Moreover, by
presenting a multiplicity of angles on a given incident, he
highlights the principle already underpinning his first-person
narratives, that 'every fact which is reported, every utterance,
every passage, is refracted in the manner of a rod plunged
into a liquid'.[307] The reader of a text by Gide, like the judge
or juror in a court case, must never forget that a critical stance
is required if we are to get at the facts behind the statements
of the protagonists. That the judicial analogy remained in
Gide's mind as he wrote *Les Faux-Monnayeurs* is borne out by
his comment, made in a letter to Roger Martin du Gard, that
studying Hans Gross's book *Le Manuel Pratique d'Instruction
Judiciaire* in 1924 was an essential factor in determining the
final shape of his novel.[308]

Gide's next narrative project after *Les Faux-Monnayeurs* was
L'Ecole des Femmes, begun in 1927, which represented a

reversion to the technique of the diary-monologue. He had great difficulty maintaining an interest in this story of a woman's disillusion with the husband she married in a naïve flush of girlish enthusiasm: he only managed to complete it, in late 1928, at the insistence of an American publisher with whom he had signed a contract for the translation. A more significant strand of work during the years 1927–30 is furnished by the succession of *faits divers* he published at regular intervals in the *Nouvelle Revue Française*. This activity culminated in *La Séquestrée de Poitiers*, published in 1930 to inaugurate the collection 'Ne Jugez Pas'. In his preface for the collection, Gide writes: 'We shall confront the facts not as a painter or novelist, but as a naturalist'. The erstwhile young symbolist can use the term which was formerly anathema to him, since it has ceased to evoke primarily a literary movement but rather the revolutions in the natural sciences which Gide had studied with such interest. He continues, 'An account is often all the more moving for being perfunctory; but we shall not be concerned for effects. We shall efface ourselves as much as possible and present documents which are as authentic as possible (by that I mean not having been subjected to any interpretation), and direct testimony' (*NJP*, p. 98). Here then is a writer seeking so far as possible to let reality speak for itself, claiming to eschew interpretative and rhetorical strategies in the interests of suspending judgement and obliging the reader to work for a conclusion. It is an obvious point to make that this in itself constitutes a narrative strategy, and in fact *La Séquestrée de Poitiers* may be seen, in some respects at least, as a development and validation of the narrative technique Gide devised for *Les Faux-Monnayeurs*. In it, Gide recounts events which occurred in Poitiers between the 1870s and 1901, when one Pierre Bastian was accused and tried for the role he played in keeping his sister shut up in the same room for twenty-five years. She had lived thus in conditions of unspeakable squalor, naked and covered only by a filthy blanket, lying in her own excrement and the remains of her food, amidst an infestation of vermin.[309] The epigraph quoted from *Les Faux-Monnayeurs*, suggesting that a 'sum which is monstrous' can be brought about by 'adding together a quantity of little facts which, taken separately, are very simple and very natural' (960; 40), indicates that Gide sees the same contingent logic at work in this *fait divers* as in his novel. In Barthes's analysis of the *fait divers*, 'les troubles de la causalité' are a major ingredient: grotesque effects from trivial causes, the intervention of chance or coincidence, are the very stuff of that reality which the *fait divers* seeks to record[310] – as they are in the world of *Les Faux-Monnayeurs*. Thus Gide gleans from the various testimonies at the trial ample evidence to show that the victim as well as her mother and father had a history of claustrophilia, a hereditary compulsion to shut themselves away; and the brother had a curious taste for filth, coupled with a defective sense of smell. The shutters of the young woman's room had had to be closed because of her tendency to exhibitionism; the windows had had to be locked and sealed up owing to her propensity for flying into demented rages and yelling obscenities. Her mental state had become unbalanced from an early age, and rather than indicating cruelty, her sequestration bore witness to her family's efforts to care for her in their home. Good food had always been provided for her, but she would eat only with her fingers and insisted on setting aside certain items which she left lying on the bed beside her until they putrefied. In short, there turned out to be perfectly logical reasons for every element in the horrific picture. 'Things had reached this point little by little, through a slow process of habituation' (*NJP*, 252, 255–6, 258). The simple truth of his conjunction of circumstances defies conventions of verisimilitude – and also of narrative logic. The appeal court, while expressing severe criticism of the passivity with which Bastian had bowed to his authoritarian mother's orders on the matter, ruled that no one had committed any crime.

In setting out the facts, Gide does resort to methods unlike those he may have used in a novel. The family history and antecedents of those involved are listed, as a catalogue (*NJP*, 235–6), rather than being narrativised as in the spoof biography of the Blafafoires in *Les Caves du Vatican* (760–4; 103–9). The chronology of events is painstakingly observed. The dialogue of the cross-examinations is frequently set out in the form of a stage script, without the interpolation of 'he said' and so on. This, however, actually repeats the technique

Gide uses in a conversation between Julius de Baraglioul and
Lafcadio (838–9; 204–5): without the narratorial interventions,
indeed, the discussions read to striking dramatic effect. They
present a telling contrast with the dialogue in the introductory
chapter, in which Gide presents the Police Commissioner's
first visit to the victim's house according to standard narrative
methods. The main effect of this sequence is in fact to
highlight the very artificiality of the devices used, including the
conventional past historic tense, and the familiar introduction
in medias res followed by a strategic use of the Commissioner's
questions to facilitate the insertion of background information
on Bastian himself (*NJP*, pp. 205–7). Elsewhere, a chapter
recounting the death of the victim's mother which ends with
the lines 'A few minutes before the doctor arrived, Mme
Bastian had called out "Ah! my poor Mélanie!"' (*NJP*, 222)
is seeking to present more, it may be felt, than a dispassionate
chronicle of events. It is true that the description of the
victim's room is presented via the Examining Magistrate's
formal report, and the catalogue of its contents comes from
the official statement of the Commissioner responsible for
seizing these items. Subsequently much of the text will consist
of extracts from depositions, as well as from newspaper articles
and records of cross-examinations. In all of this, however,
while departing from traditional narrative methods, Gide is
actually evolving techniques out of those already used in *Les
Faux-Monnayeurs*, where quotation from letters, diaries and
other documents is a staple ingredient. The documentary
technique of his narrative represents a bid for a new kind of
verisimilitude; and in authors ranging from John Dos Passos
to Georges Simenon, we see that realism is at bottom a
constantly renewed series of such bids, as each 'representation
of reality' claims to supersede the forms which have gone
before. Of equal interest is the narrative voice, which as Gide
declares, aims to avoid being intrusive in *La Séquestrée*. In fact
it has an editorial function not dissimilar to the narrator who
guides us through extracts from Edouard's diary. 'First we
shall listen to the defendants' (*NJP*, 213) has a familiar ring
to the reader of *Les Faux-Monnayeurs*, as does 'Now let us listen
to Mme Bastian senior' (*NJP*, 220). The nature of such
interventions is made slightly clearer when we read: 'Let us

interrupt for a moment the testimony of Juliette Dupuis to intercalate this astounding fragment from the deposition of Virginie Neveux, from which I shall give other equally sensational extracts later' (*NJP*, 243). The narrator of *Les Faux-Monnayeurs* interrupts his account of a conversation between Olivier and Bernard in order to eavesdrop on Georges and his companions who have appeared on the same street (1145; 235): the device appears to suggest that the characters have a life of their own, since they carry on with what they were doing while the narrator cannot be in two places at once. In both instances the effect is to foreground the practical process of assembling the stuff of the story, but if anything the example from *La Séquestrée de Poitiers* is more openly manipulative since at least the novelist's narrator is apparently following events as they occur before him, whereas the ostensibly neutral editor openly appeals to the reader's interest with this sample of 'astounding' material and the promise of more to follow shortly. The novelist, who is free to imagine the fictional reality for his story, can manipulate the plot so as to maintain the reader's interest; the documentary writer has to stick to the facts and the temptation is all the greater to find ways of injecting interest into the telling. It is true that he can have overt recourse to the hermeneutic code to maintain suspense: 'How could this case result in the acquittal of the accused? This is what you will no doubt understand by reading all that follows' (*NJP*, 204). But in the main it is by editing his material to make it centre on a succession of specific facets to the case that Gide guides and concentrates the reader's attention. In this, of course, he is selecting and shaping his material; in fact, imposing an interpretation upon it despite his disclaimers. The most striking illustration of this, to the reader familiar with the rest of Gide's work, is his insistence on 'l'inconséquence des caractères' ('inconsistency of the characters') (*NJP*, 241) – a phrase straight from *Les Faux-Monnayeurs* (1201; 295) and redolent of a theme which also looms large in *Les Caves du Vatican* and elsewhere. The psychological discontinuity implied by Mélanie Bastian's simultaneously revelling in the cleanliness and care to which she has been removed, and expressing regret for the darkness and squalor of what she called her 'chère petite grotte' (*NJP*,

277) makes of her a Gidean character par excellence. The intrusion of Gidean preoccupations in the narrative is also evident when the narrator remarks, after transcribing the Commissioner's enumeration of the items removed from the Bastian household, 'We would like to have known, for example, the titles of the thirty-seven volumes seized, and the nature of those "notes written in pencil" indicated in the report' (*NJP*, 212). This, from the author who has Julius de Baraglioul conspicuously fail to see the significance of the writing in Lafcadio's notebook, or of the presence in his otherwise sparsely furnished room of the *Novelle* of Anton Francesco Grazzini in Italian, and a copy of *Moll Flanders* with only two-thirds of the pages cut (715–17; 45–8), demonstrates the extent to which the documentary reconstruction of the *fait divers* overlaps with the exploitation within the fictional narrative of the techniques of the judicial enquiry. In both instances, Gide is seeking to convey something of the unsettling mystery of reality, the disturbing significance of the trivial, the limitless possibilities of a world which is as it is only by chance.

4

Conclusion

Gide's entire work is marked by that rivalry between the real world and the representations we make of it which preoccupies the novelist Edouard in *Les Faux-Monnayeurs*. Reality presents two problems to a writer such as Gide: first, it is unknowable in itself; and second, it is impossible to communicate our perceptions of it, since the means we use impose human patterns on what extends beyond human perception. We are like Nathanaël in *Les Nourritures Terrestres*: 'Nathaniel, you are like the man who should follow as his guide the light he holds in his own hand' (155; 18). We see what our light illuminates: but what it reveals depends not only upon its power but also upon the angle at which we hold it and the direction in which we point it.[311] Hence Gide's concern to analyse the subjective bias in human observations, and its contribution to action and relationships. Each of his characters, narrators and protagonists, is shown to have a particular vision of reality reducible to that corner of existence which his or her consciousness is capable of illuminating and absorbing. The consequence of this principle, in terms of narrative technique, is the crucial importance of point of view in Gide's narratives. His refinement of the ironic first-person narrative, as well as his manipulation of multiple viewpoints in third-person narratives, ensure that the reader is left in no doubt about the relativity of truth. Moreover, the essential concomitant of this approach to technique is our resultant awareness that every observation of reality is marked by the presence of the observer; so that reading Gide's narratives calls for a kind of stereoscopic vision, as we scrutinise simultaneously the nature of the events related and the teller's interaction with these events. The ironic first-person of *L'Immoraliste* and the self-conscious third-person of *Les Caves du Vatican* alike generate a critical awareness in the reader. We consider not only what is said, but how it came to be said that way, and in what ways it might have been reported differently.

This critical awareness is given a further dimension by means of the *mise en abyme* technique. Michel's palimpsest image, as well as the projected novels of Julius and Edouard, highlight the writing process even as we hold in our hands a product of that process. We cannot take for granted the finished work when the activity which has gone into making it emerges as aleatory, subject to human foibles just like the rest. It is a telling fact that Gide takes pains to demonstrate, notably through Julius, Edouard and Passavant, how the writer is as deeply implicated in reality, as much a victim of hypocrisy and prone to ill-considered behaviour issuing in disastrous consequences, as any 'ordinary' human being. On the other hand, the device of the novel within the novel, of the story within the story, of the work within the work, ensures that texts such as *L'Immoraliste*, *La Symphonie Pastorale*, *Les Caves du Vatican* or *Les Faux-Monnayeurs* declare their status as artefacts, self-reflexively distancing themselves from the shapeless flux of reality. In doing so they invite readings which explore their structural coherence, the sophisticated and systematic ways in which Gide has constructed an all-embracing form out of interconnected motifs, thematic echoes and intertextual allusions.[312]

We are tempted to conclude that individually and collectively human beings are immured in solipsism. The individual is trapped within his or her subjective perception of the world; and to complicate matters still further, Gide anticipates what has become known as 'the crisis of the subject' by showing how so-called individual experience reveals itself in fact to be little more than an unstable amalgam of transient states articulated in imaginary representations and linguistic structures which are second-hand, ideologically conditioned. Neither this experience nor artistic form can be assumed to have any but the most problematic link with reality. It is an awareness of this fact which seems to fuel Gide's fascination for phenomena that test the fabric of ideological constructions. Again and again his works present events and actions which not only represent the climax or culmination of misguided perceptions, but also defeat conventional patterns of representation and models of intelligibility. The spirit of the *fait divers* can be linked with Gide's formulations of the outlandish, the incomprehensible or the undecidable; but equally, an informed understanding of the contingency of reality as revealed by movements in scientific thought can be seen to be an important source of inspiration. His plots which pit human consciousness against random events undermine the traditional tenets of positivism, blur the distinctions between the real and the imaginary, the necessary and the possible, and refuse facile solutions to the issues they raise.

At the furthest extreme from the taste for the absolute which informed Gide's literary beginnings, his late work *Geneviève* has a narrator who actually addresses her narrative to Gide, challenging him to come to terms with 'contingences' and 'le relatif' (1348; 127). Artistic form and narrative structures as conventionally conceived, declares Geneviève, are inadequate to the task: 'A certain degree of perfection (which I have no desire to achieve) can only be obtained at the cost of truth. Truth, as soon as it is a matter not of abstraction but of life, is always complex, confused, indistinct, and ill-adapted to definition' (1361; 141). It would be false to assert that Gide ever really forsook or betrayed his aesthetic instincts. But something of the insight he formulates through Geneviève can be seen in the pleasure with which he contemplated what he had produced in *Les Caves du Vatican*: 'Not a "masterpiece" – but rather a bewildering book, full of holes and gaps, but also full of amusement, strangeness and partial successes'.[313] The received notion of artistic perfection gives way to the search for an aesthetic structure which encompasses – indeed cultivates – uncertainty, and reveals holes in the fabric of conventional constructions. It is clear that Gide does not belong to that family of novelists who, according to Alain Robbe-Grillet, have persisted since the nineteenth century in the construction of 'narratives codified once and for all according to the sub-balzacian realist ideology, without any contradictions or gaps in the signifying framework'. On the contrary, Gide is a precursor of those like Robbe-Grillet himself, who 'will seek to explore insoluble oppositions, fragmentation, diegetic aporias, breaks, blanks, etc., for they know that the real begins at the very instant when meaning falters'.[314] Gide's dilemma concerning the limitations of realism and the need to go beyond artistic forms which falsify the real can find a resolution in the principle that reality is what happens when meaning falters. He has Amédée Fleurissoire experience precisely this kind of reality (809; 167), and whether in the burlesque mode or not, the sense of uncertainty or perplexity is the creative centre of his narratives.

This perception arrives in the lives of his characters most notably in the form of writing. For Damoclès, in *Le Prométhée Mal Enchaîné*, it comes as an envelope addressed to him in an unknown hand, betraying an 'absolute lack of character' and defying all the specialists' efforts to trace its origin (309; 112). The document initiates existential angst as his former certainties evaporate and Damoclès becomes dominated by the enigmas which henceforth constitute his reality. It is true that Coclès owns to being the author of the lines on the envelope, but significantly, he declares 'I do not know who brought me into the world' (310; 115): which highlights the theme of a disoriginated origin, pointing to a world in which there is no anterior truth, no pre-existing meaning. Similarly, Bernard Profitendieu stumbles across a letter which puts an end to his routine existence by revealing that he is illegitimate: moreover, the signature of its author – of his author – is indecipherable (933; 11). Bernard has penetrated between the 'lames disjointes' (*'disjointed* pieces of wood') (934; 12) of a console table to find this letter, a detail curiously reminiscent of the 'pavés disjoints' which play an important role in Robbe-Grillet's fiction, suggesting (among other things) the prising apart of those forms of intelligibility which constructed previous false notions of reality as a seamless continuum.[315] For Bernard as for Damoclès, the written text itself announces a fissure in the fabric of his earlier view of reality and projects him out into the world in search of a real which will elude him, leaving him inclined to 'doubt the reality of everything' (1088; 175). The fact that these two narratives begin in this way suggests a parallel with the experience of a reader starting out on them. The written text inserts itself into the fabric of our lives, opening them to new imagined experiences, offering, in keeping with our normal expectations of narrative, a disruption to be remedied by a resolution, an enigma to be resolved by an answer. The writing points to a message contained within it. But the writing of Gide's narratives can be compared to the curious type of cloudy agate on the cufflinks which Lafcadio gives to Carola as a parting gift in *Les Caves du Vatican*. This stone '*was impossible to see anything through*, although it looked as if it were *transparent*' (731; 66). The text too offers an effect of transparency, but actually blocks our access to meaning the better to confront us with uncertainty and undecidability. The attentive reader will emerge from these works with a fuller understanding of what Gide meant when he wrote of the authentic state of mind as being one of 'passionate indecision' (*JI*, 358; *J1*, 312: 1912).

Notes

1. A comment made on 31 August 1931, quoted in *Le Journal de Robert Levesque*, in *BAAG*, XI, no. 59, July 1983, p. 337.

2. Michel Raimond, *La Crise du Roman, Des lendemains du Naturalisme aux années vingt* (Paris: Corti, 1966), pp. 9–84.

3. Quoted in A. Breton, *Manifestes du Surréalisme* (Paris: Gallimarde, Collection Idées), p. 15; cf. Gide, *JI*, 1068; *J3*, 181: August 1931.

4. Letter to Jean Schlumberger, 1 May 1935, in Gide, *Littérature Engagée* (Paris: Gallimard, 1950), p. 79.

5. Alain Goulet studies his earliest verse in 'Les premiers vers d'André Gide (1888–1891)', *Cahiers André Gide*, 1 (Paris: Gallimard, 1969), pp. 123–49, and shows that by 1892 he had already decided that prose was his forte.

6. Gide-Valéry, *Correspondance* (Paris: Gallimard, 1955), p. 46.

7. See sections of this diary reproduced in the edition by Claude Martin, *Les Cahiers et les Poésies d'André Walter* (Paris: Gallimard, Collection Poésie, 1986), pp. 181–218.

8. See Anny Wynchank, 'Métamorphoses dans *Les Cahiers d'André Walter*. Essai de rétablissement de la chronologie dans *Les Cahiers d'André Walter*', *BAAG*, no. 63, July 1984, pp. 361–73; Pierre Lachasse, 'L'ordonnance symbolique des *Cahiers d'André Walter*', *BAAG*, no. 65, January 1985, pp. 23–38.

9. 126, 127, 93; 106, 107, 79. The English translation fails to convey Walter's efforts in this direction, translating 'l'orthographie' (93) – itself a wilful distortion of *l'orthographe*, 'spelling' – by 'diction' (79), and blurring matters further on pp. 106–7. Walter proposes to replace *continuellement* by *continûment*, and *douloureusement* by *douleureusement*, for instance, the better to convey the sensation he is seeking to circumscribe.

10. Compare with the theory behind the works of Moréas and Huysmans, first-generation symbolists working in the previous decade: Ralph Freedman, *The Lyrical Novel* (Princeton, New Jersey: Princeton University Press, 1963), pp. 34–8; and Karl D. Uitti, *The Concept of Self in the Symbolist Novel* (The Hague: Mouton and Co., 1961).

11. A. Naville, *Bibliographie des écrits d'André Gide* (Paris: Guy Le Prat, 1949), p. 202.

12. For a detailed study of this process, see Vinio Rossi, *André Gide. The Evolution of an Aesthetic* (New Brunswick, NJ: Rutgers University Press, 1967).

13. *André Gide qui êtes-vous?*, Entretiens Gide-Amrouche, presentation by Eric Marty (Paris: La Manufacture, 1987), p. 160. Gide published what is in effect a manifesto of his theory concerning the correspondence between landscapes and events, for the re-edition of *Le Voyage d'Urien* in 1896; see *RRS*, pp. 1464–5.

14. Jean Delay, *La Jeunesse d'André Gide* (Paris: Gallimard, 2 vols, 1956–7), vol. 2, pp. 245–6; *The Youth of André Gide*, abridged and translated by June Guicharnaud (Chicago and London: University of Chicago Press, one volume, 1963), pp. 321–2.

15. *Si le Grain ne Meurt*, in *JII*, 535; 234.

16. Delay, vol. 2, 666–8; 487. Italics in original. The English version does not give the full text of this entry in the unpublished diary.

17. *JI*, 716; *J2*, 286. See also *JII*, 221–2; *J4*, 198.

18. See Joseph Frank, 'Spatial Form in Modern Literature', in *The Widening Gyre. Crisis and Mastery in Modern Literature* (New Brunswick, NJ: Rutgers University Press, 1963), pp. 3–62.

19. Cf. Valéry, 'Roman et poésie', in *Variété, Oeuvres*, I (Paris: Bibliothèque de la Pléiade, 1957), pp. 770–2; E. M. Forster: 'Yes – oh dear yes – the novel tells a story', *Aspects of the Novel* (Harmondsworth: Penguin, 1974), pp. 33–4; D. H. Walker, 'Subversion of narrative in the work of André Gide and John Fowles', in *Comparative Criticism*, ed. E. Schaffer, vol. 2 (Cambridge: Cambridge University Press, 1980), pp. 187–212.

20. *JI*, 751; *J2*, 319. Cf. *JI*, 788, 795, 1070; *J2*, 353–4, 359; *J3*, 183. The correspondences abound in references to these readings, as do Mme van Rysselberghe's *Les Cahiers de la Petite Dame*.

21. Gide makes the same point in a letter to Roger Martin du Gard, 1 February 1931, *Correspondance* (Paris: Gallimard, 2 vols., 1968), vol. 1, p. 442.

22. See Susan Suleiman and Inge Crosman, eds, *The Reader in the Text* (Princeton: Princeton University Press, 1980); Elizabeth Freund, *The Return of the Reader* (London: Methuen, New Accents, 1987); Gerald Prince, *Narratology. The Form and Functioning of Narrative* (Berlin, New York, Amsterdam: Mouton, 1982), pp. 16–26.

23. Manuscript note dated 18 August 1898, quoted in Claude Martin, *La Maturité d'André Gide. De 'Paludes' à 'L'Immoraliste' (1895–1902)* (Paris: Klincksieck, 1977), pp. 302–3.

24. *Prétextes* (Paris: Mercure de France, 1963), pp. 156–7; *Pretexts*, pp. 50–1.

25. See Auguste Anglès, *André Gide et Le Premier Groupe de 'La Nouvelle Revue Française'*, I. *La formation du groupe et les années d'apprentissage (1890–1910)* (Paris: Gallimard, 1978).

26. I am running together here a number of categories which narratologists choose to distinguish from each other as analytical approaches dictate. For discussions of these distinctions see S. Suleiman, 'Introduction: varieties of audience-oriented criticism', in *The Reader in the Text*, op. cit., pp. 12–14; S. Rimmon-Kenan, *Narrative Fiction: Contemporary Poetics* (London: Methuen, New Accents, 1983), pp. 86–9, 103–5; J. M. Adam, *Le Texte narratif* (Paris: Nathan, 1985), pp. 173–7.

27. On narrative as a form of contract, see Roland Barthes, *S/Z* (Paris: Seuil, Collection Points, 1970), pp. 95–6; C. Prendergast, *The Order of Mimesis* (Cambridge: Cambridge University Press, 1986), pp. 36–41, 83–7. On narrative as a transaction, see Peter Brooks, *Reading for the Plot* (Oxford: Clarendon Press, 1984), chapter 8. Brooks's psychoanalytical model, taking desire as the chief motor of the narrative transaction, seems particularly appropriate to Gide's texts, as is evident in the case of *La Tentative Amoureuse*. See below, the discussion of *Les Nourritures Terrestres*, and chapter II, the analysis of *L'Immoraliste*.

28. See R. Freedman, op. cit., pp. 137–43; D. Walker, 'The Dual Composition of *Les Nourritures Terrestres*: Autour du 'Récit de Ménalque', *French Studies*, XXIX (1975), pp. 421–33; E. Marty, 'Mythologie d'André Gide', in *André Gide, qui êtes-vous?*, op. cit., pp. 69–70.

29. For a more detailed discussion of this aspect, see my *Gide: 'Les Nourritures terrestres' and 'La Symphonie pastorale'* (London: Grant and Cutler, 1990), ch. 2.

30. Preface to the 1930 re-edition of *Les Cahiers d'André Walter*, op. cit., p. 31.

31. *Si le Grain ne Meurt*, in *JII*, 506–7; 199.

32. See Roland Barthes, 'The Structural Analysis of Narratives', in *Image-Music-Text* (Glasgow: Fontana, 1977), pp. 79–124.

33. Rossi, op. cit., pp. 127–30.

34. Preface to *Le Roi Candaule*, *OC III*, 295.

35. See Rossi, op. cit., pp. 144–61.

36. Cf. G. W. Ireland, *André Gide. A Study of his Creative Writings* (Oxford: Clarendon Press, 1970), pp. 254–7.

37. The critical literature on the *mise en abyme* is immense, as it has been taken up since Gide by very many modern writers. The best summary of its implications can be found in Lucien Dällenbach, *Le Récit Spéculaire* (Paris: Seuil, 1977).

38. See Raimond, op. cit., pp. 44–59.

39. 'L'Evolution du théâtre', lecture given in 1904, in *Prétextes*, p. 146, note 1; *Pretexts*, p. 60.

40. Letter to H. Drain, 18 July 1932, quoted in Yvonne Davet, *Autour des 'Nourritures terrestres'* (Paris: Gallimard, 1948), p. 90. Cf. also *Journal des Faux-Monnayeurs*, p. 53; 28–9.

41. Letter to Roger Martin du Gard, 27 March 1931, *Correspondance*, vol. 1, p. 471.

42. *Prétextes*, p. 168; *Pretexts*, p. 100.

43. 10 May 1894, quoted in Delay, op. cit., vol. II, p. 319; 350.

44. Cf. *Journal des Faux-Monnayeurs*, p. 103; 61: 'Opinions do not exist outside of individuals and interest the novelist only in relation to those who hold them. . . . These opinions they profess and which they believe freely accepted, or chosen, or even invented, are as predetermined and ordained as the colour of their hair or the odour of their breath.'

45. Letter to H. Drain, 18 July 1932, in Davet, op. cit., p. 90.

46. Letter to Roger Martin du Gard, 29 December 1925, *Correspondance*, vol. 1, p. 280; the same sentiment is expressed with a slightly different wording in *Journal des Faux-Monnayeurs*, p. 73; 42.

47. Cf. Genette, *Figures III* (Paris: Seuil, 1972), pp. 71–2; Mieke Bal, *Narratology*, translated by Christine van Boheemen (Toronto, London: University of Toronto Press, 1985), pp. 11–13.

48. *Journal des Faux-Monnayeurs*, p. 28; 13. Italics in original.

49. 'Feuillets', *OC XIII*, pp. 439–40. Italics in original.

50. See Elizabeth Wright, *Psychoanalytic Criticism* (London: Methuen, 1984), pp. 9–17.

51. See Peter Brooks, *Reading for the Plot*, pp. 269–83; Jonathan Culler, *The Pursuit of Signs* (London: Routledge and Kegan Paul, 1981), chapter 9, pp. 178–86.

52. This is the view of A. Oliver, *Michel, Job, Pierre, Paul: intertextualité de la lecture dans 'L'Immoraliste'* (Paris: Archives des Lettres modernes, Archives André Gide no. 4, 1979), pp. 55–6.

53. F. Jameson, *The Prison-House of Language* (Princeton: Princeton University Press, 1972). Jameson offers an interesting Derridean discussion of Michel's use of the palimpsest image, pointing out that he is caught up willy-nilly in the endless *différance* that writing inaugurates, and that he pays the penalty for 'an allegiance to the myth of some absolute and original presence' (pp. 176–8).

54. Roland Barthes, *Le Degré Zéro de l'Ecriture, suivi de Nouveaux Essais Critiques* (Paris: Seuil, Collection Points, 1972), pp. 25–7; *Writing Degree Zero and Elements of Semiology*, tr. Annette Lavers and Colin Smith (London: Jonathan Cape, 1984), pp. 26–9.

55. For illuminating comment on this declaration, see G. W. Ireland, *André Gide. A Study of his Creative Writings*, p. 191.

56. See Terry Eagleton, *Literary Theory: An Introduction* (Oxford: Blackwell, 1983), pp. 167–71; Wright, op. cit., pp. 107–22.

57. Michel Raimond traces other cases of the 'obsession du regard' in Gide's work: see op. cit., pp. 363–5. On Lacanian interpretations of the way works of art can reverse the spectator's voyeuristic fantasies, see Wright, op. cit., pp. 117–19.

58. The importance of this feature of the text emerges from Gide's own discomfiture on learning that his friend Henri Ghéon had revealed to another acquaintance the secret of his paedophile inclinations. Gide wrote to Ghéon: 'The public's gaze is so odious to me as to take away my taste for living; it removes all value from action, all worth from sincerity', and asserted that if the revelation had come earlier he would have been unable to write *L'Immoraliste*. Letter of 30 July 1902, Gide-Ghéon *Correspondance*, vol. 1, 1897–1905 (Paris: Gallimard, 1976), p. 454.

59. From Freud's definition of transference as 'a kind of intermediate region between illness and real life, through which the transition from the one to the other is made' Brooks argues: 'Those texts that dramatize narrative situation, contract, and transaction may most patently demonstrate the value of a transferential model. This is particularly the case when "framing" is an issue, for the frame of the framed tale comes to represent Freud's "real life", that outer margin that makes the life within narratable, figures it as the "artificial illness" treated for what it has to say about the story written by unconscious desire', op. cit., pp. 234–5. On the wider applicability of

transference to narrative, see Wright, op. cit., especially pp. 15–17 and pp. 122–32.

60. An extended but incomplete account of this structure, illustrated by means of a useful diagram, can be found in Henri Maillet, *'L'Immoraliste' d'André Gide* (Paris: Hachette, 1972), pp. 31–47. The further analysis I present here was first set out in my article 'Subversion of narrative in the work of André Gide and John Fowles', loc. cit., pp. 190–1.

61. Cf. Joseph Frank, loc. cit., and our discussion of spatial form in Gide's novels in Chapter 1.

62. *Si le Grain ne Meurt*, in *JII*, 547; 250. Cf. *JI*, 842; *J2*, 404: 1927: 'Suppressing the dialogue in oneself really amounts to stopping the development of life'.

63. G. W. Ireland, op. cit., pp. 189–98; G. Brée, *André Gide l'insaisissable Protée* (Paris: Les Belles Lettres, 1953), pp. 170–1.

64. 'Lettres à Angèle', 10 December 1899, in *Prétextes*, p. 79.

65. *Entretiens Gide–Amrouche*, p. 208.

66. *André Gide* (New York: E. P. Dutton, 1963), p. 117.

67. *Entretiens Gide-Amrouche*, p. 160.

68. Op. cit., p. 160.

69. Thomas Cordle, *André Gide* (New York: Twayne, 1969), p. 94, argues that the effect of the incidents involving Lucile 'is to place a severe ban on the sensual expression of love'.

70. He declared and reiterated that the two books were twinned in his mind, the one balancing the other: see *OC VI*, pp. 360–1, 469; *JI*, pp. 365–6; *J2*, p. 318: 7 February 1912.

71. See Sonnenfeld's analysis of the implications of what she leaves out of Racine's *Cantiques spirituels*, from which she quotes: 'On Readers and Reading in *La Porte Etroite* and *L'Immoraliste'*, *Romanic Review*, LXVII (1976), pp. 172–86.

72. Critics vary in their assessments of who is the most important character in the novel: Alissa commands a great deal of attention, often to the exclusion of Jérôme (see, for example, Ireland, op. cit., pp. 199–212; J. C. Davies, *Gide, 'L'Immoraliste' and 'La Porte Etroite'* (London: Edward Arnold, 1968), p. 67, note 3), though there have been attempts to argue for a 'Jérôme reading', most notably by Zvi H. Levy, *Jérôme Agonistes: Les structures dramatiques et les procédés narratives de 'La Porte Etroite'* (Paris: Nizet, 1984).

73. *Portraits of Artists: Reflexivity in Gidean Fiction, 1902–1946* (York, South Carolina: French Literature Publications Company, 1982), p. 32.

74. Maisani-Léonard, *André Gide ou l'ironie de l'écriture* (Montréal: Presses de l'Université de Montréal, 1976), pp. 106, 160ff., 180.

75. Loc. cit., pp. 172–86.

76. We read that Alissa learned Latin in order to follow Jérôme in his studies; that Jérôme in turn was reluctant to embark on new fields of study for fear that Alissa would not be able to accompany him; but that rather than inhibiting his intellectual development Alissa seemed to lead the way, since as he says 'The course my mind pursued was always shaped with reference to her' (510–11; 25).

188 *André Gide*

77. Lévy, op. cit., pp. 112–15.

78. It is also true, however, that the text we read has been edited by Jérôme: 'I here transcribe a considerable number of its pages', he says (580; 119), without explaining the grounds for the selection he has made.

79. On this concept, see Oswald Ducrot and Tzvetan Todorov, *Dictionnaire encyclopédique des sciences du langage* (Paris: Seuil, Collection Points, 1972), pp. 417–22.

80. Gérard Genette, *Figures III*, pp. 229–30, n. 2 (*Narrative Discourse*, p. 217, n. 13), invites critics to scrutinise the point, but none have so far responded to his prompting. In recent years, two critics in particular have discussed certain aspects of the question, though both leave important issues unexamined: Lorna Martens, *The Diary Novel* (Cambridge: Cambridge University Press, 1985), pp. 138–55; and John T. Booker, 'The Generic Ambiguity of Gide's *La Symphonie Pastorale*: Reading the pastor's first *cahier*', *Symposium*, 40 (1986), pp. 159–71.

81. See John T. Booker's interesting discussion of this paragraph, loc. cit., pp. 164–7.

82. See Henri Maillet, *'La Symphonie Pastorale' d'André Gide* (Paris: Hachette, 1972), pp. 31–2.

83. It is perhaps this fact which explains the unusual use of verb tenses in the French text. The pastor mingles the past historic and the perfect in his narrative in ways which are highly idiosyncratic and incorrect by normal standards. This reinforces our impression of him as a man who is unable to decide precisely what is his stance *vis à vis* the events he is recounting. See M. Maisani-Léonard, op. cit., pp. 134–48.

84. This dimension of the text is entirely omitted from John T. Booker's otherwise perceptive analysis, which accounts for the significant limitations of his study.

85. See the critical edition of *La Symphonie Pastorale*, published by Claude Martin (Paris: Lettres Modernes Minard, Collection Paralogue, no. 4, 1970), pp. 5–8. The manuscript begins with a reference to the sermon preached by the pastor on Christmas Day taking as his text a verse from Luke's Gospel, ii, 7: '[She] laid him in a manger; because there was no room for them in the inn'. He establishes a parallel with the fate of Gertrude, 'for whom my wife announced to me last week that there was "no longer any room in the house" and whom I have had to entrust to that saintly woman named Louise Jacquet, at the other end of the village'.

86. See above, note 79.

87. Lorna Martens, op. cit., p. 150, is the only critic to make this point, to my knowledge; but even she fails to see the importance for other aspects of his narrative of the life the pastor has been accustomed to leading with Gertrude: see below.

88. Booker stresses the lack of apparent provocation for this outburst and suggests plausibly that the virulence of the pastor's comments on Amélie is motivated by the memory of the incidents he is about to set down – a sort of prospective recollection: loc. cit., pp. 167–8. We cannot, however, leave out of account the factors which are contemporary with the narration: see below.

89. See R. Wellek and A. Warren, *Theory of Literature* (Harmondsworth: Penguin Books, 1973), p. 25. For versions of structuralist and post-structuralist strictures on trying to penetrate 'derrière le papier', see Roland Barthes, *S/Z*, pp. 128–9 and *passim*.

90. W. D. Wilson, *André Gide: 'La Symphonie Pastorale'* (London and Basingstoke: Macmillan, 1971), p. 38.

91. See Jonathan Culler, *The Pursuit of Signs*, pp. 178–86.

92. Cf. Barthes, 'Introduction to the structural analysis of narratives', in *Image, Music, Text*, pp. 94, 98.

93. E.g. Martin, op. cit., pp. cv–cvi; Martens, op. cit., pp. 148–52.

94. See Walker, *'Les Nourritures Terrestres' and 'La Symphonie Pastorale'*, chapter 3, (ii).

95. There is, in fact, a contradiction between his claim on 25 April not to have understood at the time the implications of his own behaviour or of words spoken to him by Amélie, and the form in which he has earlier reported these, with remarks such as 'later . . . this became clear to me' (903; 40) and 'became clear to me soon after this' (908; 45). Interpretations of these inconsistencies vary: see Martin, op. cit., pp. cii–civ; Henri Maillet, *'La Symphonie Pastorale' d'André Gide*, pp. 44–8.

96. See John Cruickshank, 'Gide's Treatment of Time in *La Symphonie Pastorale*', *Essays in Criticism*, VII, April 1957, pp. 134–43.

97. These remarks may serve as correctives to arguments adduced by Martens, op. cit., respectively pp. 154, 138; but they nevertheless owe something to her having highlighted these questions in the first place.

98. For a discussion of the pertinence of this distinction to the novel, see Wilson, op. cit., pp. 33–5.

99. The manuscript continues 'où nous nous serions enlacés' (Martin, op. cit., pp. 114–15).

100. On this important theme, see Lawrence E. Harvey, 'The Utopia of Blindness in Gide's *La Symphonie Pastorale*', *Modern Philology*, 55, February 1958, pp. 188–97.

101. Op. cit., p. 308.

102. See F. Pruner, *'La Symphonie Pastorale' de Gide, de la tragédie vécue à la tragédie écrite* (Paris: Lettres Modernes Minard, 1964), pp. 23–4; Walker, *'Les Nourritures Terrestres' and 'La Symphonie Pastorale'* chapter 6, (ii).

103. Charles Du Bos, *Le Dialogue avec André Gide* (Paris: Corrêa, 1947), p. 13.

104. *André Gide l'insaisissable Protée*, p. 161.

105. *S/Z*, pp. 187–8; 182.

106. On these two kinds of logic, see Shlomith Rimmon-Kenan, op. cit., pp. 17–18.

107. On the notion of the 'implied author', see Wayne C. Booth, *The Rhetoric of Fiction* (Chicago and London: University of Chicago Press, 1961), pp. 70–7.

108. 'Les Limites de l'Art', *Prétextes*, p. 27; 'The Limits of Art', *Pretexts*, p. 46.

109. Letter of 27 September 1901, *Correspondance 1897–1903*, p. 363.

110. Article of 1 March 1902, quoted in ibid., p. 402, n. 1. Ten years later Gide will be using the term 'empirical' to describe aspects of Dostoevsky's technique which he sought to absorb and imitate. See *JI*, 362; *JI*, 315: 1912.

111. Op. cit., pp. 355–6.

112. *JI*, 89, 'Littérature et Morale'; *JI*, 73, 'Literature and Ethics'.

113. *Si le Grain ne Meurt, JII*, 553–4; 258–9.

114. *Correspondance*, p. 193.

115. Letter to Jeanne Rondeaux, February 1894, in Delay, *La Jeunesse d'André Gide*, vol. 2, p. 307, note 3.

116. Delay, *La Jeunesse d'André Gide*, vol. 2, p. 364; *The Youth of André Gide*, p. 367.

117. Reproduced in *BAAG*, 27, July 1975, p. 53.

118. Cf. *JI*, 717; *J2*, 287: 'I have always had more understanding, more memory and more taste for natural history than for history'.

119. (London: Routledge and Kegan Paul, 1983.)

120. Cf. C. Savage Brosman, 'The Novelist as Natural Historian in *Les Faux-Monnayeurs*', *Essays in French Literature*, no. 14, November 1977, pp. 48–59.

121. See Richard Dawkins, *The Blind Watchmaker* (London: Penguin Books, 1988), p. 125.

122. *JI*, 971; *J3*, 95: 23 February 1930. See also *JI*, 1003; *J3*, 123: 2 August 1930; *JI*, 1034–5; *J3*, 151: 15 March 1931.

123. See Jean-Yves Tadié, *Le Roman d'Aventure* (Paris: Presses Universitaires de France, 1982), p. 27.

124. See Raimond, op. cit., pp. 45–7, 80.

125. C. Martin, *La Maturité d'André Gide*, p. 144.

126. Ibid., p. 519.

127. *Prétextes*, p. 59. Italics in original. Peter Fawcett argues convincingly that *The Dynamiter* influenced *Le Prométhée Mal Enchaîné* and that *Les Caves du Vatican* owes much to *The Suicide Club* and *The Wrong Box*. See 'Gide et Stevenson', in *André Gide et l'Angleterre*, ed. Patrick Pollard (London: Birkbeck College, 1986), pp. 24–9.

128. Review written for *La Revue Blanche*, May 1900; reprinted in *BAAG*, Vol. IV, no. 31, July 1976, pp. 13–14.

129. See Martin, *La Maturité d'André Gide*, pp. 299–300.

130. See *JI*, 132; *JI*, 110; March 1902 and *JI*, 255; *JI*, 220–1: November 1907. Gide declared to an interviewer after completing *L'Immoraliste* in 1902 that he was set to plunge into a very different kind of novel, wide-ranging and dense, 'a book of action and intrigue'. O'Neill, *André Gide and the Roman d'Aventure* (Sydney: Sydney University Press, Australian Humanities Research Council Monograph 15, 1969), p. 25; and Auguste Anglès, *André Gide et le Premier Groupe de la NRF*, Vol. I, 'La formation du groupe et les années d'apprentissage, 1890–1910' (Paris: Gallimard, 1978), pp. 65–6.

131. See Kevin O'Neill, op. cit., and Auguste Anglès, op. cit., and Vol. 2, 'L'âge critique, 1911–1912' (Paris: Gallimard, 1986), Vol. 3, 'Une inquiète maturité, 1913–1914' (Paris: Gallimard, 1986).

132. *Correspondance André Gide–Jacques Copeau*, Vol. 1, Décembre 1902–

Mars 1913. Edition établie et annotée par Jean Claude (Paris: Gallimard, Cahiers André Gide, 12, 1987), pp. 599–600, and note 2; O'Neill, op. cit., p. 42; Anglès, op. cit., Vol. 2, pp. 482–3.

133. Quoted in Jean-Yves Tadié, op. cit., pp. 190–1; see also O'Neill, op. cit., pp. 54–63.

134. Quoted in O'Neill, op. cit., p. 41. Charles du Bos, op. cit., p. 161, notes this remark from a conversation of 27 May 1912.

135. *Prétextes*, p. 44.

136. Helen Watson-Williams, *André Gide and the Greek Myth* (Oxford: Clarendon Press, 1967), p. 43.

137. 'The Dual Structure of the *Prométhée Mal Enchaîné*', *Modern Language Notes*, Vol. LXXIV, December 1959, pp. 714–20. See also Holdheim, *Theory and Practice of the Novel. A Study on André Gide* (Geneva: Droz, 1968), pp. 192–7.

138. In *Les Caves du Vatican* Lafcadio will similarly seek out chance events, being 'possessed by the spirit of adventure' (722; 55).

139. Compare for example with the God-novelist who intervenes to turn back the clock and play an alternative version of events at the end of John Fowles' *The French Lieutenant's Woman*.

140. C. Bremond, 'La logique des possibles narratifs', *Communications*, 8: *L'Analyse Structurale du Récit* (Paris: Seuil, Collection Points, 1981), pp. 66–83; *Logique du récit* (Paris: Seuil, 1973). This theory of narrative structure is discussed in S. Rimmon-Kenan, *Narrative Fiction: Contemporary Poetics* (London: Methuen, New Accents, 1983), pp. 22–8, and in Mieke Bal, *Narratology: Introduction to the Theory of Narrative*, translated by Christine van Boheemen (Toronto, London: University of Toronto Press, 1985), pp. 19–23. It should be noted that the model is limited to the realisation or non-realisation of a specified possibility; it does not envisage alternative possibilities from which one may be selected.

141. Umberto Eco, *The Role of the Reader* (London: Hutchinson, 1981), pp. 214–16. Postmodern fiction has made something of a speciality of narratives which strive not to sacrifice any of the alternative possibilities they would normally have to abandon. A famous example is Jorge Luis Borges' story 'The Garden of Forking Paths', in his *Labyrinths*. See also B. McHale, *Postmodern Fiction* (London: Methuen, New Accents, 1987).

142. The connections between the two are pointed out by Pierre Masson, '*Le Prométhée Mal Enchaîné*, ou du détournement d'un mythe à des fins personnelles', *BAAG*, Vol. IX, no. 49, January 1981, pp. 5–29 (23–4).

143. The exchange of letters, which dates from around 1900, is reproduced in *BAAG*, Vol. IX, no. 49, January 1981, pp. 57–9.

144. Henri Bergson, in *L'Evolution créatrice* (Paris: Presses Universitaires de France, 1948), pp. 234–6, argues this point with particular force.

145. See Elaine D. Cancalon, 'Les Formes du Discours dans *Le Prométhée Mal Enchaîné*', *BAAG*, Vol. IX, no. 49, January 1981, pp. 35–44, esp. pp. 40–1.

146. Cf. *JI*, 365–6; *JI*, 318: 7 February 1912: '*La Porte Etroite* . . . is the twin of *L'Immoraliste* and . . . the two subjects grew up concurrently in my mind, the excess of one finding a secret permission in the excess of the other and together establishing a balance'.

147. It is perhaps worth noting that Gide first conceived *Le Prométhée Mal Enchaîné* itself as a 'conte' modelled on those of Voltaire: see the diary entry for 23 December 1895, quoted in Delay, op. cit., Vol. 2, p. 576 (the passage is cut from the English version). As such the allegorical mode is not surprising.

148. 337; 169. Cf. 317; 128: 'It must increase but I must decrease'.

149. Op. cit., p. 52.

150. See David Lodge, *The Modes of Modern Writing* (London: Arnold, 1977), pp. 73–124.

151. Alain Goulet provides an illuminating survey in his article '*Le Prométhée Mal Enchaîné*: une étape vers le roman', *BAAG*, Vol. IX, no. 49, January 1981, pp. 45–52.

152. *RRS*, 1504. It is all the more odd, therefore, that Watson-Williams, op. cit., refers to the text throughout as a *récit*.

153. See Bertrand Fillaudeau, *L'Univers ludique d'André Gide* (Paris: José Corti, 1985), p. 108.

154. See Goulet, '*Le Prométhée Mal Enchaîné . . .*', loc. cit., p. 49; and below, pp. 145, 172.

155. 313; 119. On narrative as a form of contract between teller and listener, see Barthes, *S/Z*, pp. 95–6; 88–90.

156. Art. cit.

157. Goulet picks out five other quotations in art. cit., p. 52. To these should be added two more on p. 332; 156: 'What hast thou, that thou hast not received?', Paul i Corinthians, 4:7; and 'your glass eye . . . pluck it out!', Matt. 18:9. See also Fillaudeau, op. cit., pp. 178–82.

158. *Structuralist Poetics* (London: Routledge and Kegan Paul, 1975), p. 238.

159. *RRS*, 1565. Cf. *JI*, 392; *J1*, 342: 25 September 1913.

160. See Martin, *La Maturité d'André Gide*, pp. 299–300.

161. Goulet, *Fiction et Vie sociale dans l'Oeuvre d'André Gide* (Paris: Minard, Publications de l'Association des Amis d'André Gide, 1986), p. 46.

162. *JI*, 387; *J1*, 338: 24 June 1913.

163. A note states that he wrote the second chapter in the summer of 1908; *Corydon*, p. 58; 34.

164. See for example his letter of 20 June and 6 July 1911 to Jacques Copeau in their *Correspondance*, op. cit., pp. 504, 508.

165. See above, pp. 84–5. In a letter to Drouin of 24 October 1900 he admits the apparent absurdity of the exercise, but writes tantalisingly: 'It's some time now since a glimmer of it . . . but it is coming clear and satisfies me: besides, it's so simple that I am surprised not to have seen the case argued anywhere already'. Quoted in Martin, *La Maturité d'André Gide*, p. 479.

166. George Painter, *André Gide. A Critical Biography* (London: Weidenfeld and Nicholson, 1968), p. 72. See letters to Copeau, mid-November 1911, 24 November 1911, *Correspondance*, pp. 527–8, 530.

167. Daniel Moutote, *Le Journal de Gide et les Problèmes du Moi (1889–1925)* (Paris: Presses Universitaires de France, 1968), pp. 210–11.

168. For modern accounts of his work, see William J. Keeton, *Biological*

Science (New York: W. W. Norton and Co., 1967), pp. 454–6; Philip J. Pauly, *Controlling Life: Jacques Loeb and the Engineering Ideal in Biology* (Oxford: Oxford University Press, 1988).

169. Goulet, *Fiction et Vie sociale*, p. 127.

170. *L'Evolution créatrice*, op. cit., p. 35. We know that Gide read and reflected at length on this particular page since he quotes from it, and discusses the concepts of 'anagénèse' and 'catagénèse' it explains, in an important sequence of the second chapter of *Corydon*, pp. 71–7; 43–8.

171. *L'Evolution créatrice*, p. 37.

172. See note 165 above.

173. On saltationists in general and on the specific connection between such schools of thought and creationism, see Dawkins, op. cit., pp. 230–6, 248.

174. *The Origin of Species by means of Natural Selection* (London: Penguin Books, 1987), pp. 223–4.

175. Letter published in *BAAG*, no. 72, October 1986, pp. 50–1.

176. Op. cit., pp. 63–4; see also p. 24.

177. *JI*, 303; *JI*, 263: 19 June 1910. Around 1900 De Vries had rediscovered Mendel's work on genetic mutations. Gide continued to pursue his interest in the matter, reading in 1931 a study by the biologist Jean Rostand, *Etat Présent du Transformisme*: *JI*, 1097; *J3*, 208. In his *Geneviève*, a late work written over six years and published in 1936, Gide has a character refer to Mendel and the principle of 'mutation brusque' (1401).

178. *Corydon*, p. 116; 75. The reference occurs in that first third of the third chapter which Gide included in the first edition, and which Moutote in his otherwise meticulous consideration of the work's sources, op. cit., pp. 210–11, appears to have overlooked. It should be noted that Richard Dawkins pours scorn on the vogue enjoyed at the turn of the century by de Vries, Bateson, and the other prominent mutationists; op. cit., p. 305.

179. *Narcisse*, p. 6; 8. *Paludes*, pp. 96, 110, 121–2; 22, 40, 54–7.

180. Darwinism generated an interest in such transformations in English literature of the time, as Gillian Beer has shown: see op. cit., pp. 136–41.

181. This kind of conjunction on essential matters of two rival schemes within the bourgeois cosmology is a point made much of by Roland Barthes in his denunciations of *le bon sens* in *Mythologies*.

182. For a discussion of the mutual interconnections between Anthime and Julius, see Christopher Bettinson, *Gide: 'Les Caves du Vatican'* (London: Arnold, 1972), pp. 16–17, 34–5.

183. Palante was more than a little annoyed that his declaration should be used to ironic effect in this way; see *RRS*, 1574.

184. This does not prevent him from indulging in a certain coquetry over how to dress for his visitors (685–6; 8–9), nor does it preclude an awareness of the advantages he derives from having connections in the Lodge defend his interests as the owner of some land in Egypt (694; 19). Gide does not underestimate the depths and complexities of hypocrisy.

185. On this ambiguity in Anthime's transformation, a useful commentary can be found in W. M. L. Bell, 'Convention and Plausibility in *Les Caves du Vatican*', *Australian Journal of French Studies*, vol. VII, nos. 1–2, 1970, pp. 76–92 (81).

186. As Bell's analysis also confirms, loc. cit., pp. 81–2.

187. See Louis Althusser, 'Ideology and Ideological State Apparatuses', in *Lenin and Philosophy and Other Essays* (London: New Left Books, 1977), pp. 121–73. For further discussion of the concept, see Catherine Belsey, *Critical Practice* (London: Methuen, New Accents, 1980), pp. 56–8.

188. 'Verisimilitude is only ever what people say it is: it is entirely subject to public opinion': 'L'effet de réel', in Barthes, Bersani *et al.*, *Littérature et Réalité* (Paris: Seuil, Collection Points, 1982), p. 88.

189. 751; 90–2. See Goulet, *Fiction et Vie sociale*, pp. 99–104, 134–7; and A. Cobban, *A History of Modern France, Volume 3: 1871–1962* (Harmondsworth: Penguin Books, 1965), pp. 38–40.

190. Paris, Gallimard-Folio, pp. 112–13, 184–5.

191. Op. cit., pp. 44–6.

192. *Corydon*, pp. 80–5; 50–4.

193. Op. cit., p. 48.

194. *S/Z*, pp. 26, 28, 209, 267; 19, 20–1, 204, 262.

195. Op. cit., p. 235.

196. *S/Z*, pp. 183–4, 187–8; 178, 181–2.

197. Quoted in Erich Köhler, *Le Hasard en littérature: le possible et la nécessité*, tr. Eliane Kaufholz (Paris: Klincksieck, 1986), p. 13.

198. Op. cit., p. 262.

199. Painter, for example, op. cit., p. 72, offers a strikingly reductionist view of Lafcadio's crime; Bettinson, op. cit., pp. 51–8, argues a more subtle case which, however, in adducing the ungraspable complexity of Lafcadio's motivation, comes very near to accepting infinitely complex determinism, which is pretty close to chance for practical purposes.

200. *Ne Jugez Pas*, pp. 97–8. See Ireland, *André Gide. A Study of his Creative Writings*, op. cit., p. 261.

201. *Ne Jugez Pas*, p. 143. For a survey of discussions along these lines, see Roger Bastide, 'L'acte gratuit', in his *Anatomie d'André Gide* (Paris: Presses Universitaires de France, 1972), pp. 73–96.

202. *RRS*, p. 1571.

203. Bastide, op. cit., pp. 87–9, discusses the connections most productively, but does not examine Lafcadio's behaviour at length. An analysis by David Steel shows not only that the *acte gratuit* is severed from its psychological impetus, but also, a point which is directly germane to my argument, that it is 'isolated from its effects' by the way its consequences are suppressed: ' "Lafcadio ludens": Ideas of Play and Levity in *Les Caves du Vatican*', *Modern Language Review*, Vol. 66, no. 3, July 1971, pp. 554–64 (559).

204. Eric Marty best brings out this aspect of the notion: see 'Lafcadio: L'Acte Gratuit ou le Principe d'Anarchie', Chapter V of his introductory essay *Mythologie d'André Gide*, in *André Gide, qui êtes-vous?*, op. cit., pp. 81–9.

205. Paul Valéry, who was as obsessed by chance as was Gide, speculated on the possibility of a biography which avoided falling into the illusion of time as a 'conducting thread' – an illusion engendered by the combined effects of the mechanisms governing memory and language and fostered by

the standard model of narrative. ('La vie est un conte', in *Tel Quel*, *Oeuvres*, II (Paris: Bibliothèque de la Pléiade, 1960), pp. 776–7.)

206. For a full discussion of the historical elements and the implications of their use, supplemented by the relevant documents, see Bettinson, op. cit., pp. 9–12; Goulet, *Fiction et Vie Sociale*, pp. 89–90, 134–6, and Goulet, '*Les Caves du Vatican' d'André Gide* (Paris: Larousse, 1972), pp. 158–68. To the numerous historical sources assessed by these critics can be added another, pointed out by Jean Claude, the editor of the Gide–Copeau correspondence. In a letter of 1 July 1911 Gide alludes to a financial swindle involving one Dupray de la Maherie and the so-called 'Bras économique de l'église'. See op. cit., p. 384.

207. See Umberto Eco, 'Lector in Fabula', in *The Role of the Reader*, op. cit., pp. 200–60, esp. p. 214ff. We have already had occasion to highlight a related feature which occurs in the plot of *Le Prométhée Mal Enchaîné*: see above, pp. 92–3.

208. The importance of the *roman d'aventure* model has already been indicated. Gide himself referred to *Les Caves* as 'a sort of detective novel' (*Entretiens Jean Amrouche–André Gide*, in *André Gide, qui êtes-vous?*, op. cit., p. 227); in so doing he was in fact echoing remarks made by François Mauriac in 1914 (*RRS*, p. 1576).

209. Op. cit., p. 216.

210. 'Inferential walks are possible when they are verisimilar', Eco states, op. cit., p. 216.

211. Bettinson, op. cit., p. 50, says of this episode that Lafcadio 'is less the victim of chance than the master'. But objectively, precisely the opposite is the case: he does not throw a six, and does not get off the train. His choice is, in fact, nullified by novelistic chance. He controls the count, and this is indeed an act of will; but it is merely obeying the rules of the game so as to offer an opening to chance, whereas speeding up the count would have been a more obvious way of pre-empting the outcome.

212. Goulet, *Fiction et Vie sociale*, pp. 486–9; Holdheim, *Theory and Practice of the Novel*, p. 217; Fillaudeau, op. cit., p. 25.

213. Ibid., p. 104.

214. *BAAG*, XII, no. 64, October 1984, pp. 536–7.

215. Op. cit., pp. 31–2.

216. 'Introduction à l'analyse structurale des récits', loc. cit., p. 20; 102.

217. *André Gide. A Critical Biography*, pp. 63–74.

218. Cf. Germaine Brée: '(Gide) introduces into all his tales ... the question of a discrepancy between the human notion of moral consequence and the problem of chance action and retroaction which can affect a life'. 'Time Sequences and Consequences in the Gidian World', *Yale French Studies*, vol. 7, 1951, pp. 51–9 (53).

219. Ian Pickup, 'Causality and Determinism in Balzac: the "law" of diminishing possibilities', *Modern Languages*, LXII, no. 4, December 1981, pp. 196–200.

220. Op. cit., p. 52.

221. Köhler, op. cit., pp. 61–2.

222. 'Le Réalisme et la Peur du Désir', in *Littérature et Réalité*, op. cit., pp. 57–65.

223. See Eco, op. cit., pp. 217–24.

224. Bell, loc. cit., pp. 91–2, sees such allusions as strengthening the potential plausibility of the incidents they accompany by using the characters' incredulity to disarm the reader's. I am less sure that cumulatively this *is* their effect, particularly given the closing remark by the narrator.

225. See Arthur E. Babcock, *Portraits of Artists: Reflexivity in Gidean Fiction*, op. cit., pp. 79–83.

226. See Bettinson, op. cit., pp. 38–9.

227. Op. cit., pp. 41–3.

228. Ibid., pp. 26, 41.

229. 'appela à Rome', 680; 1. 'rappelait à Rome', 770; 116. 'à Rome, appelé par un congrès', 810; 167. 'à Rome, appelé par un congrès', 835; 200. 'ce congrès auquel je vais être tenu d'assister', 840; 207, etc. Similarly, the comtesse de Saint-Prix is 'appelé à Paris', p. 746; 85, and the narrator himself admits that an examination 'l'appelait', p. 760; 104, to the region where Blafaphas was born. Goulet, *Fiction et Vie sociale*, p. 88, points out the metaphorical significance of the 'congrès de sociologie' which is associated with several of the calls, referring to it as 'the hub and the point of convergence of the essential sociological revelations in the work'.

230. Du Bos, *Le Dialogue avec André Gide*, p. 161; Hytier, op. cit., p. 139.

231. Letter to Copeau, 8 June 1912, *Correspondance*, p. 622.

232. The extent of his disappointment is chronicled in O'Neill, op. cit., pp. 47–9.

233. *OC VI*, p. 361.

234. *RRS*, p. 679; also *JI*, 436–7; *J2*, 39: 12 July 1914.

235. *JI*, 420; *J2*, 24: 15 June 1914. Cf. also *JI*, 417; *J2*, 21: 11 June 1914. *JI*, 418; *J2*, 22: 13 June 1914.

236. *JI*, 29–30; *JI*, 19: 11 January 1892.

237. *Being and Nothingness*, trs. Hazel Barnes (London: Methuen and Co. Ltd., 1969), pp. 65–7. Italics in original.

238. Cf. *Journal des Faux-Monnayeurs*, pp. 47–8; pp. 24–5. Italics in original.

239. Cf. *Ainsi Soit-il, ou les Jeux Sont Faits*, in *JII*, 1187; 55: 'Nothing could be more expected, more consistent, than the remarks of Balzac's characters: most often they say just what you know in advance they are to say'.

240. 1185; 277. Such uncontrollable effusions were a characteristic of Gide's own experience to which he attached great importance. He claims to identify evidence of similar states in the life and fictional characters of Dostoevsky (*Dostoevsky*, in *OC XI*, pp. 259–64, 289–92), speaks of their significance in his own autobiography (see *Si le Grain ne Meurt*, in *JII*, pp. 438–9; 115–17), and to describe them borrows the term 'schaudern' from Goethe (*JI*, 207; *JI*, 179). Delay declares that they bear witness to a fundamental element in his makeup: op. cit., I, pp. 174–5; 80–3.

241. *Le Journal de Robert Levesque*, in *BAAG*, XI, no. 59, July 1983, p. 337: the comments were made in a conversation of 31 August 1931.

242. 'Introduction to the Structural Analysis of Narratives', loc. cit., p. 16; 95. Barthes borrows the term 'phatic' from Jakobson: see 'Linguistics

and Poetics', in *Style and Language*, ed. T. A. Sebeok (Cambridge, Mass.: M.I.T., 1960), pp. 353–9.

243. Maria van Rysselberghe, *Les Cahiers de la Petite Dame*, vol. 1, *Cahiers André Gide*, 4 (Paris, Gallimard, 1973), p. 28, 9 July 1919.

244. Op. cit., pp. 356–63.

245. N. David Keypour, *André Gide: écriture et réversibilité dans 'Les Faux-Monnayeurs'* (Montréal, Presses de l'Université de Montréal, 1980), pp. 130–1. Jean Hytier, *André Gide* (Paris: Charlot, 1946) p. 271, underlines 'la discontinuité, parfois un peu fatigante, du développement'.

246. Michael Tilby, *Gide: 'Les Faux-Monnayeurs'* (London, Grant and Cutler, Critical Guides to French Texts, 9, 1981), pp. 21–2; 75–6; 81.

247. In 1911 Gide wrote: 'The novel, as I recognize or imagine it, comprises a diversity of points of view, subject to the diversity of characters it presents; it is in essence a work of dispersion' (*OC VI*, p. 361).

248. 'Les Faux-Monnayeurs et l'art du roman', in *Hommage à André Gide* (Paris: Nouvelle Revue Française, 1951), p. 128.

249. *J1*, pp. 790, 782; *J2*, pp. 355, 348 (1924). The issue is pinpointed by Julien, loc. cit., p. 127.

250. Cf. Gerald Prince, 'Notes on the Text as Reader', in *The Reader in the Text*, ed. Susan R. Suleiman and Inge Crosman, op. cit., pp. 225–40.

251. Cf. Gerald Prince, 'Introduction à l'étude du narrataire', *Poétique*, 154 (1973), pp. 178–96. Prince cites the sentence on Vincent as one of his illustrations (p. 184).

252. This development of a narrative which mingles a *roman d'aventure* and an intrusive narrator can trace its lineage back to two major models. One is obviously Stevenson; the other is Henry Fielding, whose *Tom Jones* was a major influence during the composition of *Les Faux-Monnayeurs*. (See *Journal des Faux-Monnayeurs*, 72; 41–2: 14 February 1924).

253. Cf. Alain Goulet, 'Lire *Les Faux-Monnayeurs*', *André Gide 5*, Revue des Lettres Modernes, 1975, pp. 10–14; Arthur E. Babcock, op. cit., pp. 84–5. For a comprehensive overview and analysis, see Keypour, op. cit. The emergence of these techniques in the *récits* is examined by Maisani-Léonard, op. cit.

254. In this Gide's practice does not, of course, conform to standard conventions of free indirect speech which normally retains the 'back-shift' of tenses characteristic of indirect discourse. See Rimmon-Kenan, op. cit., p. 112. Raimond sees the feature as a 'prodigious technical success' on Gide's part: op. cit., pp. 353–4.

255. 1087; 173. The translation changes this to 'Tuesday evening', in order, presumably, to do away with the (deliberate?) metalepsis in the French.

256. It might be objected that direct speech is neutral presentation; but as Maisani-Léonard points out, 'the direct and indirect styles are always a means of marking the appropriation of one discourse by another'; and a high proportion of dialogue, 'far from revealing a calm objectivity, betrays the illusion of objectivity, precisely the illusion denounced, moreover, in the *récits*' (op. cit., pp. 192–3). Bakhtin's analysis parallels this view: see 'Du discours romanesque', in M. Bakhtin, *Esthétique et théorie du roman*, tr.

André Gide

Doria Olivier (Paris: Gallimard, Bibliothèque des Idées, 1978) pp. 82–233; 175.

257. Tilby, op. cit., pp. 90–3, holds that the tone and techniques of Edouard's narrative provide a contrast and a counterweight to the playful narrator's voice: see also his ' "Self-conscious" narration and "self-reflexivity" in Gide's *Les Faux-Monnayeurs*', *Essays in French Literature*, 15, November 1978, pp. 56–81. The argument is tenable up to a point; but the narrator's presence is constantly perceptible, even within Edouard's diary (see below). Keypour's contention is that the narrator's voice is attenuated by the discourses he quotes (but see previous note) and that in the final analysis Edouard can be viewed as the 'real' author of the novel. The subtle hypothesis of which this notion is part is built up ingeniously but on very insecure foundations, such as that the narrator cannot logically know more than Edouard about la Pérouse and the pension Vedel Azaïs (152–3) and that the epigraphs and other aspects of the editorial function must be seen as operating on a narrative level above that of the narrator (154–9).

258. See above, note 242.

259. The notion of the citational, dialogic or polyphonic novel derives from the work of Bakhtin. See 'Du discours romanesque', loc. cit.; *Problems of Dostoevsky's Poetics*, tr. R. W. Rotsel (Ann Arbor, 1973); *The Dialogic Imagination*, four essays translated by Caryl Emerson and Michael Holquist (Austin: University of Texas Press, 1981).

260. A particularly striking example of intertextual relations is provided by the story of how the actual suicide of a boy named Nény, which inspired that of Boris, found its way into *Les Faux-Monnayeurs* via a news report in the *Journal de Rouen* (reproduced in full in the *Journal des Faux-Monnayeurs*) and texts by Maurice Barrès and Jacques Copeau: see *BAAG*, X, no. 55, July 1982, pp. 335–46; no. 56, October 1982, p. 523; XI, no. 57, January 1983, pp. 107–8.

261. *Correspondance André Gide – Dorothy Bussy*, 3 vols (Paris: Gallimard, Cahiers André Gide, 9, 10, 11, 1980–1982), vol. 2, p. 27.

262. Barthes, 'Proust et les noms', in *Le Degré zéro de l'écriture, suivi de Nouveaux Essais Critiques*, p. 133. For structuralist and post-structuralist critics, the 'caractère signifiant' of language is its capacity for generating meaning, rather than for simply transcribing pre-existing meanings. The notion of language as a self-contained system of relational structures was most notably established by Saussure in his *Course in General Linguistics* (Glasgow: Fontana, 1974).

263. Op. cit., p. 236.

264. 'Lecteurs et lectures dans *Les Faux-Monnayeurs*', *Neophilologus*, 57 (1973), pp. 16–23.

265. Prince, in his 'Introduction à l'étude du narrataire', loc. cit., p. 180, writes: 'The narratee can only follow a narrative in one clearly defined direction . . . he is obliged to acquaint himself with events by proceeding from the first page to the last'. The exact status of the reader postulated here does not fall within the categories of much contemporary narrative poetics in so far as these are theoretical constructs encoded in the text, whereas the building up of this second reader for *Les Faux-Monnayeurs*

requires some pragmatic components as well as hands to turn the actual pages. Eco's 'model of a possible reader' seems the most appropriate label: see *The Role of the Reader*, op. cit., pp. 7–11.

266. It is known that this pattern was part of Gide's intention. See his letters to Roger Martin du Gard in their *Correspondance,* op. cit., vol. 1, p. 269; and to Jacques Lévy in his *Journal et Correspondance* (Grenoble: Editions des Cahiers de l'Alpe, 1954), p. 36. The *Journal des Faux-Monnayeurs* sets out the idea this structure is devised to illustrate: 'There is no act, however foolish or harmful, that is not the result of interacting causes, connections and concomitances. No doubt there are very few crimes of which the responsibility cannot be shared, to the success of which several did not contribute – albeit without their knowledge or will' (76–7; 44–5).

267. Prince indicates that textual reading signals 'may present a definition of the text that is at best superficial or off-base . . . . In this case, rather than performing as readers, they perform as counterreaders' ('Notes on the Text as Reader', loc. cit., p. 239).

268. '*Les Faux-Monnayeurs*: The Theme of Responsibility', *Modern Language Review,* 55 (July 1960), pp. 351–8.

269. *Histoire du roman français depuis 1918* (Paris: Seuil, 1950), p. 253.

270. *André Gide, l'insaisissable Protée,* op. cit., pp. 302–3.

271. On the walls are 'un tableau symbolique des âges de la vie' (1159) which Geneviève Idt comments on in her *André Gide: Les Faux-Monnayeurs* (Paris: Hatier, Profil d'une oeuvre, 1970), pp. 53–5; and a clinical picture of a horse in which 'the artist has concentrated on a single horse all the ills by means of which Providence chastens the equine soul' (1159; 251): this would appear to mirror Boris as the hapless victim of the repercussions of human weaknesses in the novel.

272. In *JI,* 1051; *J3,* 166: 16 June 1931, Gide accepts the Pascalian *pensée* as an expression of his own view of the world. See pp. 83–4 above.

273. See Jonathan Culler, *The Pursuit of Signs,* op. cit., p. 183, where Nietzsche's analysis of such tropes is considered. Barthes points out that narrative operates a related transformation of *post hoc* into *propter hoc*: 'Introduction to the Structural Analysis of Narratives', loc. cit., p. 16; 94.

274. Thematically this is underlined by the fact that the other illegitimate child, Bernard, with whom Boris is in this respect paralleled, does survive and flourish.

275. Quoted in *Journal des Faux-Monnayeurs,* p. 87; 51.

276. Cf. Gide's definition of the artist: 'he who does not believe, not completely, in the reality (in the *single* reality, at least) of the outer world . . . How much more comforting is the idea of different possibilities' (*JI,* 801, 992, 1051; *J2,* 365, *J3,* 114, 116).

277. That Gide was aware of the advances in physics evoked here seems to be hinted at in *Les Caves du Vatican* by Julius de Baraglioul's remark – clearly not to be taken seriously – 'There is no such thing as inconsequence – in psychology any more than in physics' (744; 84). We may compare with the remark by Louis de Broglie, Nobel Prize for Physics in 1924, who wrote of 'la discontinuité physique essentielle qu'on nomme aujourd'hui le quantum d'Action' (quoted in *Le Petit Robert*). See pp. 107–11 above.

278. See above, pp. 109–10.

279. See note 271 above.

280. See Roger Jones, *Physics as Metaphor* (London: Sphere Books/Abacus, 1983), pp. 117–20.

281. See G. Painter, op. cit., p. 93; Holdheim, op. cit., p. 241.

282. Edouard too claims that his novel has no plan, that nothing in it will be decided in advance (1082).

283. See Rimmon-Kenan, op. cit., pp. 17–18.

284. Holdheim, op. cit., p. 239; Tilby, op. cit., p. 27; Babcock, op. cit., pp. 87–9; Hytier, op. cit., pp. 296–7.

285. Op. cit., Chapter 9: 'Story and Discourse in the Analysis of Narrative', p. 175.

286. Barthes discusses this contradiction in *S/Z*, op. cit., pp. 183–4; 178–9.

287. See Eric Marty, '*Les Faux-Monnayeurs*: Roman, mise en abyme, répétition', in *André Gide*, 8, Revue des Lettres Modernes, 1987, pp. 95–117 (102–4).

288. *S/Z*, pp. 183–4; 178–9.

289. *Le Plaisir du Texte* (Paris: Seuil, 1973), p. 87; *The Pleasure of the Text*, tr. Richard Miller (London: Jonathan Cape, 1976), p. 55. On the production of deconstructive undecidables in fiction and philosophy, see: *S/Z*, pp. 83–4, 169–70, 183–4; 76–7, 163–4, 178–9. Vincent B. Leitch, *Deconstructive Criticism* (London: Hutchinson, 1983), pp. 110, 180, 280 n. 2. Rimmon-Kenan, op. cit., pp. 121–2. Graham Falconer, 'Flaubert, James and The Problem of Undecidability', *Comparative Literature*, vol. 39, no. 1, Winter 1987, pp. 1–18.

290. In dying as an expiatory victim of the ills of his world, Boris becomes a kind of Christ-figure, as is suggested in La Pérouse's closing comment on God having sacrificed his own son (1248; 345). Such is indeed the main thesis of Jacques Lévy, op. cit. It is therefore of considerable significance that we find Gide concerned to challenge the teleology of narrative as it applies to the story of Christ in the Scriptures. His critique of the Biblical accounts, which we have discussed earlier, pp. 82–3, is probably not unconnected with the narrative structure he devised for *Les Faux-Monnayeurs*.

291. See Raimond, op. cit., pp. 71, 80.

292. See Roland Barthes, 'Structure du fait divers', in *Essais Critiques* (Paris: Seuil, 1964), pp. 188–97.

293. See *Le Rouge et le Noir*, ed. H. Martineau (Paris: Garnier, 1960), pp. X–XII.

294. 'Les Frères Karamazov', in *Dostoïevski* (Paris: Gallimard, Collection Idées, 1970), p. 63.

295. See above, p. 106.

296. See *BAAG*, X, no. 55, July 1982, 335–46; no. 56, October 1982, p. 523; XI, no. 57, January 1983, pp. 107–8.

297. Letter to Arnold Bennett, 15 November 1920, in *OC* X, p. 553.

298. *Marxism and the Philosophy of Language* (London: Academic Press, 1973), p. 85. Italics in original.

299. See above, our remarks on ideology, p. 109.

300. Loc. cit., pp. 189, 196–7.

301. The same phrase occurs in *Souvenirs de la Cour d'Assises*, in connection with the acquittal of a girl judged guilty of infanticide; and article 66 of the Penal Code, from which it comes, is quoted in connection with the *Affaire Redureau*: *NJP*, pp. 38, 110.

302. *The Order of Mimesis*, op. cit., pp. 48–9.

303. *Mythologies* (Paris: Seuil, 1957), pp. 50–3, 102–5.

304. *NJP*, 63. Elsewhere, Gide quotes the line 'the boldness and ferocity of lawbreakers is going beyond all known limits', and adds '*(ô Flaubert!)*', an evocation of his predecessor's legendary horror of linguistic and other *bêtise*.

305. *OC VI*, 361–2.

306. See François Mouret, 'Gide à la découverte de Browning et de Hogg, ou la technique romanesque de la multiplicité des points de vue', loc. cit., pp. 224–5.

307. Letter to Roger Martin du Gard, 10 July 1934, *Correspondance*, op. cit., vol. 1, pp. 625–6. Gide went so far as to declare: 'I would even say that the *index of refraction* matters more to me than the thing refracted', letter of 29 December 1925, ibid., p. 281.

308. Letter of 21 July 1924, *Correspondance*, op. cit., vol. 1, p. 251.

309. The case is echoed in Mauriac's *Thérèse Desqueyroux* of 1927: Livre de Poche edition, p. 162. In the absence of available evidence, it is impossible, so far as I am aware, to say whether the similarity between this case and the initial plight of Gertrude in *La Symphonie Pastorale* is what drew Gide to the affair or whether in fact the case had actually contributed in some way to this text written in 1918–19. Certainly, Chanvin, the lawyer who helped Gide compile the dossier, had been a friend of his since before 1900 and may well have mentioned the story at an earlier date.

310. Loc. cit., pp. 191, 194, 195.

311. The image is picked up in *Les Faux-Monnayeurs*, in Vincent's description of fish in the deepest parts of the ocean: 'Each of these animals which people at first insisted were creatures of darkness, gives forth and projects before and around it its *own* light' (1053; 137).

312. Examples of the kind of reading this can generate are to be found in Karen Nordenhaug Ciholas, *Gide's Art of the Fugue. A Thematic Study of 'Les Faux-Monnayeurs'* (Chapel Hill: University of North Carolina Department of Romance Languages, 1974) and in Bettinson, *Gide: 'Les Caves du Vatican'*, op. cit., pp. 12–45.

313. Letter to Copeau, 8 June 1912, *Correspondance*, op. cit., vol. I, p. 622.

314. Alain Robbe-Grillet, *Le Miroir qui revient* (Paris: Minuit, 1984), p. 212.

315. Alain Robbe-Grillet, *Djinn. Un trou rouge entre les pavés disjoints* (Paris: Minuit, 1981).

Bibliography

WORKS BY GIDE

The major extensive bibliographies of Gide's works are:

Arnold Naville, *Bibliographie des écrits d'André Gide (depuis 1891 jusqu'en 1952)* (Paris: Guy Le Prat, 1949).

Jacques Cotnam, *Bibliographie chronologique de l'oeuvre d'André Gide (1889–1973)* (Boston, Mass.: G. K. Hall and Co., 1974).

Most of Gide's prose fiction is available in French in the following edition:

André Gide, *Romans, récits et soties, oeuvres lyriques.* Introduction par Maurice Nadeau, Notices et Bibliographies par Yvonne Davet et Jean-Jacques Thierry (Paris: Bibliothèque de la Pléiade, 1958).

Other sources:

André Gide, *Journal, 1889–1939* (Paris: Bibliothèque de la Pléiade, 1951).

André Gide, *Journal 1939–1949, Souvenirs* (Paris: Bibliothèque de la Pléiade, 1954).

André Gide, *Oeuvres Complètes.* Edition augmentée de textes inédits, établie par L. Martin-Chauffier (Paris: Nouvelle Revue Française, 15 volumes, 1932–9).

André Gide, *Corydon* (Paris: Gallimard, 1947).

André Gide, *Journal des Faux-Monnayeurs* (Paris: Gallimard, 1927).

André Gide, *Ne Jugez Pas* (Paris: Gallimard, 1969).

André Gide, *Dostoïevski* (Paris: Gallimard, Collection Idées).

André Gide, *Théâtre* (Paris: Gallimard, 1942).

André Gide, *Prétextes, suivi de Nouveaux Prétextes* (Paris: Mercure de France, 1963).

André Gide, *Les Cahiers et les Poésies d'André Walter.* Edition établie et présentée par Claude Martin (Paris: Gallimard, Collection Poésie, 1986).

André Gide, *La Symphonie Pastorale.* Edition critique de Claude Martin (Paris: Minard, Collection Paralogue, 1970).

André Gide, *Littérature Engagée,* textes réunis et présentés par Yvonne Davet (Paris: Gallimard, 1950).

The vast majority of Gide's fiction, as well as some works of non-fiction, is available in French paperback editions (Gallimard: Collection Folio), and

almost as much is available in English (Penguin Books). Translations to
which reference is made in this study are listed below.

Les Cahiers d'André Walter:
The Notebooks of André Walter, translated from the French and with an
Introduction and Notes by Wade Baskin (London: Peter Owen, 1968).

Le Traité du Narcisse, La Tentative Amoureuse:
The Return of the Prodigal, preceded by Five Other Treatises, with *Saul,* a
Drama in Five Acts, translated by Dorothy Bussy (London: Secker and
Warburg, 1953). *Narcissus, The Lovers' Attempt, El Hadj, Philoctetes, Bathsheba.*

Paludes, Le Prométhée Mal Enchaîné:
Marshlands and Prometheus Misbound, translated by George D. Painter (London:
Secker and Warburg, 1953).

Les Nourritures Terrestres:
Fruits of the Earth, translated by Dorothy Bussy (Harmondsworth: Penguin
Books, 1970).

L'Immoraliste:
The Immoralist, translated from the French by Dorothy Bussy (London:
Cassell and Co., 1953).

La Porte Etroite:
Strait is the Gate, translated by Dorothy Bussy (London: Secker and Warburg,
1948).

La Symphonie Pastorale:
La Symphonie Pastorale and *Isabelle,* translated by Dorothy Bussy (Harmondsworth: Penguin Books, 1963).

Les Caves du Vatican:
The Vatican Cellars, translated from the French by Dorothy Bussy (London:
Cassell and Co., 1952).

Les Faux-Monnayeurs:
The Counterfeiters, translated from the French by Dorothy Bussy (Harmondsworth: Penguin Books, 1966).

Journal des Faux-Monnayeurs:
Logbook of the Coiners, translated and annotated by Justin O'Brien (London:
Cassel and Co., 1952).

Journal 1889–1939, Journal 1939–1949:
The Journals of André Gide, translated from the French, with an Introduction
and Notes, by Justin O'Brien.
Vol. 1: 1889–1913 (London: Secker and Warburg, 1948).
Vol. 2: 1914–1927 (London: Secker and Warburg, 1948).
Vol. 3: 1928–1939 (London: Secker and Warburg, 1949).
Vol. 4: 1939–1949 (New York: Alfred A. Knopf, 1951).

Corydon:
Corydon, translated and introduced by Richard Howard (London: GMP Publishers, Gay Modern Classics, 1985).

Prétextes:
Pretexts. Reflections on Literature and Morality. Selected, Edited and Introduced by Justin O'Brien (London: Secker and Warburg, 1959).

Ainsi soit-il ou Les Jeux sont faits:
So Be It; or The Chips are Down, translated, with an Introduction and Notes, by Justin O'Brien (London: Chatto and Windus, 1960).

Geneviève:
The School for Wives, Robert, and Genevieve, translated by Dorothy Bussy (London: Cassell and Co., 1953).

CORRESPONDENCE

Gide was a prolific letter-writer, and more than 20 000 letters from him have so far been inventoried. For the complete list, see:

Jacques Cotnam, *Inventaire bibliographique et Index analytique de la Correspondance d'André Gide (publiée de 1897 à 1971)* (Boston, Mass.: G. K. Hall and Co., 1975).

Claude Martin, *La Correspondance générale d'André Gide (1879–1951): répertoire, index, notices* (Lyon: Centre d'Etudes Gidiennes, 6 vols., 1984–5).

Numerous volumes of correspondence with particular individuals have been published, including:

Francis Jammes–André Gide, *Correspondance 1893–1938* (Paris: Gallimard, 1948).

Paul Claudel–André Gide, *Correspondance 1899–1926* (Paris: Gallimard, 1949).

Paul Valéry–André Gide, *Correspondance 1890–1942* (Paris: Gallimard, 1955).

Arnold Bennett–André Gide, *Correspondance 1911–1931* (Geneva: Droz, 1964).

Roger Martin du Gard–André Gide, *Correspondance 1913–1951* (Paris: Gallimard, 2 vols., 1968).

François Mauriac–André Gide, *Correspondance 1920–1950* (Paris: Gallimard, Cahiers André Gide, 2, 1970).

Henri Ghéon–André Gide, *Correspondance 1897–1944* (Paris: Gallimard, 2 vols., 1976).

Jacques-Emile Blanche–André Gide, *Correspondance 1891–1939* (Paris: Gallimard, Cahiers André Gide, 8, 1978).

Justin O'Brien–André Gide, *Correspondance 1937–1951* (Lyon: Centre d'Etudes Gidiennes, 1979).

Dorothy Bussy–André Gide, *Correspondance 1918–1951* (Paris: Gallimard, 3 vols., Cahiers André Gide, 9, 10, 11, 1979, 1981, 1982).

Jacques Copeau–André Gide, *Correspondance*, vol. 1, Décembre 1902–Mars 1913 (Paris: Gallimard, Cahiers André Gide, 12, 1987).

WORKS ON GIDE

The critical material on Gide is enormous. A useful list can be found in:

Claude Martin, *Bibliographie chronologique des livres consacrés à André Gide (1918–1986)* (Lyon: Centre d'Etudes Gidiennes, 1987).

The following is a selective list of works referred to in the present study.

Bastide, R., *Anatomie d'André Gide* (Paris: Presses Universitaires de France, 1972).

Bell, W. M. L., 'Convention and Plausibility in *Les Caves du Vatican*', *Australian Journal of French Studies*, vol. VII, nos. 1–2, 1970, pp. 76–92.

Booker, J. T., 'The Generic Ambiguity of Gide's *La Symphonie Pastorale*: Reading the pastor's first *cahier*', *Symposium*, 40 (1986), pp. 159–71.

Brée, G., *André Gide l'insaisissable Protée* (Paris: Les Belles Lettres, 1953).

Cancalon, E. D., *Techniques et personnages dans les récits d'André Gide* (Paris: Lettres modernes Minard, Archives André Gide no. 2, 1970).

Cancalon, E. D., 'Les Formes du Discours dans *Le Prométhée Mal Enchaîné*', *BAAG*, Vol. IX, no. 49, January 1981, pp. 35–44.

Ciholas, K. N., *Gide's Art of the Fugue. A Thematic Study of 'Les Faux-Monnayeurs'* (Chapel Hill: University of North Carolina Department of Romance Languages, 1974).

Cordle, T., *André Gide* (New York: Twayne, 1969).

Cruickshank, J., 'Gide's Treatment of Time in *La Symphonie Pastorale*', *Essays in Criticism*, VII, April 1957, pp. 134–43.

Davies, J. C., *Gide, 'L'Immoraliste' and 'La Porte Etroite'* (London: Edward Arnold, 1968).

Delay, J., *La Jeunesse d'André Gide* (Paris: Gallimard, 2 vols, 1956–7); *The Youth of André Gide*, abridged and translated by June Guicharnaud (Chicago and London: University of Chicago Press, one volume, 1963).

Fawcett, P., 'Gide et Stevenson', in *André Gide et l'Angleterre*, ed. Patrick Pollard (London: Birkbeck College, 1986).

Fillaudeau, B., *L'Univers ludique d'André Gide* (Paris: José Corti, 1985).

Freedman, R., *The Lyrical Novel* (Princeton, New Jersey: Princeton University Press, 1963).

Goulet, A., 'Les premiers vers d'André Gide (1888–1891)', *Cahiers André Gide*, 1 (Paris: Gallimard, 1969), pp. 123–49.

Goulet, A., *'Les Caves du Vatican' d'André Gide* (Paris: Larousse, 1972).

Goulet, A., 'La figuration du procès littéraire dans l'écriture de *La Symphonie Pastorale*', *André Gide 3*, Revue des Lettres Modernes, 1972, pp. 27–55.

Goulet, A., 'Lire *Les Faux-Monnayeurs*', *André Gide 5*, Revue des Lettres Modernes, 1975, pp. 10–14.

Goulet, A., '*Le Prométhée Mal Enchaîné*: une étape vers le roman', *BAAG*, Vol. IX, no. 49, January 1981, pp. 45–52.

Goulet, A., *Fiction et Vie sociale dans l'oeuvre d'André Gide* (Paris: Minard, Publications de l'Association des Amis d'André Gide, 1986).

Guérard, A. J., *André Gide* (New York: E. P. Dutton, 1963).

Harvey, L. E., 'The Utopia of Blindness in Gide's *La Symphonie Pastorale*', *Modern Philology*, 55, February 1958, pp. 188–97.

Holdheim, W. W., *Theory and Practice of the Novel. A Study on André Gide* (Geneva: Droz, 1968).

Hytier, J., *André Gide* (Paris: Charlot, 1946).

Idt, G., *André Gide: 'Les Faux-Monnayeurs'* (Paris: Hatier, Profil d'une oeuvre, 1970).

Ireland, G. W., *André Gide. A Study of his Creative Writings* (Oxford: Clarendon Press, 1970).

Keypour, N. D., *André Gide: Ecriture et réversibilité dans 'Les Faux-Monnayeurs'* (Montréal, Presses de l'Université de Montréal, 1980).

Lévy, Z. H., *Jérôme Agonistes: Les structures dramatiques et les procédures narratives de 'La Porte Etroite'* (Paris: Nizet, 1984).

Maillet, H., *'L'Immoraliste' d'André Gide* (Paris: Hachette, 1972).

Maillet, H., *'La Symphonie Pastorale' d'André Gide* (Paris: Hachette, 1972).

Maisani-Léonard, M., *André Gide ou l'ironie de l'écriture* (Montréal: Les Presses de l'Université de Montréal, 1976).

Martin, C., *La Maturité d'André Gide. De 'Paludes' à 'L'Immoraliste' (1895–1902)* (Paris: Klincksieck, 1977).

Marty, E., 'Mythologie d'André Gide', in *André Gide, Qui êtes-vous?*, avec les entretiens Jean Amrouche–André Gide (Lyon: la Manufacture, 1987), pp. 11–135.

Marty, E., '*Les Faux-Monnayeurs*: Roman, mise en abyme, répétition', *André Gide 8*, Revue des Lettres Modernes, 1987, pp. 95–117.

Masson, P., '*Le Prométhée Mal Enchaîné*, ou du détournement d'un mythe à des fins personnelles', *BAAG*, Vol. IX, no. 49, January 1981, pp. 5–29.

Mouret, F. J.-L., 'Gide à la découverte de Browning et de Hogg, ou la technique romanesque de la multiplicité des points de vue', *Cahiers André Gide*, 3 (Paris: Gallimard, 1972), pp. 223–39.

Moutote, D., *Le Journal de Gide et les Problèmes du Moi (1889–1925)* (Paris: Presses Universitaires de France, 1968).

Oliver, A., *Michel, Job, Pierre, Paul: intertextualité de la lecture dans 'L'Immoraliste'* (Paris: Archives des Lettres modernes, Archives André Gide no. 4, 1979).

O'Neill, K., *André Gide and the Roman d'Aventure* (Sydney: Sydney University Press, Australian Humanities Research Council Monograph 15, 1969).

Painter, G., *André Gide. A Critical Biography* (London: Weidenfeld and Nicolson, 1968).

Prince, G., 'Lecteurs et lectures dans *Les Faux-Monnayeurs*', *Neophilologus*, 57 (1973), pp. 16–23.

Pruner, F., '*La Symphonie Pastorale*' *de Gide, de la tragédie vécue à la tragédie écrite* (Paris: Lettres Modernes Minard, 1964).

Rossi, V., *André Gide. The Evolution of an Aesthetic* (New Brunswick, NJ: Rutgers University Press, 1967).

Savage Brosman, C., 'The Novelist as Natural Historian in *Les Faux-Monnayeurs*', *Essays in French Literature*, no. 14, November 1977, pp. 48–59.

Sonnenfeld, A., 'On Readers and Reading in *La Porte Etroite* and *L'Immoraliste*', *Romanic Review*, LXVII (1976), pp. 172–86.

Steel, D. A., ' "Lafcadio ludens": Ideas of Play and Levity in *Les Caves du Vatican*', *Modern Language Review*, Vol. 66, no. 3, July 1971, pp. 554–64.

Thody, P., '*Les Faux-Monnayeurs*: The Theme of Responsibility', *Modern Language Review*, 55 (July 1960), pp. 351–8.

Tilby, M. J., ' "Self-conscious" narration and "self-reflexivity" in Gide's *Les Faux-Monnayeurs*', *Essays in French Literature*, 15, November 1978, pp. 56–81.

Tilby, M. J., *Gide: 'Les Faux-Monnayeurs'* (London: Grant and Cutler, Critical Guides to French Texts, 1981).

Walker, D. H., 'Subversion of narrative in the work of André Gide and John Fowles', in *Comparative Criticism*, ed. E. Schaffer, vol. 2 (Cambridge: Cambridge University Press, 1980), pp. 187–212.

Walker, D. H., *Gide: 'Les Nourritures terrestres' and 'La Symphonie pastorale'* (London: Grant and Cutler, Critical Guides to French Texts, 1990).

Watson-Williams, H., *André Gide and the Greek Myth* (Oxford: Clarendon Press, 1967).

Wilson, W. D., *André Gide: 'La Symphonie Pastorale'* (London and Basingstoke: Macmillan, 1971).

Index

212 *Index*

214 *Index*

Stevenson, Robert Louis 86, 190n,
197n
Dr Jekyll and Mr Hyde 86
The Black Arrow 86
The Dynamiter 86, 190n
The Suicide Club 190n
The Wrong Box 190n
Treasure Island 86
story-telling 5, 9–10, 12–13, 17, 21,
23–5, 27–8, 30, 51, 55, 64, 81,
83, 102–3, 105, 148, 150, 152,
158, 159, 169–70, 179, 200n
structure, *see under* narrative
structuralism 8, 189n, 197n, 198n
Suleiman, Susan 184n, 197n
symbol 5, 8, 15, 18, 101
symbolism 1, 2, 4, 6, 7–8, 15, 16,
18, 21–2, 54, 88, 173

Tacitus 149
Tadié, J.-Y. 190n, 191n
Taine, Hippolyte 1
tenses, *see under* narrative
Thibaudet, Albert 154
Thody, Philip 153
Tilby, Michael 145, 197n, 198n,
200n
Todorov, Tzvetan 188n
transaction, *see under* narrative
The Trial 170

Uitti, Karl D. 183n
unexpected, the *see* unforeseen, the

unforeseen, the 5, 6, 18, 85, 90,
110–12, 136, 143, 145, 153, 159

Valéry, Paul 2, 84, 130, 145, 184n,
194–5n
Van Rysselberghe, Maria 184n,
197n
verisimilitude, *see under* narrative
Virgil 102
Bucolics 102, 106
Volosinov, *see* Bakhtin
Voltaire, François-Marie Arouet
de 154, 192n
Candide 154
voyeurism 33–4, 186n
Vries, Hugo de 110, 193n

Walker, David H. 184n, 185n,
187n, 189n
Warren, Austin 189n
Watson-Williams, Helen 89, 102,
191n, 192n
Weiler, Max 108
Wellek, René 189n
Wells, H. G. 86
The War of the Worlds 86
Wilson, W. Donald 71, 189n
Wright, Elizabeth 186n, 187n
writing 15, 16, 27–30, 47, 103, 118,
131, 150, 169, 179, 181–2,
186n, 188n
Wynchank, Anny 183n

Zola, Emile 1, 21